LOST TRANSMISSIONS

Editor: David Cashion
Designer: Jacob Covey
Production Manager: Michael Kaserkie

Library of Congress Control Number: 2018958853

ISBN: 978-1-4197-3465-6
eISBN: 978-1-68335-498-7

Compilation © 2019 Desirina Boskovich

Cover © 2019 Abrams

Printed and bound in China
10 9 8 7 6 5 4 3 2 1

Abrams Image books are available at special discounts when purchased
in quantity for premiums and promotions as well as fundraising
or educational use. Special editions can also be created to
specification. For details, contact specialsales@abramsbooks.com or
the address below.

ABRAMS The Art of Books
195 Broadway, New York, NY 10007
abramsbooks.com

LOST TRANSMISSIONS

The Secret History of Science Fiction and Fantasy

DESIRINA BOSKOVICH

ABRAMS IMAGE -- NEW YORK

FOREWORD

As a twelve-year-old, lo those many decades ago, I would sneak away from my school's expeditions to the public library and set up camp in the adult section–especially the science fiction and fantasy section, where I would read through any number of pulp magazine anthologies. *The Best of Galaxy* was a particular favorite of mine because the stories were so weird, and often mysterious–a fair number of them might even be called science fantasy.

Whether it was flying coffins invading earth, a misdelivered anatomy package from the future wreaking mayhem, or a future under-earth populated with talking animals, I was transported by amazing imaginations and ingenious stories. I discovered writers that I still read to this day, some of them mentioned in this volume, like Cordwainer Smith and Jack Vance. To me, as a kid, speculative fiction was mysterious and, yes, a secret experience.

This feels like the right way to have been introduced to science fiction and fantasy, long considered low and debased genres, not at all "serious." Many of us had to sneak off to read it outside of class, which was generally bereft of such material except in the most boring and unexciting iterations. How, as a teenager, I would have loved to read a book like *Lost Transmissions*–a guide to a wealth of unusual treasures.

Because the thing about science fiction and fantasy is this: They always need more histories and more books that reclaim or examine what has been hidden or forgotten. Science fiction in particular started out as a kind of mom-and-pop genre, which lends itself to a "secret history" as well–a fan-based, pulp-book culture, a genre that allows for mash-ups of all kinds and whose collective history might be relegated at times to mentions in mimeographed fanzines.

Fantasy could always fall back on the world of myth and legend for legitimacy, but the term "science fiction" more or less came from the US pulp magazines of the 1920s that mostly published startling adventure stories set in space, by a very white and male set of authors. Within certain constraints, however, science fiction also allowed for the flourishing of unique and bizarre imaginations. In fact, the state of the field has always been more complex than memory suggests, sustaining ebbs and flows of acceptance of certain types of writers. For example, translated SF and work from outside of core genre gained more acceptance in the 1960s and 1970s, under the aegis of editors like Frederik Pohl and Damon Knight and Michael Moorcock–with the 1980s also seeing a flowering of translations of Soviet SF in anthologies published by McGraw-Hill and championed by Theodore Sturgeon. This is not to mention the rise of feminist science fiction and fantasy in the 1970s and the more recent influx of nonwhite writers into the field, both pivotal moments that utterly transformed science fiction and fantasy into something ever richer, more imaginative, and more open to all readers.

The book you hold in your hands provides an admirable introduction to the secret history of science fiction and fantasy–not just through my entry point (books!) but other media as well–guided by an able assemblage of contributors providing an abundance of points of view. (The work of those contributors could itself form an amazing speculative anthology worthy of further exploration, including wonderful creators like John Jennings, Ekaterina Sedia, and Charlie Jane Anders, to name just three.)

The joy of a compilation like *Lost Transmissions* is that it is itself a kind of secret eccentricity, cataloguing misfits and ne'er-do-wells possessed of astonishing imaginations. As an editor of reprint anthologies of science fiction and fantasy I am always struck by the unjustness of who becomes successful and who does not–the luck, bad fortune, and other factors–and thus the immense responsibility of reclaiming the underappreciated, the misunderstood, the forgotten.

This book conjures up not just a sense of wonder for its work in that regard, but also gives readers the sweet regret of might-have-beens. What if this film had been made or that book written? (We cannot, of course, know how many existing books and movies once teetered on the edge of oblivion, of never reaching an audience.) So, in a sense, *Lost Transmissions* is itself a science-fiction narrative, daring us to imagine other timelines and other universes in which things turned out differently and, for example, William Gibson made an *Aliens* movie.

And yet, no secret history can include the secret history entire. One reason for this is that one person's perception of "secret" is so different from another's. Take my treasured memories of childhood reading in the library. Cordwainer Smith was a giant in my mind, someone I just assumed everyone knew and read, while I never would have guessed, to be honest, when I first encountered Isaac Asimov, that he was practically a household name. We create by our enthusiasms and our passions the secret history we need and deserve, and, you, dear reader, are no different.

If you know nothing of science fiction and fantasy, *Lost Transmissions* will be an utter revelation; for others, it will be an affirmation of favorites you've carried a torch for, for years or even decades. Some readers may even curse and say, "What about X, Y, and Z?," for that is the joy of cultivating eccentric tastes. But what this book provides for all readers is a beautifully illustrated and edited jumping-off point for your own memory cathedral–your own secret history.

I hope you think of this book not as a destination but as part of a continuous and fulfilling journey, one of unexpected discoveries and storytelling joys that grows in the imagination and fuels your curiosity and passion. And with that good thought, I will get out of the way to let you enjoy the book before you.

Jeff VanderMeer
Tallahassee, Florida
February 2019

Galaxy Science Fiction ran from 1950 to 1980. Under the guidance of editors H. L. Gold and Frederik Pohl, *Galaxy* became possibly the most influential SF magazine of the era, publishing luminaries such as Alfred Bester, Ray Bradbury, Harlan Ellison, Cordwainer Smith, and Jack Vance.

INTRODUCTION

WHEN WE EXPLORE THE HISTORY OF SPECULATIVE STORYTELLING—science fiction and fantasy, and all the weird, magical, surreal, and uncanny threads they contain—we usually point to the landmarks that determined its course, the household names that defined the canon. But as all SFF fans know, there is always a world beneath the world, or just beyond it, or even woven artfully inside it. There are alternate dimensions and hidden doors. This book is about *that* history: the secret history.

In this book, we explore stories and projects in all genres that never saw the light of day, but if only they had—they might have changed the course of SFF storytelling forever. We tease out the hidden connections and subtle forces that pushed creators in one direction instead of another. We uncover the work of artists who, for whatever reason, did not receive their due . . . because their identities, and consequently their voices, were marginalized by the dominant demographics of the field, or because their work was too odd, too unfamiliar, too ahead of its time. We pay homage to artists, designers, architects, and fashion icons outside the "strictly genre," who nevertheless shaped SFF in their own ways, by providing the raw material of imagination and invention that seeped its way into dozens of stories to come.

What emerges is an image of science fiction and fantasy both as it is, but also as it could have been—and still might be. Speculative fiction is a genre of ideas, and the only limit to its potential is how far we're willing to eagerly and patiently explore its threads—even the ones that, like those illuminated here, are a little bit fragile and tough to unwind.

Within these pages, dozens of contributors delve into underappreciated works, discuss their own creative influences, and share their favorite obscure pieces of SFF lore. Such multiplicity is inherent and necessary. Because above all, this is not *the* secret history, but *a* secret history. For every story surfaced here, there are a dozen still buried. For every creator finally receiving their belated due, another waits patiently to be rediscovered. Our history is always evolving. And—as we discover and rediscover how we got to where we are—our genre's future is always evolving, too.

The King in Yellow by Vicente Valentine (tribute to Robert W. Chambers).

LITER—ATURE

WE ALL KNOW THE FAMOUS STORY OF HOW, IN 1816, A NINETEEN-year-old girl named Mary Shelley invented science fiction. It was a gloomy and wet summer retreat at Lake Geneva. The party included Mary's new husband, the philosopher and poet Percy Bysshe Shelley, along with their friend, famous Romantic poet Lord Byron. To amuse themselves, they began inventing ghost stories by the fire. Spurred by the dreary atmosphere, the stimulating conversation, and her vivid dreams, Shelley invented a modern twist on the classic ghost story—and a new genre was born. *Frankenstein; Or, The Modern Prometheus* was published in 1818.

But the story of science fiction hardly begins or ends there. Its seeds were planted in much earlier eras, in every culture's mythological tales of supernatural beings and otherworldly planes. Its future was shaped by many creators and influencers who, intentionally or not-so-intentionally, gave the genre a push in one direction or another. Their contributions may not be so well-known, but they are no less worthy.

And then there are the forks in the road; the inflection points whose impact on the genre is only recognized much later. What if the weather had been fine that summer in 1816, and ghost stories were abandoned for pleasant days by the lake? Through secret history, we also explore these inflection points . . . and the stories that could have been.

Fiolxhilde summons a daemon from Lavania to transport herself and her son to the moon. Original illustration by Jeremy Zerfoss, 2018.

Kepler's Proto–Science Fiction Manuscript *Somnium* and Its Legal Consequences

Johannes Kepler (1571-1630) was a German mathematician and astronomer who played an essential role in the scientific revolution of the seventeenth century. He *also* wrote a work of proto-science fiction that landed his own mother in jail.

Kepler is known today for his laws of planetary motion, which set the stage for modern astronomy. He correctly proposed that planets travel in elliptical orbits (although he incorrectly imagined these orbits all occurred on the same plane). He was the first to explain that the gravitational pull of the Moon is what causes the ocean's tides. He even coined the word *satellite*.

As a literal Renaissance Man, Kepler's scientific contributions went well beyond astronomy. He's also been called the founder of modern optics, as he developed significant theories of refraction and depth perception, and even the principle of eyeglasses.

He also wrote one of the earliest precursors of science fiction, lauded by visionaries such as Isaac Asimov and Carl Sagan. *Somnium* was written in Latin, as were most learned and scholarly works of the day; *somnium* means "the dream."

This manuscript began as Kepler's scholarly dissertation in 1593. But because of its controversial theories about the arrangement of the planets, his professors persuaded him not to publish it. In those days, insisting that the Sun was at the center of the solar system could land you in some serious trouble. Instead, Kepler continued to work on the manuscript sporadically for the next thirty-seven years.

At the core of the work is a description of what life would be like on the surface of the Moon. Of course, this was no idle flight of fancy; Kepler drew on his training as a scientist to envision the Moon's climate, flora, and fauna based on the most advanced scientific knowledge of the day–knowledge that was still considered controversial by many.

This aspect of the story might well be considered hard sci-fi, drawing as it does on the era's most accurate knowledge of natural science. But as Kepler continued to work with the manuscript, he cloaked the science fiction in myth and legend, adding the framing story of a dream and a fantastical journey to the heavens.

In 1976, science historian Gale E. Christianson wrote in the journal *Science Fiction Studies*: "There can be little, if any, doubt that Kepler selected the framework of the Dream to satisfy two major demands: First, fewer objections could be raised among the ranks of those still within the Aristotelian orbit by passing off this Copernican treatise as a figment of an idle slumberer's uncontrollable imagination; and secondly, it enabled Kepler to introduce a mythical agent or power capable of transporting humans to the lunar surface."

The dream framing begins to feel almost metafictional–perhaps Calvino-esque–in its layers of obfuscation. The story opens in first person, as Kepler writes that he was reading stories of the legends of Bohemia. Then he falls asleep and begins to dream. In his dream he reads a book. And within that book is the actual story, about a young boy named Duracotus.

One day, Duracotus makes the grievous error of angering his mother Fiolxhilde, who sells him to a ship captain. Duracotus gets seasick and the captain leaves him in the care of real-life astronomer Tycho Brahe, under whom Kepler himself studied for many years. Like Kepler, Duracotus becomes an astronomer and discovers the secrets of the celestial bodies.

After five years, Duracotus returns home to Fiolxhilde, who has regretted her impulsive child-selling and is pleased to have him back. He tells her what he's learned about the skies. In turn, she reveals that she has her own knowledge of the heavens, imparted by spirits who can teleport her wherever she pleases. She calls on one of these daemons to transport the two of them to the Moon, aka the island of Lavania and home of the spirits. Soon after, the two of them are borne on the 50,000-mile journey to the Moon. (The Moon is actually considerably farther away than that, but not an awful guess on Kepler's part, either.)

Here is where the text turns to science fiction. The rigors of the journey are described in detail. Once they arrive, Duracotus and his mother begin a detailed tour of the lunar satellite—where the extreme temperatures, low gravity, and rocky terrain suggest a very different world than our own. Kepler postulated that the extreme temperatures and low gravity on the Moon would produce totally foreign flora and fauna—for example, he imagined that creatures on the Moon would grow to massive sizes. He imagined that these large, snakelike creatures would spend much of their time roaming in the darkness, eluding the harsh, hot sun that in the unprotected atmosphere would quickly kill them.

Though now fundamental to science-fiction worldbuilding, at the time these ideas were positively groundbreaking. Christianson writes, "Nearly two centuries before Buffon, Lyell, and Darwin, Kepler had grasped the close interrelationship between life forms and their natural environment."

Then the dreamer awakes, and the story is over.

Kepler began to pass around this manuscript-in-progress to some of his friends and colleagues. In 1611, one of these manuscript copies went missing, and began circulating among people who were less friendly to him. The autobiographical elements were obvious, so, it stood to reason that his real-life mother, Katharina Kepler, probably communed with spirits and demons. One humorous aside in *Somnium* consolidated the association, as Kepler wrote of the trip to the Moon: "The best adapted for the journey are dried-out old women, since from youth they are accustomed to riding goats at night, or pitchforks, or traveling the wide expanses of the earth in worn-out clothes."

> Though the mythological aspects of the manuscript might have protected Kepler from the persecution of the Aristotelian astronomers, they exposed his mother to the machinations of the witchhunters.

In 1615, Katharina was charged with practicing witchcraft. In further damning evidence against Katharina, her aunt had also been accused as a witch and burned at the stake; it was well-known that female pacts with the devil typically ran in families.

It was a tragic, and ironic, turn of events. Though the mythological aspects of the manuscript might have protected Kepler from the persecution of the Aristotelian astronomers, they exposed his mother to the machinations of the witchhunters.

For the next five years, Kepler turned all his attention to clearing Katharina's name. She spent fourteen months in jail. Finally, she was freed, but the stress of her imprisonment had taken a toll. She died soon after.

Guilt-stricken by it all and motivated to take a stand, Kepler decided it was time to finally complete *Somnium*. Between Katharina's death in 1622 and 1630, he wrote 223 footnotes, which became the bulk of the text and expanded significantly on his scientific theories. In any case, the tides were turning and the Aristotelians didn't hold the same power they once did. The scientific community was turning toward Copernican ideas such as Kepler's.

Though he meant to publish *Somnium*, he did not have a chance. In 1630, he fell suddenly ill and died. In 1634, his son Ludwig Kepler published the work, less in honor of his father's wishes and more from financial desperation–Kepler's widow, Ludwig's mother, was in dire financial straits.

As noted, *Somnium* was originally published in Latin. To this day, English translations remain limited, obscure, and difficult to obtain. Perhaps, in the twenty-first century, this oversight will finally be rectified. ✦

Johannes Kepler was the first of many scientists to moonlight as a science-fiction writer. His research offered a scientific foundation for a speculative tale.

How Jules Verne's Worst Rejection Letter Shaped Science Fiction . . . for 150 Years

French writer Jules Verne (1828-1905) is known for his *Voyages extraordinaires,* novels that include the classics *Around the World in Eighty Days, From the Earth to the Moon,* and *Twenty Thousand Leagues Under the Sea.* In fact, Verne penned more than sixty of these adventures, laying the groundwork for the highly imaginative narratives of more than a century to come. He has even been called "the father of science fiction."

Verne's novels have inspired many successful films and been translated into more than 140 languages. And his tales of bold exploration have fueled the fantasies and ambitions of real-life adventurers and record-breakers. The famous science-fiction author Ray Bradbury once wrote, "We are all, in one way or another, children of Jules Verne. His name never stops. At aerospace or NASA gatherings, Verne is the verb that moves us to space."

So you can imagine the excitement of Verne aficionados, science-fiction fans, and lovers of French literature when in 1989, Verne's great-grandson discovered the lost manuscript: *Paris in the 20th Century,* written 126 years before. The manuscript might never have been found if not for the youthful imagination of the younger Verne, who as a child had dreamed about the contents of a locked safe that had been in the family for generations, and the treasures it might contain. "Everyone thought it was empty, but in my imagination it was full of precious stones, gold, and fabulous jewels and strange objects given to or collected by my great-grandfather," said Jean Jules-Verne.

As an adult, Jean Jules-Verne hired a locksmith to force open the old safe, revealing its contents. There were no jewels within. Instead, the safe contained *Paris in the 20th Century,* a never-before-published novel by the late, great Jules Verne. The book was published in France in 1994, and soon appeared in translation all around the world.

When manuscripts are discovered under such auspicious circumstances, it's common to doubt their authenticity. However, this one was easily proven to be a Verne original. The paper, ink, and handwriting matched other Verne manuscripts. Notes from Verne's editor, Pierre-Jules Hetzel, were scribbled in the margins, and that handwriting was also authenticated by experts. Most importantly, noted Verne scholar Piero Gondolo della

Riva already possessed a letter written by Verne's editor, rejecting the book in no uncertain terms.

Verne had already made a name for himself with the swashbuckling adventure stories that he's still known for today, arming contemporary Industrial Age heroes with futuristic technology and pitting them against the terrors of nature. *Paris in the 20th Century* was a very different kind of book: a grim vision of the future, both philosophical and prophetic. Verne scholar Arthur B. Evans writes in *Science Fiction Studies,* "Despite its frequent (very Vernian) detailed descriptions of high-tech gadgetry and its occasional flashes of wit and humor, this dark and troubling tale paints a future world that is oppressive, unjust, and spiritually hollow. Instead of epic adventure, the reader encounters pathos and social satire."

Verne's editor was unimpressed. "I'm surprised at you," Hetzel wrote. "I was hoping for something better. In this piece, there is not a single issue concerning the real future that is properly resolved, no critique that hasn't already been made and remade before." Hetzel called the manuscript "tabloidish," "lackluster," and "lifeless." He told Verne that publishing the book would be a disaster for his reputation.

Apparently convinced by this litany of discouragement, Verne put the novel

Émile-Antoine Bayard's illustrations for Jules Verne's *Around the Moon* (1870) are some of the first to depict a technological approach to space travel.

aside and returned to writing adventure stories. Instead of *Paris in the 20th Century,* Verne's next published novel was *Journey to the Center of the Earth,* which remains popular with fans even today.

Nevertheless, when *Paris in the 20th Century* was finally published in the 1990s, contemporary audiences were fascinated by the opportunity to explore Verne's vision of his future—which, as the book was set in the 1960s, now concerned a time long past. Many of Verne's predictions of the modern age turned out to be shockingly on-point, both in his depiction of future technology and his vision of future social norms. Film archivist Brian Taves writes, "Virtually every page is crowded with evidence of Verne's ability to forecast the science and life of the future, from feminism to the rise of illegitimate births, from email to burglar alarms, from the growth of suburbs to mass-produced higher education, including the dissolution of humanities departments."

Though its prescience is striking, many readers agreed that as a work of fiction, the novel leaves something to be desired. The story follows a young poet whose talents are deemed worthless by a society that only cares about business and profit. While his misfortunes are distressing, they don't quite coalesce into a coherent plot; it's a novel driven by character, written by an author for whom character development was never his strongest suit.

One thing is certain: In steering Verne away from the literary undertaking represented by *Paris in the 20th Century,* and back toward a science fiction of exploration and adventure, Hetzel did much more than shape Verne's career. *Voyages extraordinaires* became a template for the genre. Science fiction became stories of space, technology, exploration, adventure, frontiers, and conquest, a paradigm that continued for quite some time, and still shapes the genre today. Yet science fiction's greatest practitioners are often those who view it less as an opportunity for escapism, and more as a framework for imaging the world as it could be. ✦

Édouard Riou illustration from Jules Verne's
Journey to the Center of the Earth (1863).

Jane Webb Loudon's *The Mummy!: A Tale of the Twenty-Second Century*

Steam-powered lawn mowers and plows; surgical and domestic automatons; mail delivered across great distances by a system of canons and wire nets; collapsible tea service; cross-continental travel by portable balloon; irrigation using cloud-capture via electrical machine; fireproof paper and cloaks made from asbestos; the mobile home; the inflatable bed and spring-coil mattress; central air; the ceiling fan; machine-made apparel; the air compressor; the espresso machine; suborbital space flight.

These are just a few of the innovations imagined in Jane Webb Loudon's (1807-1858) 1827 novel *The Mummy!: A Tale of the Twenty-Second Century*.

Born in 1807 to a wealthy Birmingham couple, Jane Webb's mother died when she was only eight years old, after which she traveled extensively with her father, Thomas Webb. Their travels exposed young Jane to a variety of cultures, languages, and governments. A reversal of fortunes afflicted them before his death in 1824, leaving Jane orphaned and without financial support at the age of seventeen.

Jane had written some poetry, and hoped that her writing might support her. She published her first book, *Prose and Verse*, in 1826. Her second book, published anonymously in three volumes when she was twenty years old, was *The Mummy!: A Tale of the Twenty-Second Century*.

The story commences in the year 2126, under the Catholic reign of Queen Claudia– who, while presiding over a time of peace and prosperity, is not a particularly engaged ruler. England being a matriarchy in this imagined future, two cousins will vie for the future of the throne: Rosabella and Elvira, who are being courted by the sons of nobility, Edric and Edmund. Of the two, Edmund has the greater distinction, having recently returned from a successful military engagement. Edric is ashamed of his own lack of accomplishments, his passions lying in the direction of natural philosophy. Seeking to equal his brother's fame, with the help of Dr. Entwerfen and his "galvanic battery of fifty surgeon power," he resolves to reanimate the Pharaoh Cheops.

Comparisons have been made to Mary Shelley's *Frankenstein*, published nine years earlier, and while *Frankenstein* was almost certainly an inspiration, the similarities are few. In both, the dead are brought back to life via electricity, and the reanimated men certainly make for a gloomy and ostracized pair–but we spend very little time with Loudon's mummy. Romance, matchmaking, political intrigue, and melodramatic philosophizing make up much of the tale–even the resurrected mummy Cheops adds drama more in his angsty monologuing and meddling in current affairs than in revealing secrets of the grave. Loudon's future is optimistic and full of imagination, glamour, and humor in equal parts.

> *Comparisons have been made to Mary Shelley's Frankenstein, [but] Loudon's future is optimistic and full of imagination, glamour, and humor in equal parts.*

At a richly described formal ball, the women are adorned by headdresses of "capillaries of contained flame"—a precursor, perhaps, to neon. Coffee is served by "a patent steam coffee-machine, by which coffee was roasted, ground, made, and poured out with an ad libitum of boiling milk and sugar, all in the short space of five minutes," an innovation easily recognizable in every Starbucks today. A moment of slapstick comedy ensues when Dr. Entwerfen's "steam-powered valet" is sabotaged by the cook, and explodes in the process of brushing down the doctor's coat, leaving him drenched and scalded.

Forty-six years before Jules Verne sent Phileas Fogg around the world in a hot air balloon, Dr. Entwerfen made preparations to travel more quickly from England to Egypt by what today we might recognize as suborbital space flight:

> *"The cloaks are of asbestos, and will be necessary to protect us from ignition,*
> *if we should encounter any electric matter in the clouds; and the hampers are*
> *filled with elastic plugs for our ears and noses, and tubes and barrels of common*
> *air, for us to breathe when we get beyond the atmosphere of the earth."*
> *"But what occasion shall we have to go beyond it?"*
> *"How can we do otherwise? Surely you don't mean to travel the whole distance*
> *in the balloon?"*

Jane Webb's novel was a success. Her agricultural innovations caught the eye of botanist John Loudon, who wrote a favorable review of the book in a gardening journal, and arranged a meeting with the author (presuming the anonymous author to be a man) to discuss the steam-driven plow and lawn mowing machines introduced in the book. They were married shortly thereafter.

Jane Webb Loudon went on to revolutionize another field: gardening. While helping her husband with his botanical encyclopedia, she realized that no such handbook existed for the layperson, so she wrote one, opening up the hobby of gardening to the British middle class. She then turned her hand to botanical illustration, and became one of the most notable artists in the field.

She never did return to writing fiction. Today she is best known for her gardening manuals, and is credited with creating the first example of the Mummy trope. But to the science-fiction reader and writer, it's the many technological "innovations and

improvements" she imagined in *The Mummy!* that are most memorable, and their influence most recognizable in the literature that came after.

Perhaps the most prescient part of Loudon's book lies in her own Introduction, in which she shares the dream of a spirit visitation that inspired her to write *The Mummy!* The dream-spirit's reassurance to the nascent author may also serve as a guiding light for the literary genre she helped to create:

> *"The scenes will indeed be different from those you now behold; the whole face of society will be changed: New governments will have arisen; strange discoveries will be made, and stranger modes of life adopted. . . . Though strange, it may be fully understood, for much will still remain to connect that future age with the present. The impulses and feelings of human creatures must, for the most part, be alike in all ages: Habits vary, but nature endures; and the same passions were delineated, the same weaknesses ridiculed, by Aristophanes, Plautus, and Terence, as in after-times were described by Shakespeare and Molière; and as will be in the times of which you are to write—by authors yet unknown."* ✦

Jane Webb Loudon also popularized gardening as a hobby for young ladies via her accessible and beautifully illustrated horticultural manuals.

Early Feminist Utopias, From Gilman's *Herland* to Rokeya's *Sultana's Dream*

Thomas More first coined the term utopia with his eponymous work in 1516, launching a thread of speculative fiction dedicated to imagining the world as it could be. There's some controversy over whether "utopia" translates as "good place" or "nowhere." Since the perfect place is probably impossible, both feel accurate. Utopias (and their converse, dystopias) have long since been used as tools in science fiction, imagining alternate social and cultural arrangements, both good and bad.

Of course, whether a particular social arrangement is a utopia or a dystopia often depends on your perspective. Though *The Handmaid's Tale* is presented as a dystopian story of a world in the grip of abusive patriarchy and religious oppression, there will probably always be plenty of people who would be perfectly happy to see that world come into being.

Since the late nineteenth century, feminist writers have used the tool of speculative fiction to envision both dystopias–like the world of *The Handmaid's Tale*–as well as utopias free of gender-based oppression. In fact, stories such as these were among the earliest works of science fiction.

One example is *Herland*, a 1915 novella by Charlotte Perkins Gilman. Gilman is best-known for her short story "The Yellow Wallpaper" (1892), a perennial favorite of English teachers and students. A Weird classic, "The Yellow Wallpaper" remains a genuinely creepy and unsettling tale; its power has not diminished with time. Told in journal entries, the story centers on a young woman who is suffering from mental health problems, or in the parlance of the day, "hysteria." For her "treatment," her husband, a doctor, confines her to one room upstairs, where she has nothing to do but rest . . . and inspect the wallpaper. Unsurprisingly, this stint in solitary confinement does not improve her mental health.

What's most shocking about this story is how relevant it still feels, as the male-dominated political establishment still frequently tries to exert control over female bodies while simultaneously neglecting the real concerns of women's health.

Having established her feminist bona fides with "The Yellow Wallpaper," Gilman went on to write *Herland*, her vision of a world with only women. The story is initially told from

the perspective of three men, intrepid explorers who set out to "discover" this long-forgotten civilization. In the *Guardian*, feminist essayist and activist Lindy West writes, "[They] are such perfect, brutal caricatures of masculinity, they feel fresh and relevant enough to populate any sarcastic modern-day feminist blog post."

When they reach Herland, they find a peaceful paradise, free from violence and poverty and all the typical problems of modern life. The culture centers fully on the joys and responsibilities of motherhood. Everyone wears super-comfy yet attractive and androgynous tunics (see pages 204-207 for more on feminist utopian fashion). Also, everyone is vegetarian.

While this vision of a socialist utopia run by women was radical in its time, it is also highly problematic in many ways. "Being a product of its time, *Herland* is also excruciatingly antiquated–rife with gender essentialism, white supremacy, and anti-abortion rhetoric," writes West. Today, many women would find the idea of a life lived in service of maternity to be the opposite of empowering. And like the white suffragettes of the day, Gilman's brand of feminism was decidedly not intersectional.

Five years after the novella's publication in 1915, the Nineteenth Amendment to the U.S. Constitution was ratified, granting women the right to vote. Considering that in 1915–and even in 1920–the idea of women voting was extremely controversial and offensive to many, it's easy to see why imagining a world where they ran the whole government is radical, provocative, and inspiring. But despite its groundbreaking nature, *Herland* is not a particularly impressive piece of science fiction, lacking the subtlety and skill of "The Yellow Wallpaper." Which perhaps explains why it is not so well-known today.

Herland was one of a handful of similar stories published in the Western world during this very early era of women's lib. Others include *New Amazonia* (1889) by Elizabeth Burgoyne Corbett and *Millennium Hall* (1762) by Sarah Scott—both equally proto-feminist and equally problematic, if not more so.

But British and American writers were not the only ones to produce such narratives. In 1905, ten years before Gilman's *Herland,* the feminist thinker Begum Rokeya Sakhawat Hossain published *Sultana's Dream*, her own vision of a feminist utopia.

Like Kepler's *Somnium, Sultana's Dream* is presented, unthreateningly, as a fanciful dream. The sultana falls to snoozing in her chair and dreams of a world called Ladyland. She's given a tour of this amazing place, where men are confined to the home while women are given the run of the world, managing society and building a better future.

How did this state of affairs come about? Almost fatally wounded by a war they couldn't win, the men agreed to retreat and let the ladies have a try. The women won the war with a clever scientific contraption that concentrated the rays of the sun and blasted all its heat and light onto the enemy's battlefield. They then set to building a futuristic, progressive society fueled by innovations such as a floating balloon that draws water from the atmosphere above the clouds and pipes it directly down to earth, and repurposed the sun-capturing instrument as a renewable source of heat and energy.

In the highly segregated society of the early twentieth century—not just in India, where Hossain wrote, but in the West as well—women were mostly confined to the home. In India, this space was called the *zenana* and the segregation was referred to as *purdah*. Hossain skewers the irony of the fact that women are told they're confined indoors for "their own protection"—from men, of course. If men are so dangerous, perhaps it is they who should be confined?

Concept art from *Sultana's Dream,* an animated feature film directed by Isabel Herguera. The film is in preproduction as of 2019.

The story reverses the concept of traditional purdah (isolation between the sexes), and men are confined to *mardana*, an inversion of the female space zenana. Hidden out of sight, the men are content to tend to their homes and do the domestic chores. In some ways, this is less of a utopian fantasy and more of a satire, arguing that what's good for the goose is good for the gander.

Inseparable from Hossain's critique of patriarchy is her critique of colonialism. As editor and critic Mahvesh Murad writes for Tor.com, "Hossain is also very aware of living under colonisation—and not just that of women by men but that of nations." At the core of *Sultana's Dream* is the insistence that intelligence is more powerful than brute force, and none of us should submit to oppression simply because our oppressors appear to be larger and stronger than we are. "A lion is stronger than a man," says the sultana's guide through Ladyland, "but it does not enable him to dominate the human race."

Hossain's backstory is fascinating, perhaps even more so than the story itself. Her father was an orthodox Muslim, and enforced purdah when she was growing up in the 1880s, permitting the women of the family to learn only to recite the Quran. But Rokeya and her sister Karimunnesa were rebellious types, and they secretly studied Bengali and Persian, with the support of their better-educated brothers. One brother, Ibrahim Saber, also taught

Rokeya some English when she was quite young, secretly tutoring her by candlelight after their parents were in bed.

Karimunnesa shared Rokeya's affinity with language. She was a talented poet, and Rokeya admired her deeply. Karimunnesa's support remained one of Rokeya's most potent motivations throughout her life, and she dedicated one of her books to her, writing "I learned to read the Bengali alphabets only because of your affectionate care."

Rokeya married at sixteen, but her own husband–originally a friend of her benevolent older brother–was extremely supportive of her ideas and her work as a feminist activist. In fact, she wrote *Sultana's Dream* in English in part to impress him with her command of the language, which she'd been studying while he was away on a trip. She presented it to him on his return; he read the whole thing in one standing (he didn't even sit down) and was duly impressed, calling it "a splendid revenge." He also supported her work financially, saving money so that she could establish a school. The institute she founded is still one of Kolkata's most popular schools for girls. ✦

The film *Sultana's Dream* follows a Spanish film director's journey across India as she grapples with global gender inequality in the present day.

The "Timeless Green Kingdoms" of George MacDonald

George MacDonald (1824-1905) is one of speculative fiction's most influential figures; some even consider him the father of modern fantasy. Yet while his work influenced a veritable who's who of twentieth century fantasists, his own reputation has faded into undeserved obscurity.

Born in Scotland to an upper middle class and strongly religious family, MacDonald rejected his parents' more extreme version of the faith, but continued to value his Christianity. He studied Moral Philosophy and Sciences at a well-established university, where he honed his abilities as a thinker and scholar. Choosing between becoming a chemist or a clergyman, he chose the cloth, but his career as a minister was short-lived, as he was forced to resign because his liberal and eccentric ideas soon had him

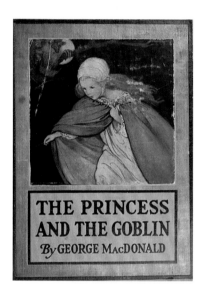

accused of "heresy." Still, as he turned to writing, his work continued to draw heavily on his Christian faith, which inspired his sense of the numinous and sublime. He went on to write more than fifty books including novels, stories, essays, and poems.

With MacDonald's body of work now considered somewhat obscure, not many fans of fantasy literature have read even his best-known books, *Phantastes* (1858), *At the Back of the North Wind* (1871), and *The Princess and the Goblin* (1872). To present-day audiences, these works can be inaccessible. But they were hugely influential for a generation of fantasy authors whose names are much better known today, including C. S. Lewis, J.R.R. Tolkien, Madeleine L'Engle, and Ursula K. Le Guin.

At the Back of the North Wind tells the story of a young boy named Diamond, a sickly child from an impoverished family. The North Wind wants to whistle around his drafty bed at night; he prefers it doesn't. They strike up a friendship, and Diamond travels–"at the back of the North Wind"–far and wide, taking in sights and experiences in a meandering

> MacDonald's books evoke the magic of hidden worlds, portals, and doors; they take for granted a world with princesses, fairy godmothers, and goblins.

story that is weak on plot. But it's also a beautiful and heartbreaking tale, especially as it eventually becomes clear that the North Wind is a metaphor for death.

The Princess and the Goblin is a somewhat easier tale to digest. The titular princess, Irene, one day climbs up a mysterious staircase, and in true fairy-tale fashion, finds an old woman spinning yarn at a wheel–whom apparently only Irene can see. Irene's friend Curdie is working class and a miner's son (though possibly descended from royalty). The miners, with their time spent underground, are particularly well-placed to eavesdrop on goblins, and find out about their evil plans. Together, Irene and Curdie navigate the goblin conspiracy . . . that the adults still deny. In her review on Tor.com, fantasy author Mari Ness writes: "The core of the book–made clear shortly after the goblins reappear–is about faith, about holding to your beliefs when you know you are right, even if others, and especially others who matter to you very much–keep telling you that you are wrong." *The Princess and Curdie* is a follow-up to this book, and focuses primarily on Curdie's adventures as he tries to stop a plague from turning a city of humans into beasts.

These works made a particular impact on C. S. Lewis. Much like George MacDonald, Lewis was a Christian whose spiritual sensibilities deeply informed the sense of awe and reverence for the sublime that infused his work. C. S. Lewis once said that reading *The Princess and the Goblin* made a difference to his "whole existence." Indeed, one of the most extensive Websites on George MacDonald is fatheroftheinklings.com, a reference to the writing and conversation club anchored by Lewis and Tolkien (see pages 26-28). An article on the site has the following to say on MacDonald and C. S. Lewis:

> *Lewis persistently acknowledged his debt to MacDonald, whom he called his 'master.' . . . Both in his autobiography and throughout his writing career, Lewis emphasized that George MacDonald was the most significant impetus in his own spiritual pilgrimage. MacDonald's writings can thus be seen as the spiritual soil out of which the faith of C. S. Lewis emerged.*

Much like C. S. Lewis's famous works, MacDonald's books evoke the magic of hidden worlds, portals, and doors; they take for granted a world with princesses, fairy godmothers, and goblins; they idolize goodness and an appreciation for the sublime.

C. S. Lewis is far from the only famous author to count MacDonald as an influence. Another is Madeleine L'Engle, best known for her beloved novel *A Wrinkle in Time*, recently made into a feature film directed by Ava DuVernay, starring Oprah Winfrey, Mindy Kaling,

Reese Witherspoon, and Chris Pine. In a thoughtful essay on L'Engle for the *Los Angeles Times*, professor and author Jonathan Alexander writes: "MacDonald, like L'Engle, was fond of the concept of mythic time, and he enjoyed detecting and reading eternal verities and spiritual truths in the present mundane world. His influence is evident in *A Wrinkle in Time*, which uses the time and space bending tesseract as a plot device to suggest the interconnectedness of all things across different planets."

Another MacDonald fan: Ursula K. Le Guin, one of our greatest contemporary writers. In an introduction to *The Princess and the Goblin*, published by Puffin Classics in 2011, Le Guin wrote of MacDonald's "timeless green kingdoms of legend and fantasy": "We learn about those kingdoms early. Our guides are the authors who began writing stories for children just about the time the timeless green world began to vanish, to become the world of the past—outside time—the country of 'There was once a little princess . . .' George MacDonald was one of the first of those authors."

By writing about working-class children who glimpsed, and grabbed at, the magical, MacDonald shephereded and developed a concept that is now essential to contemporary fantasy—the porous boundaries between worlds and the intrusion of the uncanny into the everyday. We all deserve our journeys to those timeless green worlds. ✦

Celebrated illustrator Ruth Sanderson provided magical new artwork for a 2016 publication of MacDonald's classic fairytale *The Golden Key* (1866).

Robert W. Chambers, Lesser-Known Father of Weird Fiction

CAMILLA: *You, sir, should unmask.*
Stranger: *Indeed?*
CASSILDA: *Indeed it's time. We all have laid aside disguise but you.*
STRANGER: *I wear no mask.*
CAMILLA: *(Terrified, aside to Cassilda.) No mask? No mask!*

–*THE KING IN YELLOW*, ACT 1, SCENE 2

The King in Yellow by Vicente Valentine (a tribute to the creation of Robert W. Chambers).

These lines represent what is perhaps the most terrifying known excerpt of a play that doesn't, technically, exist. This play–*The King in Yellow*–wields a distinct and horrible power: the power to drive its readers insane. Somehow, the beauties or horrors or existential truths contained within its second act are a kind of incantation with the power to haunt or possess. ". . . the writer has cursed the world with this beautiful, stupendous creation, terrible in its simplicity, irresistible in its truth–a world which now trembles before *The King in Yellow*." Once read, it cannot be unread. Governments try to ban it. Friends warn friends. Copies are seized and destroyed. And yet this forbidden fruit is all too tempting: ". . . All felt that human nature could not bear the strain, nor thrive on words in which the essence of purest poison lurked. The very banality and innocence of the first act only allowed the blow to fall afterward with more awful effect."

This play was imagined by Robert W. Chambers (1865-1933). He didn't write it (or at least he didn't publish it). He simply wrote *about* it. In a series of four linked stories, the reader is given glimpses of a world much like our own, except for the fact that a play exists with the power to break the human brain and eventually the world itself. The play is often mentioned only obliquely throughout these stories, yet the horror it represents seems to saturate everything.

In these linked short stories published under the title *The King in Yellow* (1895), Chambers reveals only the barest outlines of the play, excerpted in bits and fragments, and seen in silhouette through the haunted thoughts of those who read it. What emerges is a vision of dim Carcosa, a cursed city that feels stranded outside of space and time, black stars hung above it, the moon rising impossibly against its dark towers. A place called Hastur and the Lake of Hali. A Yellow Sign, rendered as a character in an unknown and alien language, that comes like a badge of corruption and marks its wearer for death. A stranger, who appears to wear a pallid mask–but does he? And the terrifying King in Yellow, who brings destruction, who answers to no one. "It is a fearful thing to fall into the hands of the living God."

One of the first genre authors to be influenced by *The King in Yellow* is also one of its best known: H. P. Lovecraft, who read the work in the late 1920s. His story "The Whisperer in Darkness" includes several references to signifiers such as the Lake of Hali and the Yellow Sign; it's also one of the foundational texts of the Cthulhu Mythos, a shared fictional universe with an ever-expanding pantheon of beings, creatures, and malevolent gods.

Lovecraft was well-known for all the creepy made-up words that pervaded his work, presaged by mythical and vaguely threatening terms from Chambers such as Hastur, Yhtill, Hyades, Aldebaran. Beyond that, Lovecraft perhaps drew inspiration from Chambers's method of keeping the true face of terror lurking just behind the curtain; consider the infamous Lovecraftian move of citing a horror simply too heinous for words to describe. Lovecraft's oeuvre is also threaded with tomes of mystery, arcane volumes, dangerous yet pivotal books: The Book of Azathoth, The Seven Cryptical Books of Hsan, and most enduringly, The Necronomicon. Many authors who worked within the Cthulhu Mythos– Robert Bloch, August Derleth, Lin Carter, Ramsey Campbell, Clark Ashton Smith, and others–added their own occult volumes and powerful grimoires to the pile.

But aside from specific references, the underlying assumptions of *The King in Yellow* form a major aspect of what's become weird fiction . . . the idea that the universe, beneath its mundane mask, is bizarre, terrifying, and impossible to really see without losing your mind. That's what's so poisonous about the play at the center of it all. It reveals things. It simply tells the truth. And those truths, once grasped, cannot be forgotten . . . nor can they be survived.

As an early forerunner of weird fiction, these four short stories by Chambers have inspired many of our favorite writers of genre, and not just science fiction and fantasy, but also mystery and horror. Chambers's admirers included Raymond Chandler, Robert Heinlein, Stephen King, Neil Gaiman, George R. R. Martin, Alan Moore, and Charles Stross (not to mention Nic Pizzolatto, *True Detective* producer and script writer; we'll get to that in a minute).

Many have wondered–just what is the secret of Carcosa? What mysteries are revealed in the second act of the play that remain so awful to contemplate?

Whatever's lurking in the darkness is infinitely worse in our own imaginations, so to attempt a real-life version of the cursed play is very daring indeed. James Blish (1921-1975), however, once attempted to take on the challenge in his story "More Light" (1970). Blish was a very, very good writer, one of the few writers who might pull this off, so we'll forgive him the imposition. Appropriately enough, the story appeared in print only twice and is somewhat difficult to find.

"More Light" draws on a lightweight frame story. The narrator, a fiction author, meets with an old friend named Bill Atheling, a reviewer with a "mean streak" whom he's "never trusted"; "But perhaps for the same reason, I also rather like him." This opening is a little inside joke of Blish's, as Bill Atheling was actually his own pseudonym that he used to publish literary criticism. (It also poses some interesting questions, since Atheling–himself–is the one who supplies him with the forbidden script.) Atheling is a mess. He invites the narrator to his house and relates to him the story of how he came to own the script . . . a boyhood correspondence with an aging Lovecraft, who upon his inquiries, sent him the play, which he said that Chambers had once sent to him. For various reasons, decades went by and Atheling never got around to reading the play, until just recently. There's an obstacle, though. There is something about the play that prevents the reader from finishing it. At some point, and that point varies for each person, the reader simply can't go on. Piqued by the challenge, the narrator agrees to stay over that night and give it a go.

The rest of the story is mostly devoted to the play itself, with various breaks as he considers the play and its effects on him, or lack thereof. We read with him. Blish reverse-engineered the play from the brief fragments and glancing hints revealed within Chamber's story, and the effect is, indeed, extremely creepy. The flow is purposely stilted and disjointed. Piece by piece it reveals a decaying royal family in a place outside of time, locked in an eternal stalemate of tedious incest and unchanging war. Slowly there accrues a calm yet suffocating sense of dread.

> STRANGER: *Carcosa does not sit upon the Earth.*
> *It is, perhaps, not even real; or not so real*
> *As you and I. Certainly, the Living God does not*
> *Believe in it. Then why should you?*

Wisely, Blish also spares his reader the closing lines of the play, because the narrator finds that he is not capable of finishing it, either. So the final secret remains shrouded in mystery.

My own theory is this: The horrible truth revealed in *The King in Yellow* is indisputable evidence that forces the reader to acknowledge what, on some level, we've known all along–that we have always been in Carcosa, the city that takes on the size and shape of a hostile universe; and the fact that the world itself is a garish mask.

The King in Yellow reached its largest audience yet in 2014, when Nic Pizzolatto drew on its unsettling mythology in the phenomenal first season of *True Detective*. In this installment, Louisiana detectives Rust Cohle (Matthew McConaughey) and Marty Hart (Woody Harrelson) investigate the occult murder of a young woman that reveals a much deeper conspiracy. *The King in Yellow* doesn't quite hold the key to this conspiracy; it runs in parallel with it. These references to something deep, dark, and ancient inform the threatening, despairing atmosphere of the show's Louisiana bayou setting. The Carcosa mythology is referenced by both victims and killers. "I closed my eyes and saw the King in Yellow moving through the forest," says the first victim's journal. "The King's children are marked. They became his angels." Further unexplained references abound: black stars tattooed on a girl's neck, and a flock of birds forming in the ominous spiral the show imagines as the Yellow Sign.

Meanwhile, the frequently spouted nihilist philosophy of Detective Cohle (who would be right at home in his own Cthulhu mythos story) provides a glimpse of a mind suffering deeply under the weight of its own indisputable truths: His intimate knowledge of life-changing loss and grief, coupled with his understanding that in the grand scheme of everything, life and death are just something that happens; the universe is indifferent to either. Perhaps that was the truth revealed by *The King in Yellow* all along. ✦

In the final scenes of *True Detective*'s season one finale, few answers are provided, but Cohle comes face-to-face with his own vision of Carcosa and the swirling dark between the stars.

The Inklings:
A Friendship That Changed
Fantastic Literature Forever

Some friendships begin the moment two like minds meet—a connection is made, sparks fly, and a kinship begins. This was not the case for C. S. Lewis (1898-1963) and J.R.R. Tolkien (1892-1973), who first met as faculty at Oxford University in 1926, and were not particularly impressed by each other. Lewis wrote in his diary of Tolkien: "No harm in him: only needs a smack or so."

Fortunately, first impressions were not final. They discovered they had plenty of interests in common, and began getting together for a beer every Monday morning and discussing politics, poetry, theology, and myth. "This is one of the pleasantest spots in the week," Lewis wrote. They eventually became close friends.

This friendship became the core of a local clique of contemporary thinkers made up of writers, painters, doctors, and academics. Lewis's brother Warren, or "Warnie," became a frequent member, and later, Lewis's son Christopher. The group eventually grew to nineteen, but four writers remained its core members. Along with Lewis and Tolkien, they were Charles Williams and Owen Barfield. They called themselves the Inklings: a whimsical and slightly self-deprecating pun.

The Inklings congregated frequently at Lewis's apartment, as well as at a nearby pub called the Eagle and Child, but was referred to by regulars as "the Bird and Baby." They smoked, drank beer, and argued about everything under the sun. Critic and writer Michael Dirda noted, "One evening's conversation, according to Lewis's brother Warnie, touched on 'red-brick universities . . . torture, Tertullian, bores, the contractual theory of medieval kingship, and odd place-names.'"

Most importantly, the Inklings read their manuscripts aloud to the group for comment and critique. "Listening to drafts and offering energetic feedback occupied the better part of every Inklings meeting," writes Lewis scholar Diana Glyer. "As they met through the 1930s and '40s, extraordinary things began to happen. They generated enormous creative energy. . . . Together, they helped bring to light some of the greatest literary works of this past century."

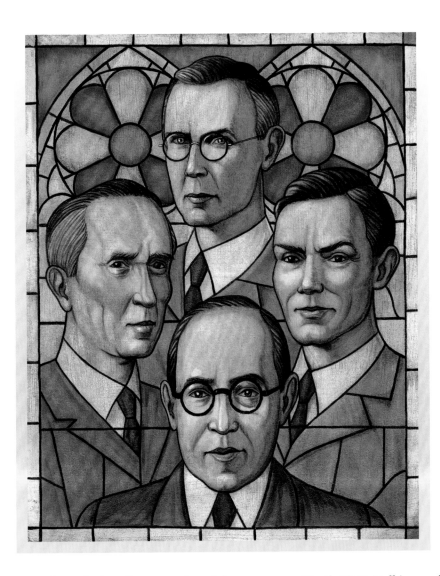

These works include, of course, the mighty oeuvres of both J.R.R. Tolkien and C. S. Lewis. Their books have sold more than three hundred million copies and been translated into forty-plus languages around the world. Films based on *The Chronicles of Narnia, The Hobbit,* and *The Lord of the Rings* have earned billions of dollars. But beyond that, the work of these two essential fantasists shaped the entire field of fantasy for generations. "Without the Inklings there would be no *Dungeons & Dragons* (and the whole universe of online fantasy role-playing it produced), no Harry Potter, no Philip Pullman (in his role as the anti-Lewis)," wrote Philip Zaleski and Carol Zaleski, the authoritative Inklings scholars.

The Inklings by Marc Burckhardt for the *Atlantic.* Clockwise from top: Charles Williams, Owen Barfield, C. S. Lewis, and J. R. R. Tolkien.

We can also add to that list Lev Grossman's Magicians trilogy, which directly engages the idea of Narnia and the portal fantasy, as well as the SyFy television series that the books inspired.

Did Tolkien and Lewis influence each other's work? The writers themselves did not think so. They drew from the same well of interests, influences and inspirations–the foundation of their friendship in the first place–but their work remained very different.

Tolkien wrote of Lewis, "The unpayable debt that I owe to [Lewis] was not 'influence' as it is ordinarily understood but sheer encouragement. He was for long my only audience."

Lewis shared this view. "I don't think Tolkien influenced me, and I am certain I didn't influence him," he wrote. "That is, didn't influence what he wrote. My continual encouragement, carried to the point of nagging, influenced him very much to write at all with that gravity and at that length." They shared most of their work with each other and exchanged manuscripts in progress, cheering and supporting each other through the creation of the famous works we love today.

Of course, all four of the core writers in the Inklings–and the group as a whole–influenced and inspired one another in their avid and voracious exploration of a dozen different disciplines. In the *Los Angeles Times*, fantasy novelist Elizabeth Hand wrote of Williams and Barfield that they were "minor writers who nonetheless had considerable influence on their friends, especially Lewis, a literary magpie who made liberal use of images and ideas from the other Inklings in his work."

Though nowhere near as successful as Lewis and Tolkien, Williams and Barfield were also relatively influential in their day. Williams wrote poetry, plays, literary scholarship, and spiritual thrillers. Barfield wrote a well-received children's fantasy, *The Silver Trumpet*, as well as significant books on language and linguistics. He later taught in the United States, including at Brandeis, where he became a friend to the American literary figure Saul Bellow, another intriguing ripple in the pond of literary history.

Zaleski and Zaleski impressively describe the broad and massive reach of the Inklings' influence: "By the time the last Inkling passed away, on the eve of the 21st century, the group had altered, in large or small measure, the course of imaginative literature (fantasy, allegory, mythopoeic tales), Christian theology and philosophy, comparative mythology, and the scholarly study of the *Beowulf* author, of Dante, Spenser, Milton, courtly love, fairy tale, and epic." ✦

The iconic Eagle and Child continues to operate today, serving up drinks and pub food along with a hearty helping of history.

Henry Dumas's Foundational Afrofuturism

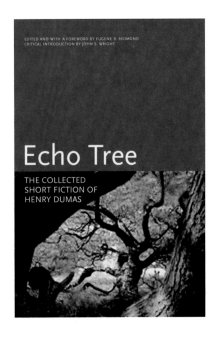

I magine that you're in a lush, green rural space. The sky is full of billowing clouds and the air is sweet. You are listening to the life of the forest and the song of the lake nearby. Suddenly, to your awe and dismay, you witness a giant sailing ship wafting in from that once peaceful sky; its masts strutting like trees into the air.

The ship's massive sails block out the sun. What mysteries would such a vessel have in its hold? In this case, if you had the courage to venture below decks, you'd find millions of bones stacked neatly and carefully catalogued. This ship carries all of the bones of the slaves who died in the Middle Passage and finally made it to the shores of America to collect the rest. These bones resonate with the trauma, pain, and diabolical legacy of chattel slavery in our country. It's a legacy that still haunts our country to this day.

This narrative is the plot of the short story by Henry Dumas (1934-1968) called "Ark of Bones." It is just one tale told by this tragically unsung genius.

Born in Sweet Home, Arkansas, Dumas was a prolific poet and short story writer, political activist, educator, and one of the foundational creators in what would later be called Afrofuturism. Dumas was a powerful contributor to the Black Arts Movement; the sister aesthetic movement to the Black Power Movement.

Dumas's writing fused the hope and pain of the southern American black experience with the promise and broken dreams of the urban landscape. He used the metaphorical affordances of the speculative to unpack the tensions of being black in America, the peculiar tragedies beset upon black citizens by systemic oppression, and the sometimes magical joys of simply surviving to tell the tale.

Dumas's stories showcased allegorical aspects like a little boy witnessing God and the Devil play a card game for his grandfather's soul, a mystical tree that houses ancestral spirits, and a magical horn that has dire consequences for particular people who hear it. His poetry vibrated with the voices of the age and was heartbreakingly moving. Each of his carefully crafted short stories were soaked in the sorrow and excitement of the era.

Dumas taught at Southern Illinois University with the poet Eugene Redmond. The two would become close friends and collaborators. This friendship is what would make Dumas an immortally tragic figure in literature. Dumas was also a close friend of the experimental Afrofuturist jazz musician Sun Ra. Dumas was in Harlem in May of 1968, coming from one of Sun Ra's rehearsals. On his journey back to his space he unfortunately had an argument with a police officer that ended with his death. He was thirty-three years old. Dumas's work was posthumously edited and shepherded by his friend Eugene Redmond and the amazing Toni Morrison.

Morrison cites Dumas as one her influences and has called him an "absolute genius."

Unfortunately, his work has yet to reach a larger audience.

As of now, I can imagine his specter guiding that wondrous and terrible magical ark, picking up the pieces of history to show us when we are truly ready to see. ✦

Dumas used the metaphorical affordances of the speculative to unpack the tensions of being black in America . . . and the sometimes magical joys of simply surviving to tell the tale.

The Author of the Narnia Books Worked on a Mega-Creepy Time Travel Story . . . Probably

C. S. Lewis is the author of *The Chronicles of Narnia* and iconic characters like the cruel White Witch, the noble lion Aslan, and the pessimistic marshwiggle Puddleglum. Lewis also wrote science fictions for adults: *Out of the Silent Planet*, *Perelandra*, and *That Hideous Strength*. Though less popular than the Narnia books, this Space Trilogy still received substantial acclaim.

When an incomplete manuscript of a time-travel novel surfaced in 1966–three years after Lewis's death–fans were ecstatic. A story about inter-dimensional time travel, created by one of the most imaginative minds of the twentieth century?! Yes, please. The unfinished story, titled "The Dark Tower," was published in a 1977 collection by the same name, assembled by Lewis's literary executor, Walter Hooper.

Though obviously not as polished a published work, "The Dark Tower" still possesses plenty of raw appeal; it's an uncanny and compelling read that seizes attention from the very beginning. The story centers on a group of academics performing experiments with a "chronoscope" that its inventor believes allows them to see to other times–whether past or future, they aren't sure. The world they observe is geographically similar yet also utterly alien, frequently terrifying and grotesque, ruled by a "Stinging Man" with a poisoned horn to slay his sacrificial victims. The professors begin to believe they're looking not at a future or a past, but an alternate reality.

During one of these viewing sessions, as the scholars watch–equally entranced and horrified–a mishap occurs and the inventor's assistant, Scudamour, is actually drawn into that other world, which they've taken to calling "the Othertime." As he navigates this bizarre reality, he learns about a society with far more advanced time-science than our own, a theory of time that flows "eckwards" and "andwards" as well as backward and forward, and features parallel and perpendicular timelines that occasionally touch.

Then–right as the story is really picking up steam–it ends. Right in the middle of a scene. And even though I knew I was reading an incomplete manuscript, I felt disappointed and frustrated . . . maybe even a little cheated. Like every C. S. Lewis fan,

I wanted that story! As *Kirkus Reviews* commented on the collection, "the groundwork of the plot is laid out with such confidence that one wonders how Lewis could have borne not to finish it."

But . . . there's more. The plot thickens, because the drama surrounding the story may be even more intriguing than the story itself.

Hooper claimed to have discovered this unfinished manuscript and several others in 1964, when he rescued it from a pile of Lewis's old papers that Lewis's brother was about to burn as he tidied up the Lewis estate. All was well until 1978, when Kathryn Lindskoog, a prominent C. S. Lewis scholar, dramatically accused Hooper of fabricating the manuscript for his own personal gain. The explosive accusations ripped

C. S. Lewis fandom apart. For years a bitter and acrimonious battle of words raged among Lindskoog, Hooper, and their various supporters. Journalist Jim Washburn wrote in the *Los Angeles Times*, "Given the way the Lewis community has responded to her book, one would think that Lindskoog had been guilty of letting flies into heaven. . . . At times the exchanges seem less like a scholarly debate than a playground brawl."

Lindskoog's evidence for the accusation was wide-ranging. She pointed to the extreme control that Hooper had exerted over Lewis's estate and his tendency to make editorial decisions that contradicted Lewis's living preferences as well as the wishes of Lewis's brother. She insisted that Hooper's story about rescuing the work from a fire was not believable, nor supported by testimony from the gardener. She also believed that the quality of the writing was simply too poor to be Lewis's, its rough draft status notwithstanding. And, she pointed out some similarities she saw between this text and Madeleine L'Engle's

The Lion, The Witch, and the Wardrobe by C. S. Lewis, illustration by Pauline Baynes. © C. S. Lewis pte. Ltd. 1950. Reprinted by permission.

A Wrinkle in Time, which didn't come out until 1962. (L'Engle and Lewis counted many influences and inspirations in common, including Christian theology and the writings of early fantasist George MacDonald, so a resemblance between their writings is not unexpected.)

According to Lindskoog, through Hooper's desire to completely own Lewis's legend and legacy, he'd begun to blend Lewis's identity with his own, even studying Lewis's handwriting and replicating it to forge manuscripts, "The Dark Tower" being just one of these.

Some scholars sided with Lindskoog, agreeing that Hooper's possessive behavior surrounding the Lewis estate was suspicious. Others thought her claims lacked any concrete evidence.

So much time had passed since Lewis had ostensibly drafted the manuscript that contemporary recollections from his peers were patchy. However, several of Lewis's friends said they did remember hearing Lewis read passages from the work in progress. Most significantly, Lewis's former student Alastair Fowler recalled the horrifying "Stinging Man" character from a work in progress that Lewis shared with him in 1952. Still, as Fowler conveyed these memories in 2003–a full fifty years later–some still found their veracity open to question.

Lindskoog remained unconvinced, and furthering her accusations against Hooper became a major focus of her scholarship and career. She wrote and published three books expanding on these allegations: *The C. S. Lewis Hoax* (1988), *Light in the Shadowlands: Protecting the Real C. S. Lewis* (1994), and *Sleuthing C. S. Lewis: More Light in the Shadowlands* (2001). For some, her fervor in pursuing the argument began to undermine her credibility on the topic. Still, the discussion remains fascinating to follow–both for the critic-on-critic drama and the issues of authorship, authenticity, and legacy.

Lindskoog passed away in 2003. Today, most Lewis scholars tend to believe that "The Dark Tower" is, in fact, an authentic C. S. Lewis manuscript, both because of the distinctive handwriting on the original manuscript and the recollections of Lewis's contemporaries. As academic Sanford Schwartz wrote in his 2009 book *C. S. Lewis on the Final Frontier: Science and the Supernatural in the Space Trilogy*, "Lindskoog's case was compelling enough to have kept the controversy alive, but most scholars who have seen the manuscript regard it as genuine, and after the recent testimony of Lewis's student, Alastair Fowler, the burden of proof is increasingly on those who question its authenticity."

Thus, the controversy has settled. But alas, the sinister and suspenseful story of the "The Dark Tower" itself remains abandoned mid-sentence, forever unresolved. ✦

[FOLLOWING SPREAD] In the parallel dimension of the Othertime, the White Riders arrive to storm the sinister Dark Tower. Original illustration by Jordan Grimmer, 2018.

The Weird World of
Mervyn Peake's *Gormenghast*

T he brilliant Gormenghast trilogy has been deeply influential on every speculative
fiction writer to encounter it, but perhaps due to its dense, surreal, and cerebral
nature, it remains a work primarily read by writers and neglected by fans.

Titus Groan (1946), *Gormenghast* (1950), and *Titus Alone* (1959) were authored by Mervyn
Peake (1911-1968), an English writer and illus-
trator. He was born in China to missionary
parents and spent much of his childhood in
what's now known as the Lushan District,
Jiangxi, China. His youthful cross-cultural
experiences deeply influenced his work, as did
the class-conscious novels of Charles Dickens
and the swashbuckling adventure stories of
Robert Louis Stevenson. (Incidentally, Peake
also illustrated a 1949 edition of *Treasure
Island*, Stevenson's best-known work.)

Peake's art school education, his dedicated study of famous artists and illustrators
from Albrecht Dürer to Francisco de Goya,
and his own talent as an illustrator undoubtedly shaped the highly visual and evocative
nature of his work. Even more significantly,
his role as a war correspondent and artist,
depicting the later events of World War II
for civilians back home, exposed him to the

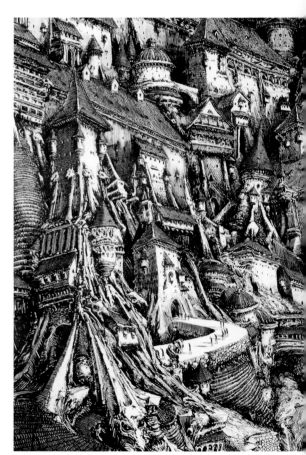

Gormenghast I by Ian Miller (b. 1946). Miller
is a British fantasy illustrator who brings a
wonderfully macabre yet playful aesthetic to
his work.

unbearable excesses of both human cruelty and human suffering. He traveled as a reporter to cities devastated by the war, a former concentration cramp, and a trial for war crimes. The trauma of witnessing these evils permanently infiltrated his work.

In a letter to his wife back home, Peake wrote of Germany's Cologne Cathedral, surrounded by destruction:

> *It is incredible how the cathedral has remained, lifting itself high into the air so gloriously, while around it the city lies broken to pieces, and in the city I smelt for the first time in my life the sweet, pungent, musty smell of death. . . . But the cathedral arises like a dream—something quite new to me as an experience—a tall poem of stone with sudden, inspired flair of the lyric and yet with the staying power, mammoth qualities and abundance of the epic.*

Later, Peake would turn these descriptive powers to Gormenghast Castle, and its gothic and decadent world:

Over their irregular roofs would fall throughout the seasons, the shadows of
time-eaten buttresses, of broken and lofty turrets, and, most enormous of all,
the shadow of the Tower of Flints. This tower, patched unevenly with black ivy,
arose like a mutilated finger from among the fists of knuckled masonry and
pointed blasphemously at heaven. (Titus Groan)

As novelist and playwright John Spurling wrote glowingly in *The Spectator,* "There is surely no other novel in the English language so rich in the sheer visibility of its characters and their movements, as well as of its landscape: endless towers, roofscapes and courtyards, labyrinthine corridors, decaying rooms and furniture, its surrounding environment of mountain, marsh, forest and lake, its weather and seasons, its very atmosphere."

These utterly weird works, presaging science fiction's inventive New Wave by decades (see pages 39-42 for more on New Wave SF), were perhaps too far ahead of their time to find success. The first, published in 1946, came eight years before *The Fellowship of the Ring,* the first novel in J.R.R. Tolkien's much better-known trilogy. Superficially, the Gormenghast novels share some common ground with *Lord of the Rings:* Each is a second-world, mythic fantasy depicting an ancient kingdom and fanciful land, and a royal legacy in disrepair. But where Tolkien is romantic and grandiose, Peake's work is tragic and surreal, a sometimes nightmarish fever-dream.

The Gormenghast books went in and out of print and never really claimed a strong literary foothold. Peake, suffering from early onset dementia that claimed his health and eventually his life, died in 1968 at only fifty-seven. His wife and children continued to advocate for his work, in part to earn money to manage the debts incurred throughout his illness.

In time, the impact of this unparalleled work has became clear. Some of the most interesting and inventive speculative fiction writers working today have paid tribute to Gormenghast's influence on their work, including K. J. Bishop, Neil Gaiman, M. John Harrison, China Miéville, and Jeff VanderMeer. Gene Wolfe's brilliant *Book of the New Sun* seems to draw on Peake's influence as well. Michael Moorcock, himself a massively influential figure in the genre through his work as editor of *New Worlds* magazine, readily acknowledged his novel *Gloriana*'s debt to Gormenghast—he even dedicated the book to Peake's memory. It seems that the Gormenghast trilogy laid the groundwork for the New Wave and later the New Weird—a shocking achievement for work that remains all too obscure. ✦

> These utterly weird works, presaging science fiction's inventive New Wave by decades, were perhaps too far ahead of their time to find success.

The New Wave and New-Metal Men: The Almost-Forgotten Brilliance of David R. Bunch

T he 1940s and 1950s were excellent years for science fiction, often referred to as its Golden Age; in the lull of postwar prosperity, the dominant voice of the American public tended toward optimism–about the promises of technology, the wonders of the future, the galactic call of American destiny. Science fiction reflected these visions.

But as the dreams of science fiction began to be realized–Man actually set foot upon the Moon!–and the sweeping social changes of the 1960s set in, both readers and writers grew discontented with science fiction's same old stories. In the *Encyclopedia of Science Fiction*, literary critic Peter Nicholls writes, "Traditional Genre SF had reached a crisis point . . . both the style and content of SF were becoming generally overpredictable. Many young writers entering the field came to feel . . . that genre SF had become a straitjacket; though widely supposed to emphasize change and newness, SF had somehow become conservative."

A different kind of science fiction began to emerge, one that expressed the mindset and the milieu of 1960s and 1970s counterculture. In a significant, almost scandalous, break with the science fiction of simpler times, these stories contained plentiful amounts of drugs, sex, and rock 'n' roll, set against the backdrop of a darker and more dystopian world. These New Wave authors, as they came to be called, also aspired to more ambitious literary heights than their predecessors. Their stories drew on experimental and postmodern techniques like stream of consciousness, fragmented narratives, meta-narratives, and other ways of playing with language.

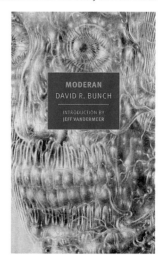

This revolution produced a surge of inventive and innovative work: bolder, more daring and literary than its forebears in the field. The new aesthetic was solidified between 1964 and 1971 in the pages of *New Worlds* magazine, mostly under the editorial guidance of the legendary Michael Moorcock, and celebrated in Harlan Ellison's two seminal anthologies,

Dangerous Visions (1967) and *Again, Dangerous Visions* (1972). A number of these stories are still recognized as some of the greatest ever written in the genre–think Samuel R. Delany's "Aye, and Gomorrah," Joanna Russ's "When It Changed," Ursula K. Le Guin's "The Word for World Is Forest." Brian Aldiss, J.G. Ballard, Thomas M. Disch, and Roger Zelazny were also associated with the New Wave.

Yet, conversely, some of the most exceptional of this New Wave work–a prolific output of short stories by David R. Bunch (1925-2000)–has received very little notice in the decades since.

Bunch was the only contributor to appear twice in *Dangerous Visions*. At the time, Ellison called him "possibly the most dangerous visionary of all those assembled here" (rivaling Philip K. Dick, J. G. Ballard, and Samuel R. Delany) and also wrote that Bunch had, "oddly enough, barely received the acclaim due to him." Unfortunately, this state of affairs continued. Bunch's stories rapidly fell out of the print. Writing in 2014, Ted Gioia–who runs an ambitious and comprehensive Website dedicated to Conceptual Fiction–said Bunch "may be the best kept secret in New Wave sci-fi."

But, with a new and expanded collection just released in 2018 by the *New York Review of Books*, Bunch is back in print for the first time in decades, finally giving a new generation of SFF fans the opportunity to read and enjoy his work. And despite being primarily written in the 1960s, Bunch's stories of the cybernetic world of Moderan feel shockingly current and unsettlingly timely. *Kirkus* reviews the new collection: "Almost a half-century after these stories were originally released, the thematic power of Bunch's vision still resonates, the narrative equivalent of a new-metal alloy punch to the gut."

The stories in this collection are loosely connected and vaguely chronological. Many of them center on the same character, Stronghold #10–a New-Metal Man who is nearly entirely mechanical, but for a few pesky "flesh-strips." He shares his name with the impenetrable fort he rules and commands, from which he makes war. He is by turns regretful and triumphant, anxious and boasting, because while his cyborg condition has freed him from the threat of physical mortality, it has not removed his humanly mortal fears. He receives a variety of visitors–some from Moderan, although not of his elevated stature–and others from the lands beyond, where "flesh people" still eke out some kind of meager existence in a permanently toxic world.

The world of Moderan is simultaneously sadistic and masochistic, violent and bleak; its culture represents the ultimate endgame of toxic masculinity and zero-sum power games. The most repugnant traits in this world are those of compassion and mercy. In Moderan, the military-industrial complex is taken to its final conclusion, with life lived in service of never-ending war at every level–between sexes, between nations, between neighbors, an all-out rush to the last man standing. So too is ecological indifference extended to its breaking point; the ecosystem has been rendered as synthetic as the people who inhabit it. The earth is encased in a layer of plastic, poked through with holes so the metal flowers can bloom, while the metal birds wheel overhead. The artificial sky can be any color of the rainbow. The seasons are programmed.

Original illustration by Jeremy Zarfoss.

Yet despite the unmitigated horror of the world portrayed, Bunch deploys a lighthearted, almost jocular tone, lyrical in the gonzo, singsong way of future-forward 1960s admen. The primary narrator's cheerful pragmatism about very ugly things brings to mind the inspired satirical dialogue of a George Saunders short story. At times the language verges on invented; not only through the invented words and odd neologisms, though there are those, but also in the awkwardly self-conscious syntax of a metal death monster who was once a man.

In his foreword to the new edition, Jeff VanderMeer posits that "this clash between subject and style" is intentional, provoking in the reader a special kind of unease. "To relax would be to normalize the future the stories depict, to accept foundational assumptions that no one should accept, even as we as a society have accepted so much that is bizarre and unhealthy."

Moderan is often compared to Anthony Burgess's *A Clockwork Orange,* another 1960s work that vividly portrays a violent future as a means to condemn it, and experiments with language as a form of worldbuilding. "Like Burgess," writes Gioia, "Bunch realized that the conceptualization of a different kind of society ideally involves the creation of a different kind of language, a new body of speech patterns. . . . [Bunch's] futuristic metal men sometimes remind me of medieval chroniclers in their language, at other times their words resemble the belligerent taunting of skinheads at a British football match right before the rioting and hooliganism get out of control."

While the language is transcendent, it's fair to say the collection, as a group of linked short stories, suffers a bit from a lack of overarching narrative. There is an eventual arc, but it's the kind that emerges over seasons of a highly episodic television show. Most of the stories are quite short, and some begin to feel a little repetitive. There is a static quality to immortality, after all. Moderan is best experienced as it was written, and published–dipping in and out in fragments, a few chapters at a time, the better to savor each page.

What's indisputable is that there has never been anything quite like these stories. They are so unusual it's hard to even find the right comparisons. In the *Los Angeles Review of Books*, senior editor Rob Latham speculates that Bunch may have found inspiration in the work of the Beat poets–particularly Jack Kerouac and Allen Ginsberg. Kerouac's work, Latham writes, "in its rambling prosody, its spastic goofing, wise-ass parody of techno-cratic jargon . . . offers something of a stylistic model for Bunch's febrile speculations." In the *Encyclopedia of Science Fiction*, esteemed SFF writer and critic John Clute compares Bunch's best work to R. A. Lafferty "at *his* best, though it is far more exclamatory, and rhetorically pixilated, than Lafferty's work." Bunch, he says, "resembles a diced, gonzo Walt Whitman, sampling (in a frenzy) the body electric." VanderMeer calls the Moderan stories "a seamless meld of the eccentric poetics of E. E. Cummings, the genius level invention of Philip K. Dick, and the body horror of Clive Barker."

The variety–and yet inadequacy–of these comparisons suggest that Bunch may be that rare specimen . . . a writer without peers. You simply must experience his work for yourself. ✦

The Continuous
Katherine Mortenhoe

T hough his writing appeared in the same era as J. G. Ballard and Philip K. Dick, and in some ways explored similar themes, D. G. Compton (b. 1930) has been much less widely known and admiringly read. This oversight should be rectified immediately. Compton's 1974 novel *The Continuous Katherine Mortenhoe* is strikingly ahead of its time, both in its prophetic depiction of a society corrupted by its addiction to voyeurism, and its sensitive, sophisticated portrayal of a complex female character who is simply allowed to be herself.

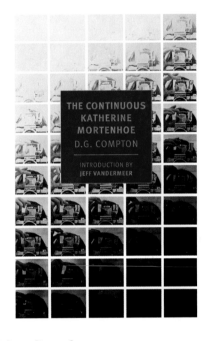

In a future where death by illness has been all but defeated, almost no one dies from anything except old age. Disease is such a rare calamity that it's viewed with a sense of hungry ownership by the media-addled, "pain-starved" public. This is the same contemptuous entitlement to other people's stories—and other people's pain—that today supports an entire wing of the reality television industry; the same impulse that drives social media mobs.

The story begins when Katherine Mortenhoe is informed by her doctor that she's suffering from an incurable disease, a degenerative condition caused by her brain's inability to properly filter outside stimuli. The symptoms include rigor, paralysis, coordination loss, sweating, double vision, incontinence, and eventually death.

Katherine is an independent, self-sufficient woman with a complex inner life. (She works as a programmer of romance novels, which means adjusting and overseeing the algorithms the computer uses to generate a never-ending supply of fresh stories.) She accepts her fate with a mixture of bafflement, disappointment, and resigned dignity. What she can't accept is the public's feeling of entitlement to her story, or the media moguls' confidence they should be allowed to create a melodramatic spectacle out of her death. From the moment of her diagnosis they hound her mercilessly to sign the release forms that will allow them to begin broadcasting her decline.

But the producers also have an ace up their sleeve. Their inside man, Rod, has undergone a new and experimental operation that has transformed his optic nerves into cameras. He's recording 24/7, broadcasting everything to his handlers–a decidedly cyberpunk body modification, appearing well before its time. As Katherine goes on the run from her rapacious public, Rod is with her all the way, posing as a friend–while unbeknownst to her, the show goes on.

Structurally, the novel alternates between their two points of view. Despite his unforgivable purpose, Rod becomes an increasingly sympathetic character, pressed into this ugly task by both his bosses and the baser parts of his own nature. He is weak in a way that Katherine isn't. Simply by pursuing a career in these broken times, he's become a tool of the everyday dystopia, while she steadfastly holds herself against it, even as this sense of "outrage" (as the doctor describes it) becomes the feedback mechanism that tears her down.

As Katherine attempts to savor the last days of her existence, a bond forms between them. There is something so naked and honest about this natural bond of friendship, two lost people grasping at the threads of their humanity. For a novel about a woman with only four weeks to live, this story is surprisingly joyful, finding in the end a note of bittersweet grace.

The novel is undoubtedly a critique of a media machine that destroys human dignity for fleeting entertainment, but it's also more than that. As speculative fiction author Lisa Tuttle writes in her introduction to the SF Masterworks edition (2012), "Compton's real interest here is not issues of privacy, or the future of the media, or whether watching TV is bad for you . . . but rather with the eternal question of how we are to live, how to be true to ourselves, whatever happens." Along similar lines, Jeff VanderMeer writes, "At its heart . . . Compton's book is about two essential predicaments of the human condition: mortality and love." And *GQ's* Kevin Nguyen comments, "It also reads like something written today, which is impressive for something written yesterday about tomorrow."

The Continuous Katherine Mortenhoe is a subtle and lovely novel, occasionally funny, often tense, written in spare but potent prose that provides a quietly factual account of the world as it almost is. It's a masterful work of science fiction whose time for acclaim has come. ✦

Harlan Ellison's
Legendary Lost Anthology

M uch as Jodorowsky's *Dune* holds the uncontested and incontestable title of the greatest movie never made, a similar artifact reigns supreme in the literary world. The saga of *The Last Dangerous Visions*—an anthology so magnificent it could never be made—reached its final chapter on June 27, 2018, with the passing of its erstwhile editor, Harlan Ellison. The cautionary tale lives on.

Ellison was a supremely talented writer whose massive contribution to the genre is indisputable. Primarily a short fiction writer, his best-known works include the classic shorts "I Have No Mouth, and I Must Scream" and "Jeffty is Five"; the novella "A Boy and His Dog" (the basis for the 1975 film); and the *Star Trek* episode "The City on the Edge of Forever." His accolades include eight Hugo Awards, four Nebula Awards, and two World Fantasy Awards.

Equally influential was his work as an editor and anthologist. His groundbreaking anthology *Dangerous Visions* (1967) delivered a knockout punch to the genre's stuffy preconceptions, with a New Wave-defining assortment of brilliant stories by all-time greats such as Brian Aldiss, Philip K. Dick, Carol Emshwiller, Theodore Sturgeon, J. G. Ballard, and Samuel R. Delany. In 2002, fantasy writer and *New Worlds* editor Michael Moorcock observed in a foreword to the anthology's newest edition, "Single-handedly [Ellison] produced a new benchmark, demanding that in future nothing *anyone* of any ambition did should fall below that mark. He did what we had, as visionaries, wanted to do. He changed our world forever."

In 1972, Ellison followed up the first anthology with an equally well-received installment, titled *Again, Dangerous Visions*, released in two

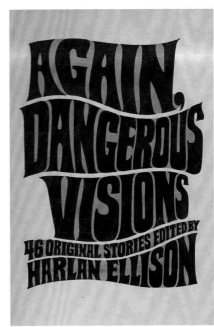

volumes. Part of the conceit for this follow-up anthology was that no authors included in the first would be invited to contribute to the second, thus exploring the cutting edge of the genre in greater breadth. The result is another breathtaking collection of stories: The assembled authors include Gene Wolfe, Thomas M. Disch, M. John Harrison, and James Tiptree Jr. The collection also included Ursula K. Le Guin and Joanna Russ, with their award-winning classics "The Word for World is Forest" and "When It Changed."

Having laid such a lofty foundation, Ellison was determined to follow up with the anthology to end all anthologies. When *Again, Dangerous Visions* was released in 1972, Ellison was already promising a third installment to be called *The Last Dangerous Visions*, to be published in 1974. In fact, it would never be published, but Ellison continued to promise this incredible anthology for at least another decade.

The history of the project was charted in extensive detail via the dedicated journalistic efforts of writer Christopher Priest, who published his report first as a fanzine titled "The Last Deadloss Visions" (1987) and later as a chapbook titled *The Book on the Edge of Forever* (1994), a play on the title of Ellison's own famous *Star Trek* episode. For a lengthy report on bombastic correspondences, failed deadlines, and broken promises, Priest's pamphlet offers surprisingly entertaining reading. Even more entertainingly, it was nominated for a Hugo in the nonfiction category (an interesting parallel with *Jodorowsky's Dune*, both the subject and title of an award-winning documentary).

In 1973, Ellison announced a table of contents for *TLDV* that included sixty-eight stories. He promised the book would be out soon—as soon as he wrote the 60,000 words of accompanying introductions. Perhaps penning those 60,000 words proved more onerous than expected, and the timeline dragged on, and in the meantime he acquired several more stories, announcing an expanded table of contents in 1974. Priest writes, "Assuming that the non-fiction matter still amounted to 110,000 words, the book has now reached over 600,000 words in prospect: equivalent to seven and a half normal-length novels."

In mid-1974, Priest became personally involved in the project, as Ellison solicited a contribution from him with the persuasive words, "It would be a terrible omission were there not to be a story by you in this landmark trilogy, now being taught in over 200 colleges and universities." Priest later learned that an almost identical letter had been sent to a colleague, whose work Ellison also termed "*sui generis*," or "one of a kind."

Obviously, Ellison was still buying stories for the anthology. In 1976, he announced a change in publishers and a table of contents that now included more than one hundred stories . . . about sixteen novels' worth.

TLDV had become a kind of black hole, voraciously sucking in the best stories of the decade, never to release them, while growing ever more lumbering and unwieldy. In 1979, the anthology again changed publishers, and now numbered three volumes and 110 stories. In June of that year, *Locus* published what has become *TLDV*'s most complete and definitive table of contents; it can easily be found today in various online sources, offering a story-by-story breakdown of the project's proposed 700,000 words.

To this day, many of the stories Ellison purchased have never been published, and likely never will—a true loss to the genre, considering they once represented the best work of the era's best writers. One author wrote in 1983, "Another way not to write is to sell a story to Harlan Ellison and wait for it to be published in [*TLDV*]."

To this day, many of the stories Ellison purchased have never been published, and likely never will—a true loss to the genre, considering they once represented the best work of the era's best writers. One author wrote in 1983, "Another way not to write is to sell a story to Harlan Ellison and wait for it to be published in [*TLDV*]. . . . I heard the book will be out real soon now. It's only thirteen years later, so I really shouldn't complain. You don't hear me complaining, do you?"

This state of affairs was allowed to continue for so long because many authors were in fact afraid of Ellison. He was known as a mercurial, volatile, and occasionally violent person, who usually managed to get his way via a combination of flattery, bribery, pleading, and threats, along with a penchant for lawsuits. "Fear of reprisal from Harlan Ellison is a very real phenomenon," wrote Priest, and later editions of his report included letters he received from *TLDV* contributors attesting to this claim. One remarked pithily: "I hope you're still alive when you receive this. I don't think it's likely that Ellison has hired a gunman, but if you're dead when you get this, or soon after, that will establish how little I've learned about Ellison over the years."

To his dubious credit, Ellison never gave up on *TLDV*. In a 1995 magazine column, David Langford wrote, "I talked to Harlan Ellison myself last year, and he managed to sound genuinely hurt and surprised that, despite minor delays since 1972, anyone could doubt that *TLDV* would soon appear. We must have faith." In 2007, Ellison remarked in an interview with *Newsarama*, "For . . . my piece of mind, and to have people stop sniping at me, of course, I'd like to get *The Last Dangerous Visions* out of here. It's this giant Sisyphean rock that I have to keep rolling up a hill, and people will not stop bugging me about it."

By that interview in 2007, a sizable portion of the anthology's authors had already passed away, making publication an even less likely proposition. In 2018, Ellison joined their ranks.

The Last Dangerous Visions persists in myth, perhaps grander in our imagination than it could ever have proven in real life. Tamed by the decades, no longer dangerous, a vision it remains. ✦

The Otherworldly Visions of Philip K. Dick

This brings me to my frightening premise. I seem to be living in my
own novels more and more. I can't figure out why. Am I losing touch
with reality? Or is reality actually sliding toward a Phil Dickian type of
atmosphere? And if the latter, then for god's sake why? Am I responsible?
How could I be responsible? Isn't that solipsism?

I f you're at all familiar with the works of Philip K. Dick, then you know that a "Phil Dickian type of atmosphere" is one saturated with paranoia, mystery, symbolism, shifting realities, and hallucinatory vision. You may not know that the words above were written by Philip K. Dick (1928-1982) himself, one tiny fragment of an 8,000-page document he created over the last decade of his life in an attempt to grapple with a hallucinatory experience of his own.

This very strange document is called the Exegesis. It has never been published in full; considering its length, it probably never will be. But about 1,000 pages were recently collected in a volume edited by Pamela Jackson and Jonathan Lethem. The book offers a fascinating glimpse into a fascinating mind, though it never comes close to solving the mystery at its heart, the mystery that drove Dick to write obsessively through the night: What exactly happened to him in February of 1974?

As a writer, Dick is an interesting case. He was massively prolific, publishing forty novels and around 120 short stories. His writing encompasses decidedly literary themes, grappling philosophically with the fundamentals of human existence and offering unflinching explorations of drug abuse, mental illness, and the dark side of human nature. Nevertheless, his high reputation in literary circles is a fairly recent development. Throughout his lifetime, he was considered decidedly pulpy, and embraced by science-fiction fans alone. His cult following eventually morphed into a much broader recognition of his irreplaceable contributions to both literature and the culture at large. This change in status has no doubt been helped along by the fact that his work seems to be ideal for adapting to screen. We can thank Phil K. Dick for *Blade Runner* (1982), *Total Recall* (1990; 2012), *Minority Report* (2002), *A Scanner Darkly* (2006), *The Adjustment Bureau* (2011), and *Blade*

Runner 2049 (2017), as well as *The Man in the High Castle* (2015-unfinished) and of course, Amazon Video's ten-part anthology series *Philip K. Dick's Electric Dreams*. Dick also wrote the remarkable novels *Flow My Tears, the Policeman Said*; *Ubik*; and *VALIS* (a trilogy). Like the Exegesis, the *VALIS* trilogy was also an extended attempt to understand the events of February-March 1974, or as Dick typically referred to it, 2-3-74.

The years immediately preceding 2-3-74 were difficult ones for Dick. He spent some time in a psychiatric hospital in 1973. In *The Divine Madness of Philip K. Dick*, perhaps the most authoritative book on the subject, biographer Kyle Arnold writes of this time, "The IRS, who seized his car in 1971, continued to hound him for back taxes. Dick was afraid they would seize his assets again. Also, his relationship with Tessa, his fifth wife, was turbulent. Dick was afraid that Tessa might suddenly abandon him, and on bad days he became enraged if she left him alone for more than a half hour. Dick's phobias and paranoid fears had become so paralyzing that he was rarely able to leave the house."

On February 20, 1974, Dick visited the dentist to receive treatment for an impacted wisdom tooth; while there, he received a dose of sodium pentothal, a barbiturate that's used as an anesthetic and also has a reputation as a "truth serum." Soon afterward, he was convalescing at home when a delivery arrived from the pharmacy bearing more pain-re-lieving narcotics. The delivery girl had "black, black hair and large eyes very lovely intense." The description of her appearance is relevant; Dick was always preoccupied and perhaps even obsessed with dark-haired, dark-eyed girls, who represented for him an image of his twin sister as she might have been if she'd lived. Instead,

Futuristic street scene inspired by Philip K. Dick's *Ubik*. Illustration by Aleksandr Dochkin. Mentally, Dick connected *Ubik* and 2-3-74, believing the novel—published four years earlier—in some ways predicted or presaged his hallucinatory revelations.

she died when the twins were infants, a loss at the center of Dick's life that never stopped haunting him.

On that February afternoon, Dick stood there a moment, loopy from the drugs, "thinking I'd never seen such a beautiful girl, and why was she standing there?" The girl wore a gold necklace with the Christian fish symbol, recently repopularized. A ray of sun glinted off her necklace, and according to Dick, the fish began to emanate a pink laser beam. Contained within that beam was a sudden flood of knowledge. So much raw, unfiltered knowledge that it was impossible in the moment to understand or even process it all. Later, Dick writes, "Her appearance at the door had that effect only as a mere triggering release and because of manifold almost infinite preparatory steps. This was a life time process, not a single event."

Over the next several weeks these visions continued. He saw visual hallucinations; he felt that he was communicating with an otherworldly entity, somehow tapped into his consciousness: "A gold and red illuminated-letter like plasmatic entity *from the future*, arranging bits and pieces here: arranging what time drove forward." He saw a local playground transformed suddenly into a scene from ancient Rome, complete with Christian martyrs being fed to lions for the entertainment of the masses. In true poltergeist fashion, his radio played threatening messages whether or not it was plugged into the wall.

Inexplicably, one vision also alerted Dick to the fact that his infant son was suffering from an undiagnosed hernia. According to Tessa Dick, the baby's mother, this insight proved invaluable for getting their son medical care. "I had taken our baby to the doctor about a week before Phil told me about the hernia, but the doctor did not take me seriously," Tessa said in an interview with dickien.fr, a French Philip K. Dick fan site. "When I took him back to the doctor and told him that Christopher had a hernia, he took me seriously and referred me to a specialist." The doctor confirmed that the baby had an inguinal hernia, a condition that could be life-threatening without prompt surgical intervention.

But in time the visions departed. Dick was despondent, and attempted suicide. The attempt was serious; the method brutal and, Dick presumed, foolproof. Reportedly, he swallowed forty-nine tablets of his blood pressure medication, slit his wrist so deeply the spurting blood sprayed the ceiling, and then staggered off to his car that was parked in the garage with the engine running. But as miraculously as he'd survived the infant neglect that killed his twin sister, he lived once again. He vomited up the pills, the cut coagulated and the bleeding stopped, and the car stalled out. Accounts differ on how the paramedics arrived, but they did. Afterward, he was admitted to a psychiatric hospital for another month.

In the aftermath of 2-3-74, he devoted himself to trying to figure out what had happened, both in the private journaling that would become the Exegesis and in the VALIS trilogy, as well as many letters to friends and colleagues. This analysis and exploration had no particular object and certainly no end; it was simply a knot he couldn't stop worrying. As Jackson and Lethem write in their introduction, "Dick's pursuit of the truth of 2-3-74 was destined, like Zeno's arrow, for no destination. Years before his death, it became apparent that these activities would not cease until the pen fell from his hands, no matter his periodic attempts at closure."

The obsessive writings of the Exegesis are often preoccupied with thoughts of good and evil, religion and philosophy, consciousness and metaphysics. They're filled with references to Plato, Jesus Christ, and other Greek and Roman historical and mythological figures. One thought connects restlessly to another. These prolific nights of frantic free association were often fueled by methamphetamines, which Dick habitually abused throughout his life, fueling his productivity as well as his paranoia.

Dick considered all the options, opining variously that he'd had some kind of temporary psychotic break; that he had in fact been touched by the Divine; that the universe and the nature of time itself are not as they seem; that entities from other times or dimensions were reaching out to him; that he'd suffered some kind of neurological event; or that his years of drug use were finally catching up with him. Others have theorized that perhaps he experienced a temporal lobe epilepsy, or seizures of the brain, which can cause both graphomania (obsessive writing) and pre-occupations with religious themes. Dick's friend, or perhaps frenemy, Tom Disch (who wrote, among other things, *The Brave Little Toaster*) mockingly suggested that perhaps Dick had been possessed by the Old Testament prophet Elijah.

According to another of Dick's eventual theories, the world as we perceive it is a Black Iron Prison. Arnold writes, "The Black Iron Prison is not localized to our time period or even ancient Rome, Dick says. It exists in all times and places, cutting through the laminated layers of reality . . . The Black Iron Prison casts a disguise over itself, placing life forms in

an illusory bubble of a reality that conceals its true nature. We journey through our lives perceiving the world as ordinary and normal, when in fact the ordinary world is merely a facade papered over the iron bars of the Black Iron Prison."

Referencing such conceptions, philosopher Simon Critchley in the *New York Times* gets to the heart of what links the Exegesis with Philip K. Dick's fiction, and so much of the SF genre it indelibly shaped: "This is the idea that reality is a pernicious illusion, a repressive and authoritarian matrix generated in a dream factory we need to tear down in order to see things aright and have access to the truth." It's impossible to deny how thoroughly this idea pervaded the next three decades of science fiction.

Of course, Dick himself contributed with the VALIS trilogy, an autobiographical series of novels based on both the experience and his interpretations of it. In an analysis on his conceptual fiction site, writer Ted Gioia notes, "Sci-fi novels are rarely autobiographical, but *VALIS* is not your typical sci-fi book. Indeed, it is the strangest work of genre fiction I've ever read. Even if you're familiar with Dick's other major books, nothing in them prepares you for this one."

The Exegesis continued as long as Dick was alive to write it. It fed into itself, an ouroboros of meaning, interpretation, reinterpretation. Dick often summed up everything he'd theorized so far, came to a conclusion of a sorts, and then was off and running in an entirely new direction.

Somewhere in the middle of all that, Dick wrote: "What I have shown . . . is that our entire world view is false; but, unlike Einstein, I can provide no new theory that will replace it. However, viewed this way, what I have done is extraordinarily valuable, if you can endure the strain of not knowing, and knowing you do not know." Though not speculative fiction itself–though certainly speculative–the Exegesis taps into some of speculative fiction's truest pleasures and terrors: both the strain of not knowing, and the certainty of the universe as infinitely unknowable. ✦

Cityscape inspired by Philip K. Dick's *Ubik*.
Illustration by Aleksandr Dochkin.

The Empress of the Sensual: Kathy Acker

K athy Acker (1944-1997) did not write science fiction; she *was* science fiction. Acker was fantasy as well. Specifically, she was a cyberpunk, a cyborg, and one of the Endless. If speculative fiction is an exploration of unknown worlds, of places beyond the borderlands, Kathy Acker is that tempting, forbidden space we cannot yet comprehend.

Acker's own work—mostly fiction for lack of a better word, but also essays and other pieces—was intensely personal and formally rigorous. Even before she was a published writer, her great subject was her own self. She and scholar/musician/artist Alan Sondheim made a pornographic video of sorts with early half-inch black-and-white reel-to-reel videotape in 1974. *Blue Tape* features the least sexy blowjob ever, and in-depth power struggles as the pair chat, write one another letters, and contend

with power, memory, the limitations of the brand-new personal medium, and one another. *Blue Tape* calls to mind Victorian-era epistolary romances, while presaging the amateur porn boom of the 1980s. *Blue Tape* wasn't a work of science fiction so much as it was an *act* of science fiction, with new technology overdetermining human relationships.

With her prose, Acker combined the memoirist's focus on the agonies of the family with the postmodern technique of appropriation, i.e., she wrote about her tempestuous childhood and sexual hang-ups, and "stole" stuff from other writers ranging from Dickens to William Gibson. As Acker's primary subject was herself; unusually for novelists, her own face appeared on the front covers of many of her books. But if you have not seen them, don't worry, just recall Delirium from Neil Gaiman's *Sandman* comic. Acker, with her buzz cut, huge eyes, and ferocious makeup, was Gaiman's model, and Acker's work is often as delirious as the character–"Cynthia lays down on the street and sticks razor blades vertically up her arm. The bums ask her if she needs a drink" is a typical line from her novel *Great Expectations*. Incidentally, that book begins in a familiar way: "My father's name being Pirrip, and my Christian name Phillip, my infant tongue . . ."

Acker was a fairly obscure author in the United States, where she was more often assigned in college classrooms than read for pleasure, but in the 1980s she was huge in the United Kingdom. There, Acker appeared on television, performed alongside industrial artist-provocateur Genesis P-Orridge, had her work reviewed in music magazines, and ran with a crowd that included Gaiman and Alan Moore. Literary critic Roz Kaveney, who knew Acker during this period, said of the author in an extensive remembrance on her old LiveJournal account (of all things): "Kathy was never all that interested in science fiction, but she saw in William Gibson's work a corpus of techno-myth it would be fun to draw on. Falling in with a bunch of people who talked about cyberpunk and its roots with familiarity was as handy as being given a canary when you are planning to visit a coalmine."

What Acker was interested in were manipulations–of her flesh (tattoos, bodybuilding), the flesh of others (she was pansexual and prolific), and texts. Her time in London was cut short when one of her manipulated texts, *Young Lust*, was "found" to contain a two thousand-word passage from novelist Harold Robbins's *The Pirate*. The resulting public kerfuffle and legal wrangle sent Acker back to the U.S. She was forced to sign an apology to Robbins, but also wrote a defiant summary of events called "Dead Doll Humility." It reads, in part:

CAPITOL MADE A DOLL WHO LOOKED EXACTLY LIKE HERSELF.
IF YOU PRESSED A BUTTON ON ONE OF THE DOLL'S CUNT LIPS
THE DOLL SAID, "I AM A GOOD GIRL AND DO
EXACTLY AS I AM TOLD TO DO.

One of the more remarkable of Acker's plagiarisms, as she called them, can be found in her 1988 novel *The Empire of the Senseless*. Entwined like a helix with dizzying and occasionally horrifying sexual adventures of pirates is an extended riff on William Gibson's *Neuromancer*. Gibson had first borrowed a line of Acker's for *Mona Lisa Overdrive*; Acker returned the favor by liberating a significant hunk of Gibson's plot, Wintermute (now Winter), and the Panther Moderns (now the Moderns). Unlike Acker's more obvious, straightforward appropriations of sentences and paragraphs, Acker kidnapped *Neuromancer's* DNA, separated it out from the literal "cyberspace," and created a transgressive pulp thriller about the reclamation of the self, herself, Kathy.

Empire of the Senseless reads like what cyberpunk would be, divorced from the conventions of traditional publishing and instead married to Black Mountain poetry and pornography. "Round revolving cars emitted sonar waves. Certain sonar vibrations blinded those not in the cars; other levels numbing effectively chopped off limbs; other levels caused blood to spurt out of the mouths nostrils and eyes. The buildings were pink. Preferring mutilation the families who lived in bed-sits ran out into the streets," is a scene of middling intensity. Later, a chapter is entitled "Me Equals Dead Cunt."

One will not find the pleasures associated with cyberpunk, even at its most noir-inflected, in *Empire of the Senseless*. The book is instead about the *results* of cyberpunk—mash-ups of autobiography, fiction, and well-founded political paranoia; the persistence of malevolent authority in supposedly value-free artifacts of rational society (i.e., computer programs); and sensualized body horrors. There's no three-act structure, no moral victory at the book's climax, and no traditionally well-rounded characters or even characters with coherent motivations.

What Acker was interested in were manipulations—of her flesh (tattoos, bodybuilding), the flesh of others (she was pansexual and prolific), and texts.

Acker wasn't just messing about with what was popular at the time. She read deeply and widely, and was familiar with the antecedents of cyberpunk, as can be seen from her introduction to the Wesleyan University Press edition of Samuel R. Delany's *Trouble on Triton*. In it, she frames Delany as an Ackeresque—albeit more humanistic—figure, which is reasonable enough as Acker was clearly influenced by Delany. She says of him, and by extension herself: "For the poet, the world is word. Words. Not that precisely. Precisely: the world and words fuck each other."

And that was Acker—fucking the world with words, and being fucked by it. ✦

NEIL GAIMAN

On Viriconium:
Some Notes Toward an Introduction

Neil Gaiman is one of the most influential figures in contemporary fantasy. His books include *Neverwhere* (1995), *Stardust* (1999), the Hugo and Nebula Award-winning *American Gods* (2001), *Anansi Boys* (2005), and *Good Omens* (with Terry Pratchett, 1990), as well as the short story collections *Smoke and Mirrors* (1998) and *Fragile Things* (2006). He's also celebrated for his innovative work on comics and graphic novels, including the groundbreaking series *Sandman*. His honors include four Hugos, two Nebulas, one World Fantasy Award, four Bram Stoker Awards, six Locus Awards, two British SF Awards, one British Fantasy Award, three Geffens, one International Horror Guild Award, and two Mythopoeic Awards. In the essay below, Gaiman offers an appreciation of the Viriconium cycle by M. John Harrison.

People are always pupating their own disillusion, decay, age. How is it they
never suspect what they are going to become, when their faces already contain
the faces they will have twenty years from now?
–"A YOUNG MAN'S JOURNEY TOWARD VIRICONIUM"

And I look at the Viriconium cycle (1971-1985) of M. John Harrison and wonder whether *The Pastel City* knew it was pupating *In Viriconium* or the heartbreak of "A Young Man's Journey Towards Viriconium" inside its pages, whether it knew what it was going to become.

Some weeks ago and halfway around the world, I found myself in the center of Bologna, that sunset-colored medieval towered city which waits in the center of a modern Italian city of the same name, in a small used bookshop, where I was given a copy of the the *Codex Seraphinianus* to inspect. The book, created by the artist Luigi Serafini, is, in all probability, an art object: there is text, but the alphabet resembles an alien code, and the illustrations (which cover such aspects of life as gardening, anatomy, mathematics, and geometry, card games, flying contraptions, and labyrinths) bear only a passing resemblance to those we know in this world at this time: in one picture a couple making love becomes a crocodile, which crawls away; while the animals, plants, and ideas are strange enough that one can fancy the book something that has come to us from a long time from now, or from an extremely long way away. It is, lacking another explanation, art. And leaving that small shop, walking out into the colonnaded shaded streets of Bologna, holding my book of impossibilities, I fancied myself in Viriconium. And this was odd, only because until then I had explicitly equated Viriconium with England.

Viriconium, M. John Harrison's creation, the Pastel City in the Afternoon of the world; two cities in one, in which nothing is consistent, tale to tale, save a scattering of place-names, although I am never certain that the names describe the same place from story to story. Is the Bistro Californium a constant? Is Henrietta Street?

M. John Harrison, who is Mike to his friends, is a puckish person of medium height, given to enthusiasms and intensity. He is, at first glance, slightly built, although a second glance sug-

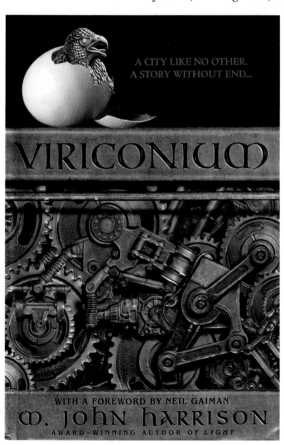

gests he has been constructed from whips and springs and good, tough leather, and it comes as no surprise to find that Mike is a rock climber, for one can without difficulty imagine him clinging to a rock face on a cold, wet day, finding purchase in almost invisible nooks and pulling himself continually up, man against stone. I have known Mike for over twenty years: in the time I have known him his hair has lightened to a magisterial silver, and he seems to have grown somehow continually younger. I have always liked him, just as I have always been more than just a little intimidated by his writing. When he talks about writing he moves from puckish to possessed: I remember Mike in conversation at the Institute for Contemporary Art trying to explain the nature of fantastic fiction to an audience: he described someone standing in a windy lane, looking at the reflection of the world in the window of a shop, and seeing, sudden and unexplained, a shower of sparks in the glass. It is an image that raised the hairs on the back of my neck, that has remained with me, and which I would find impossible to explain. It would be like trying to explain Harrison's fiction, something I am attempting to do in this introduction, and, in all probability, failing.

There are writers' writers, of course, and M. John Harrison is one of those. He moves elegantly, passionately, from genre to genre, his prose lucent and wise, his stories published as SF or as fantasy, as horror or as mainstream fiction. In each playing field, he wins awards, and makes it look so easy. His prose is deceptively simple, each word considered and placed where it can sink deepest and do the most damage.

The Viriconium stories, which inherit a set of names and a sense of unease from a long-forgotten English Roman City–*English antiquaries have preferred Uriconium, foreign scholars Viroconium or Viriconium, and Vriconium has also been suggested. The evidence of our ancient sources is somewhat confused,* a historical website informs us–are fantasies, three novels and a handful of stories which examine the nature of art and magic, language and power.

There is, as I have already mentioned, and as you will discover, no consistency to Viriconium. Each time we return to it, it has changed, or we have. The nature of reality shifts and changes. The Viriconium stories are palimpsests, and other stories and other cities can be seen beneath the surface. Stories adumbrate other stories. Themes and characters reappear, like Tarot cards being shuffled and redealt.

The Pastel City states Harrison's themes simply, in comparison to the tales that follow, like a complex musical theme first heard played by a marching brass band: it's far future SF at the point where SF transmutes into fantasy, and the tale reads like the script of a magnificent movie, complete with betrayals and battles, all the pulp ingredients carefully deployed. (It reminds me on rereading a little of Michael Moorcock and, in its end of time ambience and weariness, of Jack Vance and Cordwainer Smith.) Lord tegeus-Cromis (who fancied himself a better poet than swordsman) reassembles what remains of the legendary Methven to protect Viriconium and its girl-queen from invaders to the North. Here we have a dwarf and a hero, a princess, an inventor and a city under threat. Still, there is a bittersweetness to the story that one would not normally expect from such a novel.

A Storm of Wings takes a phrase from the first book as its title and is both a sequel to the first novel and a bridge to the stories and novel that follow and surround it: the voice of this book is, I suspect, less accessible than the first book, the prose rich and baroque. It reminds me at times of Mervyn Peake, but it also feels like it is the novel of someone who is stretching and testing what he can do with words, with sentences, with story.

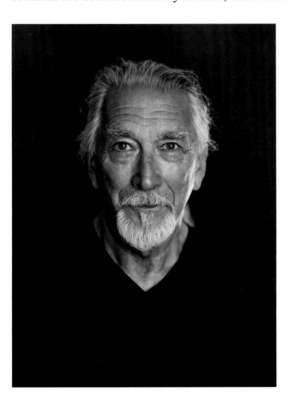

And then, no longer baroque, M. John Harrison's prose became transparent, but it was a treacherous transparency. Like its predecessors, *In Viriconium* is a novel about a hero attempting to rescue his princess, a tale of a dwarf, an inventor, and a threatened city, but now the huge canvas of the first book has become a small and personal tale of heartbreak and of secrets and of memory. The gods of the novel are loutish and unknowable, our hero barely understands the nature of the story he finds himself in. It feels like it has come closer to home than the previous stories—the disillusion and decay that was pupating in the earlier stories has now emerged in full, like a butterfly, or a metal bird, freed from its chrysalis.

The short stories which weave around the three novels are stories about escapes, normally failed escapes. They are about power and politics, about language and the underlying structure of reality, and they are about art. They are as hard to hold as water, as evanescent as a shower of sparks, as permanent and as natural as rock formations.

The Viriconium stories and novels cover such aspects of life as gardening, anatomy, mathematics, and geometry, card games, flying contraptions, and labyrinths. Also, they talk about art.

Harrison has gone on to create several masterpieces since leaving Viriconium, in and out of genre: *Climbers*, his amazing novel of

[OPPOSITE] Neil Gaiman, photo by Kyle Cassidy.
[ABOVE] M. John Harrison, photo by Hugo Glendinning.

rock climbers and escapism takes the themes of "A Young Man's Journey to Viriconium" into mainstream fiction; The *Course of the Heart* takes them into fantasy, perhaps even horror; *Light*, his transcendent twining SF novel, is another novel about failed escapes–from ourselves, from our worlds, from our limitations.

For me, the first experience of reading *Viriconium Nights* and *In Viriconium* was a revelation. I was a young man when I first encountered them, half a lifetime ago, and I remember the first experience of Harrison's prose, as clear as mountain-water and as cold. The stories tangle in my head with the time that I first read them–the Thatcher Years in England seem already to be retreating into myth. They were larger-than-life times when we were living them, and there's more than a tang of the London I remember informing the city in these tales, and something of the decaying brassiness of Thatcher herself in the rotting malevolence of Mammy Vooley (indeed, when Harrison retold the story of "The Luck in the Head" in graphic novel form, illustrated by Ian Miller, Mammy Vooley was explicitly drawn as an avatar of Margaret Thatcher).

Now, on rereading, I find the clarity of Harrison's prose just as admirable, but find myself appreciating his people more than ever I did before–flawed and hurt and always searching for ways to connect with each other, continually betrayed by language and tradition and themselves. And it seems to me that each city I visit now is an aspect of Viriconium, that there is an upper and a lower city in Tokyo and in Melbourne, in Manila and in Singapore, in Glasgow and in London, and that the Bistro Californium is where you find it, or where you need it, or simply what you need.

M. John Harrison, in his writing, clings to sheer rock faces, and finds invisible handholds and purchases that should not be there; he pulls you up with him through the story, pulls you through to the other side of the mirror, where the world looks almost the same, except for the shower of sparks . . . ✦

DARRAN ANDERSON

The Salvage Yard: Real-Life Experiences Revisited in Science Fiction

T he end of the world took place in 1944 for the monks of Monte Cassino. The Bene-dictine abbey occupied a hilltop near the German Gustav Line. When Allied recon-naissance reported that Axis soldiers were occupying the site, it was relentlessly bombarded from the sky. Onboard one of the bombers was the twenty-one-year-old gunner Walter M. Miller Jr. Years later, he would write his sole novel *A Canticle for Leibowitz* (1959); a tale of monks keeping the memory, or even myth, of civilization alive in a postapocalyptic future, after mankind had almost rendered itself extinct in a nuclear war. Miller would claim that it "never occurred to me that *Canticle* was my own personal response to war until I was writing the first version of the scene where Zerchi lies half buried in the rubble. Then a lightbulb came on over my head: 'Good God, is this the abbey at Monte Cassino? This rubble looks like south Italy, not the southwest desert. What have I been writing?'"

Rarely is the real world explicit in sci-fi, but rarely too is it absent. Few writers are alle-gorists, but nevertheless it is present in fragments, shadows, echoes, and elements within the atmosphere. Writers are always providing a curious refracted form of autobiography in their writing, as well as a survey of their environment. However warped or subliminal, it contains their fixations. We can learn a great deal from the webs of mythology in Samuel R. Delany and Roger Zelazny's books or the issues of sovereignty, freedom, and fluidity in Ursula K. Le Guin's, provided we don't lean too heavily into literalism; they remain fiction writers after all. We do not need to know that Arkady and Boris Strugatsky survived the Siege of Leningrad before working as professionals in Soviet institutions or that Liu Cixin grew up during the Cultural Revolution to value their writing, but context deepens our appreciation of the texts and the worlds they emerged from.

Given the science component of science fiction, there is still a tendency to see the genre as a vehicle for rationalism, which would be true perhaps if humans were entirely rational agents. Certainly, there have been SF writers, like H. G. Wells, who have followed existing threads and human tendencies into the future (while displaying their own predilections and prejudices) or, grounded in physics like Arthur C. Clarke and Isaac Asimov, have speculated on the probable impact of technological, biological, and environmental developments. SF has had something of a symbiotic relationship with actual progress; a significant number of leading rocket scientists and submariners, for example, began because of reading Jules Verne.

Our understanding of reason has its limits however. The processes of the imagination, whether a collage or some dialectic development, are still obscure. Chance plays a major part. Russell Hoban was moved to write his postapocalyptic masterpiece *Riddley Walker* upon one day discovering a medieval painting of a Christian martyr at Canterbury Cathedral: "There are places that can heighten your responses, and if you let your head go its own way it might, with luck, make interesting connections. On March 14th, 1974, I got lucky." The dazzling airships that reoccur in Philip José Farmer's books came from a single inexplicable blimp that passed over his head as a child. Meteor showers and comets gave us alien invasions and global pandemics. A mistranslation and a distortion through a telescope gave us canals on Mars and the ancient civilizations that built them.

In the writing of M. John Harrison, we find the mechanics exposed for our benefit.

Barrel vaulted ceiling of Canterbury Cathedral, photographed from below in 2009. Credit: Edo Tealdi/iStockPhoto.

His is the messy, unmappable salvage yard. A living thing that we are already part of. The preservation of the past not as an inert museum but as a teeming, shifting, dangerous form of geology that intrudes and continually alters the present. Too often popular visions of the future become relics of what the future used to be (the Raygun Gothic style of the 1950s or the rain-drenched neon of 1980s cyberpunk). Our love of them is not progressive at all, but nostalgic, and nostalgia is not what it used to be. The past, we should not forget, is a perilous place. When China Miéville conjures the river of New Crobuzon, he is writing of the Victorian-era Thames and London: "Sewers riddling the earth like secular sepulchres, a new landscape of wasteground, crushed stone, libraries fat with forgotten volumes, old hospitals, towerblocks, ships, and metal claws that lift cargoes from the water." There are ghosts to be found in his work, the ghosts of real-life places like rookeries, markets, and red-light districts. It would be easy to discern overtly-divided cities like Belfast in his *The City & the City*, but really it demonstrates how we inhabit all metropolises, via our blind spots and cognitive dissonances, surrounded by inequities and periodic glimpses of bedlam.

Perhaps the most intangible entity we can conceive is the tabula rasa–the truly blank slate. Even obliteration leaves traces. When Billy Pilgrim time-travels in *Slaughterhouse-Five*, he is doing so through the memories of his creator Kurt Vonnegut, who was once imprisoned in a subterranean meat locker while the citizens of Dresden burned and melted in their thousands above him. There are many writers who never forgot their experiences of war, such as Brian Aldiss, whose extraterrestrial jungles have more than a hint of the Burmese rainforest he once fought in. When people forget or pass away, the environment remembers. The dreaded area known as the Cacotopic Stain in Miéville's Bas-Lag books, legendary in fearful rumor, mirrors our own Chernobyl. Yet even nature's memory is finite. Frank Herbert's *Dune* evolved from a real-life study of the spread of the Oregon Dunes, titled "They Stopped the Moving Sands," the kind of conditions that might one day cover a planet and erase a civilization.

The impulse to write is rarely for a singular reason, but escape is certainly a major factor. Writers dream up scenarios in defiance of experience even while being shaped by it. There is Mary Shelley, inventing Frankenstein, in a parlor game turned visionary nightmare, stuck indoors in Byron's Swiss villa while volcanic ash blocked out the sun. There is Jack Vance, bored below decks in the Merchant Marine, somewhere in the South Seas. There is Octavia Butler, writing in the hours before dawn before going to a string of dead-end jobs. There is Thomas Disch, working as a night watchman at an undertaker's before writing his mortality-fixated tales. There is Iain M. Banks working on an oil rig off the Scottish coast, yet to dream up a city built from rusting hulks and oil platforms tied together. Where were they escaping *to*? Their imaginations firstly, and then, via their creative abilities, a different future. William Gibson's line, "The future is already here–it's just not very evenly distributed," is endlessly quoted, but it's much more than a perceptive pithy remark. It is an admonition and an exhortation to go out there and, sifting through the wreckage and the refuse, find the future and shape it, before it finds us unawares. ✦

The Dark Fairy Tales of Angela Carter

Fairy tales are fundamental to the fantastic tradition, and yet for many decades they were neglected by speculative storytellers, viewed as irrelevant and auxiliary, more bedtime story than serious literature. Through her seminal collection *The Bloody Chamber,* Angela Carter (1940-1992) did more to challenge this misconception than any other author. Her explorations of these ancient tales, through the multiple lenses of Surrealism, feminism, Freudian psychoanalysis, and Symbolist poetry, are erotic, dark, and dangerous. Yet despite her massive influence on writers both of her own generation and ones to come, Carter remains a rather obscure name to many.

One of her better-known fans is bestselling author Neil Gaiman, who has spoken of the huge influence Carter's work had on his own: "*The Bloody Chamber* is such an important book to me," Gaiman told the *Guardian.* "Angela Carter, for me, is still the one who said: You see these fairy stories, these things that are sitting at the back of

Beauty and the Beast illustration by Walter Crane (1845-1915). Angela Carter's fairytale retellings often blur the line between person and animal, human and creature.

[OPPOSITE] A brave and fierce young girl might find herself surprisingly at home in the company of wolves. Original illustration by Dea Boskovich, 2018.

the nursery shelves? Actually, each one of them is a loaded gun. Each of them is a bomb."

While critics often described the stories in *The Bloody Chamber* as "fairy tales for adults," Carter herself decried this simplistic reduction. She did not see her project as retelling these stories, but more as mining them, sampling from their imagery and archetypes, finding flow from their dark undercurrents.

Carter repeatedly revisits that common fairy tale trope of an innocent girl menaced by both men and beasts (with a quite intentionally ambiguous overlap between the two). But her tellings subvert the traditional moralities and unsubtle warnings these patriarchal tales deployed. Instead, as critic and cultural historian Marina Warner writes in *The Paris Review*, "[Carter] rewrites the conventional script formed over centuries of acclimatizing girls–and their lovers–to a status quo of captivity and repression, and issues a manifesto for alternative ways of loving, thinking, and feeling."

This approach is most evident in "The Courtship of Mr. Lyon" and "The Tiger's Bride," which both find their base material in the story of Beauty and the Beast, as well as "The Werewolf" and "The Company of Wolves," which trace their ancestry to Little Red Riding Hood.

And yet to discuss the philosophical underpinnings of these stories does not fully do justice to Carter as a writer, whose most formidable talent was as a prose stylist. The searingly erotic and terrifying language of her tales; the haunting and vivid imagery; the beautiful brutality. Carter's facility with language is what gives these stories their staying power, elevating them from mere retellings to singular works of art. Critically acclaimed novelist Margaret Atwood writes in *The Observer*, "She was, among other things, a quirky, original, and baroque stylist, a trait especially marked in *The Bloody Chamber*–her vocabulary a mix of finely tuned phrase, luscious adjective, witty aphorism, and hearty, up-theirs vulgarity."

Consider this passage from "The Company of Wolves":

> *You are always in danger in the forest, where no people are. Step between the portals of the great pines where the shaggy branches tangle about you, trapping the unwary traveler in nets as if the vegetation itself were in a plot with the wolves who live there, as though the wicked trees go fishing on behalf of their friends–step between the gateposts of the forest with the greatest trepidation and infinite precautions, for if you stray from the path for one instant, the wolves will eat you. They are grey as famine, they are as unkind as plague.*

Here, through the power of Carter's prose, the fairy tale becomes again what it once was: a metaphor for the frailty of human civilization, the terror lurking just beyond the firelight's edge. And yet, what might seem maudlin is continually undercut by Carter's wisdom and practicality; lines such as "My father, of course, believed in miracles; what gambler does not? In pursuit of just such a miracle as this, had we not traveled from the land of bears and shooting stars?" ("The Tiger's Bride") and "The wolf let out a gulp, almost a sob, when it saw what had happened to it; wolves are less brave than they seem"

("The Werewolf"). And then, also, there is her frank indecency, unflinching at human physicality: "The moon had been shining into the kitchen when she woke to feel the trickle between her thighs and it seemed to her that a wolf who, perhaps, was fond of her, as wolves were, and who lived, perhaps, in the moon? must have nibbled her cunt while she was sleeping, had subjected her to a series of affectionate nips too gentle to wake her yet sharp enough to break the skin" ("Wolf Alice").

Along with *The Bloody Chamber*, Carter's best-known works include the novels *The Infernal Desire Machines of Doctor Hoffman* (1972), *The Passion of New Eve* (1977), and the short story collection *Saints and Strangers* (1985), all of which combine fantastic and speculative elements with a deeply literary sensibility. Despite–or perhaps because of–her utterly unique and original voice, Carter was not hailed as a major talent of British literature during her own lifetime. Her body of work was not small, encompassing novels, short stories, drama, and nonfiction. Yet she was never nominated for the Man Booker Prize, the UK's most prestigious novel award, an oversight that rankled her friends and supporters at the time and appears more egregious with every passing decade.

Carter died from lung cancer in 1992, only fifty-one years old. Shortly after her death, Salman Rushdie, internationally renowned author of *The Satanic Verses,* wrote: "In spite of her worldwide reputation, here in Britain she somehow never quite had her due. Of course, many writers knew that she was that rare thing, a real one-off, nothing like her on the planet . . . But for some reason she was not placed where she belonged–at the center of the literature of her time, at the heart."

Rushdie predicted that her passing would secure her "place in the pantheon," saying that with her death, "I have no doubt that the size of her achievement will rapidly become plain." His assessment proved correct–at least among a dazzling literary cohort that includes David Mitchell (*Cloud Atlas, The Bone Clocks*) and Jeanette Winterson (*Oranges Are Not the Only Fruit, The Stone Gods*), both of whom count Carter among their influences. In *The Infernal Desire Machines of Angela Carter*, Jeff VanderMeer writes that "Carter stands among the greatest of all twentieth century fantasists, eclipsing lesser talents such as Bradbury or Ellison."

And yet, among readers, Carter remains somewhat obscure. Few speculative fiction fans cite her as one of their favorites. Her short stories are not reprinted nearly as often as they should be. And her novels are more often taught in English courses than mentioned in top twenty lists and the like. This iconic author's star still has plenty of room left to rise. ✦

Beauty and the Beast illustration by Walter Crane (1845–1915).

Funny Fantasy's Myth Conceptions

When I was in third grade, my best friend told me I had to read the Myth books by Robert Asprin. As class was starting one day, he handed me the second book in the series, *Myth Conceptions*, which he had borrowed (I suspect without asking) from his older brother. He said he hadn't been able to find the first book, *Another Fine Myth*. (Every book in the series has the word *myth* in the title, used as a pun.) The cover showed a blond boy, a tiny dragon, a scaly demon, and a green-haired woman in a miniskirt facing off against a military general holding a giant axe. It was the sort of cover that thrilled me beyond all imagination and that, I was already starting to discover, sent my teachers into paroxysms of rage. I opened the book, holding it under my desk so the teacher couldn't see it, and read the first sentence: "Of all the various unpleasant ways to be aroused from a sound sleep, one of the worst is the noise of a dragon and a unicorn playing tag." I could not possibly have been more excited.

"What are you reading?" my teacher asked. I showed her the cover, and she gave a long-suffering, world-weary groan. "Oh, that," she said. "Well, put it away." I put the book away . . . for about five seconds, then as soon as her back was turned I opened it up again and kept reading. This process was repeated several times, until she finally threatened to confiscate the book. The thought of losing my newfound treasure was like a dagger through my heart, and I did finally put the book away, though I didn't pay any attention to anything that happened in class. All I could think about was the book. At the end of the day I ran home as fast as I could so I could keep reading it.

Before long I'd read all the Myth books—of which there were about eight—countless times. The series relates the adventures of a naive young wizard named Skeeve who finds himself apprenticed to a demon named Aahz. This was long before Harry Potter, at a time when reading stories about young wizards was a fringe interest that marked you as an outsider and a nerd. Fantasy was a ghetto that attracted a lot of misfits and iconoclasts, and unlike today's YA fantasy, which generally seems pretty bland and safe and librarian-approved, the Myth books had an anarchic streak a mile wide. Aahz is rude and horny and greedy, and he lies constantly. Harry Potter learns magic from tenured professors; Skeeve learns magic from a degenerate demon whose scheming quickly gets them strung up by a lynch mob, and things only go downhill from there. Aahz teaches Skeeve about magic, but more importantly he teaches him about the way the world really works, and I absorbed those same lessons. In a way, Aahz was like the "bad influence" older brother that I–an only child–never had.

The seventh book in the series, *M.Y.T.H. Inc. Link*, contains a foreword by Asprin in which he relates the story of how the Myth books came to be written. In those pre-Internet days there was simply no information available anywhere about what it was like to be a working fantasy and science-fiction writer. A few authors like Isaac Asimov, Harlan Ellison, and Larry Niven included brief essays about their process, and I hoarded these, reading them over and over, but Asprin's was by far the funniest and best. (His afterword to the first *Thieves' World* anthology is almost as good.) As much as I was interested in reading fantasy and science fiction, I was just as interested–if not more interested–in learning about how people *wrote* fantasy and science fiction. I now host the *Geek's Guide to the Galaxy* podcast, and have interviewed hundreds of fantasy and science fiction authors, and it would not be much of an exaggeration to say that that whole project is about trying to capture that same thrill I first experienced hearing Robert Asprin talk about how he created the Myth series.

Starting around 1990, the Myth books lost their magic for me. Years passed between volumes, and the books that did appear seemed half-hearted. In his introduction to *M.Y.T.H. Inc. in Action*, Asprin apologized for the delay, citing a bad case of writer's block. In these volumes Skeeve increasingly descends into alcoholism, which seemed out of place and was hard not to interpret as the author working through some personal issues. I also heard vague rumors that Asprin was having problems with the IRS, further hampering his ability to write. In 2003, Asprin took on a cowriter, Jody Lynn Nye, who continues to write new Myth books. I haven't read any of these, so I can't really comment on them. I'll probably check them out at some point.

But those early Myth books, wow they're good. I reread *Another Fine Myth* a few years ago and still found it laugh-out-loud funny. When it comes to humorous fantasy, people think Terry Pratchett, and everything else seems to get no respect. I still remember a time when I was competing in a high school science fair, and I was talking to the girl who eventually became our class valedictorian. We were each holding a book. "What are you reading?" I asked her, and she showed me her book, *War and Peace*. "How about you?" she asked. "It's a funny fantasy," I explained, showing off my copy of Craig Shaw Gardner's *A Multitude of Monsters*, which I was reading for the fifth time. She sort of rolled her eyes and said something about how our respective reading choices said a lot about our personalities. That's what I mean about the no respect thing, same as my teacher in third grade. Of course I know that none of those people have ever actually read any funny fantasy books. But if they did, I'm sure they'd love them just as much as I do. ✦

It's a Man's, Man's, Man's Apocalypse

U nderneath the bleachers of the early eighties, men's adventure fiction had a quickie with science fiction and birthed a generation of what Professor Paul Brians of Washington State University calls "Radioactive Rambos." These tough guys starred in numerous books set in the postapocalyptic ashes of the United States of America after the missiles flew, fighting Commies, biker gangs, and mutants (or "muties", or "mutates" depending on the series) with a lovingly described arsenal of subguns, shotguns, Minimi M249's, and Madsen 380 ACPs.

Science fiction has always embraced the apocalypse, all the way back to the very first postapocalyptic novel, Mary Shelley's *The Last Man* (1885), which attributed the death of humanity to a plague. By the late fifties, the Soviets were to blame. Whether by accident (*On the Beach*, 1957), or by design (*Alas, Babylon*, 1959) we assumed the Commies were going to kill us all in a nuclear hellfire. Or even worse, as both books posited, they'd leave a few survivors scrounging around in the ruins, trying to pathetically piece the world back together out of glowing scraps.

The eighties didn't have time for depressing reality, and Jerry Ahern figured out what became the formula for postapocalyptic men's adventure in *The Survivalist: Total War* (1981). Ahern's Survivalist series owed a massive debt to Don Pendleton's Executioner series, as did pretty much every paperback writer churning out men's adventure novels in the seventies and eighties. In 1968, World War II vet Don Pendleton had written *War Against the Mafia*, his first Executioner novel, which introduced the world to his hero, Mack Bolan, who would feature in 453 Executioner paperbacks, and sell 200 million copies.

Judge Gerard Goettel, in his opinion in the case of Harlequin v. Warner Books, one of several lawsuits surrounding Pendleton's creation, summed up the template as succinctly as anyone, "The constant element was killing on a massive scale. Terse dialogue spiced the violence. Each killing was described in explicit and gory detail. Paramilitary tactics, weaponry, and terminology were heavily emphasized."

Jerry Ahern's 1981 stroke of genius was to graft science fiction's preoccupation with nuclear war onto the Mack Bolan template, in this case introducing readers to John Thomas Rourke, a hard man and survivalist prepper who emerges from his bunker after the missiles fly and battles Commies and mutants, with his woman by his side, for twenty-nine volumes that ultimately sold 3.5 million copies and only ended in 1993.

The Survivalist's success spawned at least eighteen other postapocalyptic men's adventure series, and whether the world ended by natural disasters (The Warlord, six volumes, 1983-1987), or nuclear war (Doomsday Warrior, nineteen volumes, 1984-1991); whether the series took place immediately after a first strike (C.A.D.S., twelve volumes, 1985-1991), or a hundred years later in the ashes of the old world (Endworld, twenty-nine volumes, 1986-1991) the drill was always the same. Our lone Mad Max manly man roamed the ruins on a motorcycle, in powered armor, a supertank, or on foot, either searching for his wife and children in the chaos or just kind of randomly blowing away Commies, mutants, bikers, and the occasional feminist

First published in 1987, the Phoenix book series by David Alexander comprises five volumes: *Dark Messiah, Ground Zero, Death Quest, Metalstorm,* and *Whirlwind.* The books are out of print, but the full set is available for e-readers.

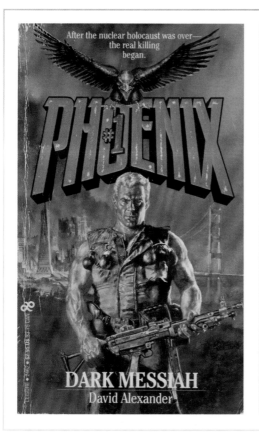

Our lone Mad Max manly man roamed the ruins... kind of randomly blowing away Commies, mutants, bikers, and the occasional feminist war tribes stealing man sperm and murdering the donors.

war tribes stealing man sperm and murdering the donors (*Doomsday Warrior #3: The Last American*, 1984).

Written under numerous house names (Jason Frost, D. B. Drumm, Ryder Stacy) by authors ranging across the political spectrum—from a punk rocker like John Shirley to a military vet like Len Levinson, who railed against the women controlling what he called the "New York Publishing Cartel"—these books delivered fantasy scenarios for weekend warriors who thought America was falling apart and kids today were wimps. Peaceniks were inevitably part of the problem and numerous novels kick off when a spineless U.S. president sells America out in the interests of appeasement. But despite being set in the aftermath of nuclear mass murder, the postapocalyptic landscapes were high-caliber playgrounds where nukes were off the table and conventional weapons ruled, where radiation was limited to a few danger zones, where there was no nuclear winter, rarely any radiation sickness, plenty of food, lots of sex, and where the main characters usually repaired to ultra-comfy man caves in hardened bunkers between action climaxes.

Ironically, for a genre heavy on the gun porn, one of the last publishers standing was Gold Eagle, an imprint of Harlequin, best known for its romance novels. The genre's sales had peaked around 1988 and steadily declined thereafter, but Gold Eagle enjoyed a direct distribution deal with PX's on military bases around the world and was able to hold on until 2014 when HarperCollins acquired Harlequin and shut down Gold Eagle, bringing to an end their postapocalyptic series Deathlands (125 volumes since 1986), and its spin-off Outlanders (75 volumes since 1997). Today, the closest thing publishing has to a postapocalyptic men's adventure series is the long-running *Walking Dead* comic book (177 issues since 2003) that features a one-handed former cop and a stoic, female, African American lawyer with a katana, rebuilding civilization after the zombie apocalypse. ✦

Foreword to John Shirley's
City Come a-Walkin'

William Gibson's first novel, *Neuromancer*, won the Hugo Award, the Philip K. Dick Award, and the Nebula Award in 1984. He is also the *New York Times* bestselling author of *Count Zero*, *Mona Lisa Overdrive*, *Burning Chrome*, *Virtual Light*, *Idoru*, *All Tomorrow's Parties*, *Pattern Recognition*, *Spook Country*, *Zero History*, *Distrust That Particular Flavor*, and *The Peripheral*. In science fiction's alternate history, Gibson also penned a screenplay for *Alien III* (which you can read about on pages 122-128). Though widely credited as the founding father of the influential 1980s SF genre of cyberpunk, in this foreword to *City Come a-Walkin'* by his friend and fellow author John Shirley, Gibson suggests there's plenty of credit to go around.

John Shirley was cyberpunk's Patient Zero, first locus of the virus, certifiably virulent, a carrier. *City Come a-Walkin'* is evident of that and more. (I was somewhat chagrined, rereading it recently, to see just how much of my own early work takes off from this novel.)

Attention, academics: The city-avatars of *City* are probably the precursors both of sentient cyberspace and of the AIs in *Neuromancer*, and, yes, it certainly looks as though Molly's surgically-implanted silver shades were sampled from City's, the temples of his growing seamlessly into skin-stuff and skull. (Shirley himself soon became the proud owner of a pair of gold-framed Bausch + Lomb prescription aviators: Ur-mirror shades.) The book's near-future, post-punk milieu seems cp to the max, neatly predating *Blade Runner*.

So this is, quite literally, a seminal work; most of the elements of the unborn Movement swim here in opalescent swirls of Shirley's literary spunk.

That Oregon boy with the silver glasses.

That Oregon boy remembered today with a lank forelock of dirty blond, around his neck a belt in some long-extinct mode of patient elastication, orange pigskin, fashionably rotted to reveal cruel lengths of rectilinear chrome spring. "Johnny Paranoid," convulsing like a galvanized frog on the plywood stage of some basement coffeehouse in Portland. Extraordinary, really. *And,* he said, he'd been to Clarion.

Was I impressed? You bet!

I met Shirley as I was starting to try to write fiction. Or rather, I had made a start, had abandoned the project of writing, and was shamed back into it by this person from Portland, point-man in a punk band, whose day job was writing science fiction. Finding Shirley when I did was absolutely pivotal to my career. He seemed totemic: There he was, lashing these fictions together, and propping them in the Desert of the Norm, their hastily-formed but often wildly arresting limbs pointing to the way to Other Places.

The very fact that a writer like Shirley could be published at all, however badly, was a sovereign antidote to the sinking feeling induced by skimming George Scithers's *Asimov's Science Fiction* at the corner drugstore. Published as a paperback original by Dell in July 1980, *City Come a-Walkin'* came in well below the genre's radar. Set in a "near future" that felt oddly like the present (an effect I've been trying to master ever since), spiked with trademark Shirley obsessions (punk anti-culture, fascist vigilantes, panoptic surveillance systems, modes of ecstatic consciousness), *City* was less an SF novel set in a rock demi-monde than a *rock gesture* that happened to be a paperback original.

Shirley made the plastic-covered Sears sofa that was the main body of seventies SF recede wonderfully. Discovering his fiction was like hearing Patti Smith's *Horses* for the first time: The archetypal form passionately reinhabited by a debauched yet strangely virginal practitioner, one whose very ability to do this *at all* was constantly thrown into question by the demands of what was in effect a shamanistic act. There is a similar ragged-ass derring-do, the sense of the artist burning to speak in tongues. They invoke their particular (and often overlapping, and indeed she *was* one of his) gods and plunge out of downscale teenage bedrooms, brandishing shards of imagery as peculiarly-shaped as prison shivs.

Mr. Shirley, who so carelessly shoved me toward the writing of stories, as into a frat-party swimming pool. Around him then a certain chaos, a sense of too many possibilities–and some of them, always, dangerous: that girlfriend, looking oddly like Tenniel's Alice, as she turned to scream the foulest undeserved abuse at the Puerto Rican stoop-drinkers, long after midnight in Alphabet City, the visitor from Vancouver in utter and horrified disbelief.

"*Ignore* her, man," J.S. advised the Puerto Ricans, "She's all keyed up."

And, yes, she *was*. They tended to be, those Shirley girls.

I looked at Shirley today, the grown man, who survived himself, and know doing that was *no mean feat*. A cat with extra lives.

What puzzles me now is how easily I took work like *City Come a-Walkin'* for granted. There was nothing else remotely like it, but that, I must have assumed, was because it was *John's* book, and there was no one remotely like John. Fizzing and crackling, its aura, an ungodly electric aubergine, somewhere between neon and a day-old bruise, *City* was evidence of certain possibilities which had not yet, then, been named. It would be a couple years before whatever it was that was subsequently called cyberpunk began to percolate from places like Austin and Vancouver. Shirley was by then in whichever stage of sequence of relationships (well, marriages actually; our boy was nothing if not a plunger) that would take him from New York to Paris, from Paris to Los Angeles (where he lives today), and on to San Francisco (hello, *City*). He gave me vertigo. I think we came to expect that of him, our tribal Strange Attractor, and blinked in amazement as he gradually brought his life in for a landing. Today he lives in the Valley, writing for film and television, but for several years now he has been rumored to be at work on a new book. I look forward to that. In the meantime, we have Eyeball Books to thank for reissuing the Protoplasmic Mother of all cyberpunk novels, *City Come a-Walkin'*.

Vancouver, B.C.

March 31, 1996 ✦

An Interview with John Shirley

John Shirley, an early architect of the cyberpunk movement, has written novels, short stories, TV scripts, screenplays, lyrics, poetry, songs, and various forms of nonfiction. More than forty of his novels have been published. Many of his 200 or so short stories have been compiled in eight short-story collections. As a musician, Shirley has fronted his own bands and written lyrics for Blue Öyster Cult and others.

DB: *Cyberpunk is sort of the quintessential example of a political landscape merging with a literary landscape to birth a new genre. Do you see any parallels between the political and cultural atmosphere of the early 1980s and the world of today? I guess another way of saying that—could a literary SF movement with the same political underpinnings arise today, even if the aesthetics were different?*

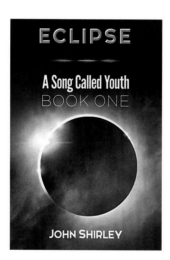

JS: There are always going to be parallels because there will always be young people redefining the world to their own preferences, their own evolving values, against a backdrop of some constraining—sometimes oppressive—status quo. Angry Young Men of the early twentieth century, Beats, and so on. Not that all constraints are needless—I haven't been an anarchist since I was nineteen–but cultural forms, for example, are going to be set in terra cotta . . . even though that concrete has only just dried and hardened! It's the duty of one generation to model forms; it's the duty of the next one to break them down to some degree, so that real choices can be made. Artistically it's constantly happening, sometimes with good results, sometimes with unintended absurdity. Punk rock was necessary; cyberpunk, as we understood it (now it means something else to most people) was necessary. The latest trend, excessive political correctness, is absurd. When cyberpunk started, science fiction was still largely Heinleinian, John

Campbellesque, despite the occasional Michael Moorcock and Ballard. We had to bring it down to the street reality, because that's where meaning was for us. So yes, a new mold-breaking literary SF movement can and will arise. Some sort of transhumanist (ugh!) variant, perhaps.

DB: *You used to describe yourself as "the Lou Reed of cyberpunk and Gibson as the David Bowie." Would you expand on this analogy?*

JS: A very loose analogy, and hubris was involved. But Gibson is more refined than I am, though I've learned a great deal about consistent style and cogent writing over the years. He got a review in *The New Yorker*! Also, while Gibson had his drug experiments, I got quite carried away, and was occasionally literally carried away, and had to go through a struggle, after relapses thirty years ago, to really get clean (see my novel *Wetbones*). So that's like Lou Reed–he was never a heroin addict, as some people imagine, despite his song about it. He was an amphetamine addict, for sure, big time. I was a cocaine addict. I identified with the underclasses, the demimonde he described in "Sister Ray," in "Street Hassle," in many other works. He was the unofficial poet laureate of those largely abandoned people. I tried to do something like that in some of my stories–e.g., the stories in *Black Butterflies*–and in some of my science fiction. Misfit science fiction . . .

DB: *I was delighted to discover that you're also a Clarion alum. (And incredibly jealous that you were lucky enough to have Ursula Le Guin as one of your instructors.) What was your experience at Clarion like (BESIDES dropping acid and jumping out of a tree onto Harlan Ellison)?*

JS: I was a very young, very unpolished, often unbathed mess of a kid there, but Harlan and Ursula Le Guin and Frank Herbert and Avram Davidson and Robert Silverberg and Terry Carr at Clarion, all thought I was talented and they gave me hope. Before then I felt like the great misfit of the western world, hopeless . . . They helped me get my first professional publication and that kept me out of the reach of suicide. I remember that I was prolific but, of course, sloppy. The pressure of these various professionals scrutinizing young Clarion writers, and our scrutinizing of one another, was enormously helpful. I began to get a sense of . . . editing!

DB: *Did the Clarion workshop play a role in shaping and influencing your work? Did any of your classmates share your literary and aesthetic inspirations and goals?*

JS: It shaped my writing by helping me to see it more objectively. There were one or two guys at Clarion who read the avant-garde writers, like I did, who read decadent poets and listened to Dylan and the Doors and Alice Cooper and Stones' *Exile on Main Street* and Zappa and the Blue Öyster Cult and Patti Smith as well as having read heaps of science fiction and horror . . . A lot of people there were more sophisticated than I was. I was semi-feral. It was later, when I met Sterling and Rucker and Gibson and Shiner and Cadigan that I found fellow travelers. I was more influenced by the weirder rock and by filmmakers like Fellini and Buñuel and by painters like Max Ernst and Duchamp than the others at Clarion . . .

DB: *You've cited Beat writers and poets like Baudelaire and Rimbaud as influences on cyberpunk, which absolutely fascinates me. How do you find that these authors influenced cyberpunk, and your own work?*

JS: I think they're influences on cyber-punks because they were underground writers of their time; they were the "alter-

native," they accepted that whores and drug addicts and drunks and dirt could have a place in their writing. And they in turn influenced people like Dylan and Bowie and Lou Reed. I know for a fact Rucker was influenced by Beat writers, like Kerouac and Gary Snyder . . . "The street has its own uses" for technology, I think Gibson said that. So those people were "street" writers like we were, but we brought technology and "outside" scientific ideas into it. I wasn't so very nihilistic, at heart, though I sneered at mainstream SF a good deal, along with all "square culture"–I was influenced by reading the Transcendentalists, like Emerson and Thoreau, and also by meta-physical thinkers like William James and Ramakrishna and Alan Watts. I was always in search of transcendence–something I had in common with Rudy Rucker. The other cyberpunks are gritty realists, in terms of philosophy. Perhaps high-tech existentialists. As for the Beats, I liked some of them–I liked their boldness, the wild flow of their writing.

DB: *As a musician and lyricist yourself, it makes sense that rock music is a huge theme throughout your work, from* City Come a-Walkin' *to* A Song Called Youth. *Can you talk a little about the connections and inter-play between your work in these two different creative mediums? And what role did music play in birthing and defining the cyberpunk genre overall?*

JS: I tried for a long time to find a way to truly fuse these forms. I wanted to write lyrics that evoked science fiction/urban fan-

give up. And my new SF novel *Stormland* is now looking for a publisher. "The present-day composer refuses to die."

DB: *If there was one memory (time, place, show) that evoked for you the cyberpunk scene of the 1980s . . . what would it be?*

tasy/horror, as well as other scenes, and I wanted to write prose that called up the visceral, libidinous, angry energy of hard rock and punk rock. "Anger is an energy," John Lydon said . . . I tried to write stories that structurally had opening verses, a chorus, and a guitar solo, somehow, in the prose. I described futuristic concerts in many of my books—in *Eclipse*, in *City Come a-Walkin'*, elsewhere. These were my passions and I was aware that a lot of great artistry is about fusing things that hadn't been fused before. It didn't work for many editors and it didn't work for all readers. To me it's like what someone said about the Velvet Underground, that they weren't a big hit but spawned a generation of bands. I know I've influenced a lot of people . . . I particularly found that rock people were NOT impressed by science-fiction writers! But I persisted as a writer and a songwriter—Blue Öyster Cult has recorded many songs with my lyrics. And I'm STILL in a rock band—the Screaming Geezers—and I have another project coming out—someone's described it as Lou Reed meets prog-rock—called Spaceship Landing in a Cemetery. I never

JS: Sterling, Rucker, Shiner, and I walked out of a panel at a convention in Austin in protest to the jeers of the backward staid science fiction status quo—and that was solidarity, you see. It was the recognition that we represented something in particular, together. We were not all the same but, still, it was a movement as real as the Beats.

DB: *You've mentioned that in the 1970s and 1980s, you, William Gibson, and Bruce Sterling used to correspond via letters. Those sound like they would make for some interesting reading. What kind of ideas, observations, stories did you exchange back then? Do you think those letters influenced your (collective) work?*

JS: I constantly use email but regret it has destroyed the literature of epistles, of real letter writing. I regret, too, that I did

John Shirley (far right) fronted the post-punk funk-rock band Obsession in the 1980s, with guitarist Chris Cunningham and bassist Jerry Antonias. Photo courtesy of Paula Guran.

not take care of those letters as well as I might've. In our letters we were like other young writers, bitching about the field, muttering about editors, flailing about trying to impress one another, but also observing the world at large. We talked of concerts we'd seen, shared strange observations of the world, comparisons of technology, suggestions about writing–I got lots of those suggestions from Gibson and Sterling and Shiner! In my letters you could find something puerile, something deeply insecure, but a relentless seeking after creativity.

DB: *One of our favorite "secret history" topics is projects that were aborted or abandoned, or for one reason or another never came to fruition. Since you've done a fair amount of work on television and movies, I imagine you have some stories. Are you at liberty to share details on any of your favorite pieces that never made it all the way to the screen (or the page)?*

JS: Sometimes, when it came to television and film, things didn't happen because someone stole them. I have a SF-horror novel called *Crawlers* that was originally an elaborate movie pitch. A young studio producer at a small outfit asked to read the treatment, then said no to it–then went on to steal the idea, even the title! And he wrote a script. It wasn't made into a movie but its existence prevented me from selling my novel as a movie, later. Gibson and I wrote an adaptation of Gibson's "New Rose Hotel" story. This was taken up, and I guess we got paid something–and then the script was sucked into Abel Ferrara's buzzed world, and our adaptation was basically discarded. A movie was made–but it wasn't ours. Gibson and I wrote a script called *Black Glass*, together. Cyberpunk in a pulpy sort of way. Detective stuff, tech ideas. It went hither and thither about LA, and then was back-burnered. Gibson let me have the story so I turned it into a novel by that name.

DB: *Let's talk unsung heroes of science fiction and fantasy (via any medium). What are your favorite "cult classics?" What works or creators do you believe should get more credit and attention than they do–and why?*

JS: I think Cordwainer Smith and R. A. Lafferty and Phil Dick and James Tiptree were influences on me and Rucker and other writers of avant SF. I think Smith did some of the earliest true cyberpunk. Delany's novel *Nova* was an influence on cyberpunk–brain/tech fusion inspiringly envisioned. Phil Dick's later SF novels were an influence, I'm sure. Michael Moorcock's Jerry Cornelius stuff had to influence some of us. Alfred Bester's *The Demolished Man*. Certainly John Brunner's *The Sheep Look Up* affected me personally–environmental concerns show themselves in much cyberpunk, especially mine–and his *Shockwave Rider* influenced cyberpunk. Harlan Ellison's "Repent, Harlequin . . ." piece was an influence on me–and his *A Boy and His Dog*. Certainly, Ballard is prescient (just wait!): *The Drowned World* and his surreal *The Crystal World* should be rediscovered. Ballard's *The Concrete Island* is a dirty gem of a book . . . And now we most of us live on a "concrete island." ✦

An Interview with Thomas Olde Heuvelt

Thomas Olde Heuvelt (b. 1983) is a Dutch novelist who works in the realms of the fantastic. His critically acclaimed horror novel *HEX* (2016) became a worldwide bestseller with editions in twenty-six countries, including the United States, China, Japan, and Brazil, and was called "totally, brilliantly original" by Stephen King. Screenwriter Gary Dauberman (*It*, *Annabelle*) is currently working on the first season of a TV series based on *HEX*. Olde Heuvelt's short fiction has been nominated for several Hugo and World Fantasy Awards. In 2015, his story "The Day the World Turned Upside Down" became the first ever translated work to win a Hugo Award.

DB: *Your influences include big names in genre like Neil Gaiman and Stephen King, but also a number of writers who are more associated with literary fiction. Can you talk about your varying inspirations and what they bring to your work?*

TOH: Whenever I finish reading a horror novel, I pick up a work of literary fiction. I do this because I both love scary fiction and well-crafted, stylized writing. Not to say that these can't go hand in hand, of course. But I love strong voices, the kind of writers when you read one sentence, you immediately know it's them, like Chuck Palahniuk or Jonathan Safran Foer. As an author, you learn so much from reading a varied spectrum of genres and authors. When I was younger, I even used to completely write out a page from a random novel, word-for-word, and the act of doing so made me aware of how other writers put words in a different order than I was naturally inclined. I'd then try to write a page of my own in their style, and I did this with everyone, ranging from Stephen King to Isabel Allende to Vladimir Nabokov. That's how I developed my own voice–by picking up what I liked, and dropping what I didn't. Today, my only condition for the books I pick out to read, is they have to invoke a sense of wonder. A few of my favorite novels–for exactly that reason–are *Life of Pi* by Yann Martel, *The Raw Shark Texts* by Steven Hall and, yes, *Pet Sematary* by Stephen King.

DB: *What works or creators do you believe should get more credit and attention than they do–and why?*

TOH: Since I have an outside perspective, I'll leave the discovery of new talented U.S. writers to others who are closer on top of that. But as for published works, I think everyone in the world–both fans of the fantastic and literary fiction–should read Chuck Palahniuk's novel *Lullaby*, because it's outrageously funny and so cleverly crafted. As for King's work, *Revival* is very much underrated. It's one of his more recent novels, and marks a turn back to the really dark stuff he was writing earlier in his career . . . but it's also a fantastic gem about the span of a lifetime.

DB: *HEX is an amazingly creepy novel, and the English version clearly has some influences of the New England Gothic. What resources did you draw on as you crafted this sinister setting in upstate New York?*

TOH: I studied American literature at the University of Nijmegen in the Netherlands and at uOttawa in Canada, and was introduced to all the good stuff there–Nathaniel Hawthorne, Washington Irving, Edgar Allan Poe, and the lot. When I was looking for a U.S. setting for *HEX*, I thought it was quite fitting to use the breeding ground of the American gothic. The original 2013 edition of the book sets in a small Dutch town in the hills, so geographically, it showed some resemblance. Of course, I physically went there as well. The town of Black Spring, New York, is fictional, but the location is very real. It's right in the Black Rock Forest, two hours up the Hudson from

New York City, near the West Point military academy. All these assets were of great use to the story.

DB: *You've talked about how Dutch literature doesn't have a long history of the fantastic. Do you think your own work has a Dutch essence? What would a uniquely Dutch fantastic look like?*

TOH: It's true, we don't have a tradition of the fantastic. Dutch culture is very Calvinistic in nature, and our literature is as well. It's originally not plot-driven, but driven by interior monologue. One of the all-time classics of Dutch literature is a novel called *De Avonden* (*The Evenings*) by Gerard Reve. It's a book about nothing. It spans ten days of nothingness. Nothing happens in it. Then you read on, and still nothing happens. I was forced to read it in high school at the age of fifteen, and my literature teacher called it "an exploration of boredom, a celebration of nothingness." And I was like, wait a minute. This is where I draw the line. Give any fifteen-year-old this book and it kills their joy in reading. I wanted to celebrate *something*, not nothing. By then, I was already reading quite a bit of American fiction, and I discovered that it, contrary to Dutch literature, was always plot-driven. Not only the horror novels, but also literary novels. Stuff *happened* in these books. And I loved it. Nowadays, Dutch literature is much more international than it used to be, but there's still not a lot of the fantastic. Still, I use our Dutch, down-to-earth nature to my advantage, because it's part of who I am. The key element that makes *HEX* work, is that the people in town aren't really afraid of the supernatural element that's haunting them, they're used to it and frankly, kind of annoyed by it. I always say: If a sane person sees a seventeenth-century disfigured woman appear in the corner of their living room, they'd probably run and scream. If a Dutch person sees a seventeenth-century disfigured woman appear in the corner of their living room, they'd hang a dishcloth over her face and read the paper. And maybe sacrifice a peacock to get on her good side. I feel this take on it makes the book uniquely Dutch, and that's why it is such a success in my home country.

DB: *As your followers on social media no doubt know, you've done a lot of world traveling. How do these experiences show up in your work?*

TOH: A lot–like any life experience you gain. The people you meet, the emotions you feel, the journeys you make, it's all part of the tantrum of the writer's life, and therefore, the writer's fiction. For any writer, life and fiction go hand in hand. As for the influence of traveling on my fiction in particular, I can name a few examples aside from the Americanization of *HEX*. After spending a few months with my uncle and aunt in northern Thailand, I wrote "The Ink Readers of Doi Saket," a short story that was nominated for a World Fantasy and a Hugo Award a few years back. It's about the myths and magic and mysteries of Thai culture. After being the guest of honor in a convention in Croatia, I used one of their local urban legends in my story "You Know How

the Story Goes," which is about a mountain tunnel near Opatija on the Adriatic Sea. And my new novel is about a mountaineer and leans heavily on my own experiences as a mountain climber in the Swiss Alps. But then, it's also a story about love, and I draw on my own experiences with love. It's all tangled.

DB: *Do you have any abandoned novels you don't mind telling us about? Or temporarily shelved novels you hope to return to one day?*

TOH: I do. It was a big deal for me when *HEX* became so successful around the world. It's now been published in twenty-six countries, and for a relatively unknown Dutch author, it's not an everyday thing when

suddenly Stephen King tweets about how "brilliant" he thought it was, nor when the *Guardian* and the *Wall Street Journal* write rave reviews. It was all I ever wanted, but it also put huge pressure on the next one. I found myself thinking with every new paragraph I was writing: What will the *Guardian* say about this? Will King actually like this? Which is, of course, the stupidest thing you can do. So it took me a while to find the ability to write freely again, and in the process, I abandoned a horror novel called *November*. It's about a group of really good people who are forced to do really bad things to prevent something worse from happening. It was a really dark story, and I loved it, but somehow, the time wasn't ripe for it. I'm pretty sure I'll get back to it after I finish the novel I'm currently working on.

DB : *Are there plans to publish more of your novels in English? I'd love a chance to read PhantasAmnesia.*

TOH : Ha—*PhantasAmnesia* was my second novel, and I wrote it when I was nineteen and twenty. It's a 600-page brick that could well have done with 400 pages. It was published with a small imprint in the Netherlands and before I had my first tough editor. Looking back at your early works, it always feels you're cringing. Like looking at pics from puberty, and you go: Ouch, I remember, that's what I looked like back then. My first two books are out of print and I'm not sorry for it. Every now and then some Dutch fans show up with secondhand copies of them, but I currently don't have any plans to reissue or even rewrite them. I'd rather look forward and

write new stuff. So, no—these early works will not be available in English for a while. I would love to have my fourth novel published around the world, though—the one that came before *HEX*. It's called *Sarah*, and it's not a horror novel but a work of magical realism and humor. It's a very personal story, and I think it's one of the best things I've ever written.

DB : *What are you working on now?*

TOH : I'm still promoting *HEX*—it's amazing how this book has such a long life. In 2018 I'll be touring countries like Brazil, China, Ukraine, Poland, and France for my publishers in these countries. Aside from that, I am currently finishing my next novel. The way *HEX* was my twist on the witch archetype, this one is my possession novel. What gets old in possession novels is the religious aspect. There's always a demon or a devil or an evil spirit who possesses a person and a priest comes to exorcise it. We all know the story. I'm not a religious or very spiritual person, but as I said earlier, in my spare time I'm a mountaineer, and whenever I'm in the mountains, I feel like mountains are elevated, living beings. Like they have a soul. Other mountaineers have come down with similar stories. And each mountain has a very specific, different soul that is unique to that particular mountain. They are places of power. So I thought, wouldn't it be great to have a mountaineer who has a horrible accident way up during a climb, and comes down possessed by the soul of the mountain? To have this force-of-nature-gone-bad raging inside of him? That's the premise of the new book. ✦

An Interview with Karen Joy Fowler

Karen Joy Fowler is the author of six novels and three short story collections. Her 2004 novel, *The Jane Austen Book Club*, spent thirteen weeks on the *New York Times* bestseller list and was a *New York Times* Notable Book. Fowler's previous novel, *Sister Noon*, was a finalist for the 2001 PEN/Faulkner Award for fiction. Her debut novel, *Sarah Canary*, won the Commonwealth medal for best first novel by a Californian, was listed for the *Irish Times* International Fiction Prize as well as the Bay Area Book Reviewers Prize, and was a *New York Times* Notable Book. Fowler's short story collection *Black Glass* won the World Fantasy Award in 1999, and her collection *What I Didn't See* won the World Fantasy Award in 2011. Her most recent novel, *We Are All Completely Beside Ourselves*, won the 2014 PEN/Faulkner Award for fiction and was shortlisted for the 2014 Man Booker Prize.

DB: *Your work has always existed in this kind of liminal area between science fiction, fantasy, literary, historical, slipstream . . . a good place for secret history to exist. What fascinates you so much about the liminal space between genres?*

KJF: This is not something I think about as I work, so my attraction to the liminal spaces is not so much a conscious choice as a gravitational pull. If I try to step back and see it from the outside, my best guess is that I find the most freedom there. Solidly in the center of genre are conventions and expectations and contracts with the reader and other annoying constraints. Those demands tend to weaken as you head to the edges. In my opinion, genuine science fiction is really, really hard to do well. My gifts are better suited to the slippery slopes.

DB: *Your story "What I Didn't See" sparked a controversy when it won the Nebula in 2003–because it was so liminal, some readers didn't see it as science fiction at all. In fact, the words "What I Didn't See" feel like a perfect summation of much of your work, which often withholds information or draws on an unreliable narrator. As a writer, how do you find a balance between what is revealed and what is the engine behind the scenes?*

KJF: I spend as much or more time thinking about what I don't want a reader to know as what I do. I think of this as the negative space in my stories. I focus a lot on that negative space. The trick for me is not in revealing too much too soon–I rarely do that–but in still wanting the reader to understand the story clearly at the end, which I am less good at. Readers are smart and wily. And cranky. It's hard to keep them off balance, but also leave them satisfied.

I think "What I Didn't See" exemplifies another thing I do often, i.e., that I write a lot of stories that are not really science fiction, but are written for people who read science fiction. The kind of readers I want–engaged, puzzle-solving, thoughtful, and smarter than I am–are thick on the ground in science fiction.

DB: *One of your many contributions to the genre was helping found the James Tiptree Jr. Award, a prize given to science fiction and fantasy that "expands or explores our understanding of gender"–which has been a tremendous opportunity to highlight work that the canon may have previously overlooked. To which (perhaps underrated) works would you like to award a retrospective Tiptree?*

KJF: One of Pat Murphy and my main motivations for starting the Tiptree Award was our desire to see Carol Emshwiller's novel,

Carmen Dog, win a bunch of prizes, even if we had to make those prizes up. In the intervening years, Emshwiller has gotten more attention and if it still isn't as much as she deserves, I'm not as upset about it as I once was.

It's been fascinating to watch the conversation on gender move along through the lens of the Tiptree Award–to see what things we were talking about when we started it, as opposed to the things we are talking about now. I can't even guess where the conversation will go next, but I'm excited to see it.

DB: *I loved this line of yours from a previous interview: "I always say that I write history as it might have been reported in the* National Enquirer.*" Can you expand a bit on what that means to you?*

KJF: I think that we tend to be pretty conscious of the insanity of the time we actually are living through. (I say that, well aware that we are currently mired in the most insane time I can remember, and I have been alive a good long while. Every morning's headlines beggar belief.) But as the past recedes, it ends up sepia-toned. Those history books that focus on the movement of troops and the speeches of politicians leave out all the parts that I prefer–the immortality cults, the Elvis and UFO sightings, the dance marathons, picnics to see Civil War battles, streaking, phone booth-stuffing, rains of fish and toads, toad licking, bizarre medical treatments, fasting girls, etc., etc., etc.

Though now that the *National Enquirer* has become a genuine player in our political

in the footnotes of some book or paper that I'm reading (Always read the footnotes!). Sometimes, but less frequently, they arise out of something I'm told. I live in a university town and go to lectures on campus. These are good sources for arcane information. When the Smithsonian used to publish the *American Heritage* magazine, I got a lot of ideas out of it, and I still have a number of back issues that I turn to when I'm fresh out of ideas.

I'm attracted to the bizarre. If my response is "WTF?" it's likely I'll want to write about it. I like the nineteenth century because I can go and read the contemporaneous newspapers. I'll be writing a story and I'll pull the articles and headlines up on microfiche and be reminded that Jack the Ripper was working London at the same time that my story takes place. Or else that San Francisco was being menaced by a ghost train. Or that the whole city was obsessed by a custody case. I like to look at the advertisements and read the letters to the editor.

I also like nineteenth-century science, which is almost science, but sometimes not quite. I try to think of something contemporary that would pose the same paradigm-shifting challenge to our worldview as fossils did during the 1800s. I haven't found it yet. I'm fascinated by how people negotiated that shift.

world, mostly through the stories they suppress, I may have to find a new reference. Although the *National Enquirer* version of the *National Enquirer* story is an intriguing thing to think about.

DB: *Your work also explores our world's own secret history by delving deeply into the less familiar corners of our past, particularly the nineteenth century. One example is the "Sweetwheats Sweethearts," a women's baseball team in 1947 Minnesota, explored in your novel* The Sweetheart Season. *How do you stumble on these tidbits, and what makes you think "Hmm, that would make a good story?" And is there something about the nineteenth century that is particularly powerful for you?*

KJF: I think your configuration is perfect. I stumble on to them. Sometimes they're

DB: *Your speculative fiction is powerful in part because of how deeply it's grounded in*

> As the past recedes, it ends up sepia-toned. Those history books that focus on the movement of troops and the speeches of politicians leave out all the parts that I prefer—the immortality cults, the Elvis and UFO sightings, the dance marathons, picnics to see Civil War battles, streaking, phone booth–stuffing, rains of fish and toads... etc., etc., etc.

realism and verisimilitude; the speculative parts are made authentic by the attention given to real-life detail. You spoke at a Clarion writing workshop about how extensive your research process is for your historical novels, and the dedication of that work made a big impression on me. Can you talk a little here about how you go about researching a historical novel?

KJF: Again, I rarely set a story so far back there isn't a massive written record. So I've yet to work in the time period where there's a shortage of material. I read newspapers, which is great for giving you a sense what people were talking about at their dinner tables and what the general mood in a city might've been. I read nonfiction about the time, the place, the people, but I also try to find novels that were published just before, books my characters might've been reading. I'm very happy if I can find letters or diaries. I haunt the special collections rooms in libraries. I read other novels set in the same time period, even if their locations are different. I usually read for about a year before I begin to write. It's a very happy time for me.

DB: *Speculative fiction is often a tool for imag-*

ining the future. You have a particular talent for using it to imagine the past. Why do you think it's important to reexamine the past through this lens?

KJF: The past is never dead. It isn't even past. You can quote me on that. You can quote me quoting Faulkner.

DB: *A lot of secret history depends on shifting our focus from the traditional protagonists to the peripheral characters, and seeing things from their perspective. In your opinion, how does this project intersect with the project of speculative fiction?*

KJF: One of the things speculative fiction is especially suited for is destabilizing an accepted narrative. Changing perspective from the one readers probably expect is also a destabilizing strategy. So the two fit together very neatly.

Speculative fiction often focuses, just as historical fiction also often does, on the extraordinarily consequential character. Realism is more likely to look at characters whose lives impact the large story less. I tend toward more ordinary characters, but I'm also greatly interested in the context of a specific political, legal, scientific, and ecological moment. A focus on more peripheral characters allows me to indulge both those desires.

DB: *You've expressed an idea that I share as well, which is that our actual reality is far too strange, messy, horrific, and unlikely to be accurately represented by "realistic" fiction. What are your favorite works of "realistically unrealistic" fiction—and how, or why, do you think they work?*

KJF: I'm going to try to avoid the obvious suspects here and also to stay in that liminal territory we already talked about. I love Susanna Clarke's *Jonathan Strange & Mr. Norrell*; that one's probably not so liminal. There was a book out last year called *The Epiphany Machine*, by David Burr Gerrard, that I thought was extraordinary. I love the short stories of Alice Sola Kim and Kelly Link and Sofia Samatar.

Often what I love about science fiction and fantasy are the settings. This is the only genre in which a story can take place absolutely anywhere. If I'm deeply immersed in a strange (or even slightly tipped) world, then the story is likely to work for me on that basis alone. I most love that reading experience in which the writer's imagination is producing things you could never have dreamed up yourself. In which you were constantly asking yourself, how does someone think of that?!!

DB: *Who are your most obscure influences? Which creators of speculative stories, whether now or in the past, do you think should receive more attention than they do?*

KJF: I think I read a lot in those liminal spaces when I was a child. Books like *The Pink Motel*, *The Trouble with Jenny's Ear*, *Castaways in Lilliput*, and *David and the Phoenix*. I went through a long period in which all the books I read had dog protagonists or else protagonists who worked with dogs—most memorably *The Green Poodles*, *Follow My Leader*, *A Dog for Davie's Hill*, and *A Dog on Barkham Street*. These all turned out to be appetizers for the completely fabulous novel *Fifteen Dogs* by André Alexis, published in 2015.

I recently reread *Lolly Willowes* by Sylvia Townsend Warner and remembered how much I love it. I often talk in interviews about T. H. White's *Once and Future King*, but far less often about his wonderful *Mistress Masham's Repose*. Doris Lessing's *The Golden Notebook* had a powerful impact on me when I first read it in college, and my father's favorite book, pressed upon me, but I'm grateful for it, was Herbert Read's *The Green Child*. I loved *Green Mansions* as a child, but I'm terrified to reread it. Maxine Hong Kingston's *The Woman Warrior* completely transported me. I was particularly struck by all the different strategies she employs in telling her story. Different voices, different texts, different tones. There was a freedom she allowed herself that, when I began to write, I wanted, too.

Fifteen Dogs is a book I'd like more people to pay attention to. Also *The Epiphany Machine*. Brian Doyle's *Mink River*. Ruth Ozeki's *Tale for the Time Being*. I would have included Andrew Sean Greer's *Less*, but since it just won the Pulitzer Prize, I guess I can shut up about that one. And Molly Gloss should be on the bestseller list every time she writes a book. ✦

FILM—AND TELEVISION

IN MANY WAYS, FILM AND TELEVISION ARE AS FOUNDATIONAL to science fiction and fantasy as is the more ancient art of literature. Through visual spectacle, inventive set design, and special effects, moving pictures spark the imagination in their own unique way.

This chapter explores some of the earliest entries in the one hundred-plus year-old tradition of SFF cinema; the work of ambitious filmmakers who through their nascent visions of a genre not yet defined, laid the groundwork for the field that would eventually bring us *Star Wars*, *Star Trek*, and *Doctor Who*.

We also imagine a few of the films that could have been–from *Jodorowsky's Dune* to William Gibson's *Alien III*, from an erotic "film noir" take on aliens in Manhattan to a horror-movie precursor to *E.T.* While they never made it to the big screen, these visions live on in screenplays, concept art, storyboards, and more; and their raw inventiveness influenced Hollywood and spawned many imitators.

Finally, we pay tribute to the unsung all-stars of moving pictures–concept artists. Though they seldom get the red carpet treatment reserved for directors, producers, and actors, concept artists have played a particularly essential role in SFF cinema, inventing the memorable and arresting characters and creatures, landscapes and planets, futures and pasts that make science-fiction storytelling so delightful.

Bonus: The science fiction movie that shaped American military policy; why *Star Wars* got slapped with a lawsuit for ripping off a Buck Rogers serial from the 1940s; the scientific discoveries of James Cameron; and a couple not-quite-canon films that shaped the genre.

Though wildly influential, the 1927 film
Metropolis has existed in a fragmented and
incomplete form for most of its history.

Le Voyage dans la Lune, the First Science-Fiction Film Ever Made

Science fiction's first film is a surreal twelve-minute extravaganza created by a magician turned filmmaker. *Le Voyage Dans la Lune* (or *A Trip to the Moon*) was made in 1902 by French filmmaker Georges Méliès (1861-1938). No doubt fueled by his practice of the magical arts, Méliès brought an incredible sense of the surreal and fantastic to his visual storytelling. The short film's most recognizable image—a makeshift space capsule landing in the eye of the Moon—remains one of the most iconic visuals in cinema history. The same image is often referenced in art and graphic design, particularly to evoke the retrofuturistic aesthetic of steampunk, H. G. Wells, and Jules Verne.

Indeed, Verne and Wells were both influential to the filmmaker and the film, Verne with *From the Earth to the Moon* and *Around the Moon* (Méliès called these major influences) and H. G. Wells with *The First Men in the Moon,* which was published in French just a few months before Méliès made *Le Voyage Dans la Lune.* He was quite likely also influenced by an operetta by Jacques Offenbach, also titled *Le Voyage Dans la Lune,* which parodied the works of Jules Verne.

Méliès starred in the film as Professor Barnenfouillis, leader of the voyage. The story follows the professor and his colleagues, a group of six astronomers (fancifully named Nostradamus, Alcofrisbas, Omega, Micromegas, and Parafaragaramus) who build a cannon-propelled, bullet-shaped space capsule, along with an appropriately sized cannon to launch it to the Moon. The six astronomers are loaded in and fired off by young women playing the role of flight attendants, dressed in sailors' outfits. The Moon watches benevolently as the capsule courses toward it, sinking into its eye, in the image that's become so iconic.

There are plenty of other striking and beautiful visuals in the film, which is done in a highly theatrical, stage-play influenced style (as film, in its early days, still sought its own voice). Each shot is packed full of action and visuals, with many actors in each scene, moving both individually and together in a complex choreography that occasionally becomes chaotic. The imagery is surreal and baroque, and the storytelling is racuous and slightly comedic, tongue in cheek.

The astronomers disembark from their capsule and bed down on the surface of the Moon. They watch Earth rise as they fall asleep; mythological celestial bodies frolic overhead. It begins to snow. They run to hide in a cave filled with giant semi-sentient mushrooms. There, the astronomers encounter a lunar inhabitant called a Selenite, who they promptly kill–pretty effortlessly, as the Selenites explode when struck. But many more Selenites soon appear, and the astronomers are captured and taken to the court of the Selenite king. One of the astronomers body-slams the Selenite King, who disintegrates into a puff of colored dust.

The Selenites pursue the astronomers as they run back to their capsule in a hasty attempt to escape. With no cannon to launch them back to Earth, Professor Barbenfouillis

Built in 1897, Méliès's film studio in Montreuil, Seine-Saint-Denis was modeled after a greenhouse, inviting plenty of sunlight through the glass walls and ceiling to aid in filming.

ties a rope to the space capsule to tip it off a Moon cliff and into the void of space. An attacking Selenite stows away at the last moment and makes it back to Earth with them. The capsule lands in a sea and is towed to shore. The Selenite ends up a captive in their celebratory parade.

The story sounds simple, but this film was one of the earliest narrative movies ever made. In that sense, its twelve-minute story was a groundbreaking achievement for film. Technically, it was also impressive, drawing on a larger budget than usual, a longer filming schedule (three months), and an unusually lavish and detailed film set. The film studio Méliès worked in had a large glass roof, which appears in the film as the astronomers build their spacecraft. The film's special effects drew particularly on substitution splices–the cameras would stop rolling for a second, they'd switch up some stuff in the shot, and then splice the two shots together to create the visual illusion. That's how Méliès achieved the shocking and delightful shot of the astronomer's umbrella suddenly transforming into a giant mushroom. The iconic sequence of the capsule in the eye of the Moon was also created using this early special effects technique. Here, Méliès's background as a magician no doubt came in handy, as he was already accomplished in the art of redirecting the eye to create the illusion of magic.

The original film is silent, though when shown to contemporaneous audiences, it was usually accompanied by a narrator as well as live music and other sound effects. In the century since, many composers have tried their hands at creating music for it. The French band Air (see page 190-192) created a composition for it that offers a great accompaniment to the 2011 color-restored version.

Méliès made hundreds of short films over his career, leaving an indelible mark on the history and art of the cinema. Wildly popular at the time of its release, *Le Voyage Dans la Lune* remains his best known work today. The film can be seen in its entirety online, and at just twelve minutes, it's a worthwhile and enjoyable watch for anyone who is interested in the history of SFF cinema! ✦

Metropolis:
The Long Shadow of the Never Seen

ilm historian David Bordwell calls *Metropolis* (1927) "one of the great sacred monsters of the cinema." As one of the seminal texts of science fiction, Fritz Lang's famous silent film is both holy and profane. Visually, it's a groundbreaking work whose production set standards in the still-youthful medium of film, and whose arresting aesthetic has been one of the most influential in shaping our conception of the future. Narratively, its story has been almost wholly incoherent for most of its ninety-year history, thanks to a botched editing job and lost footage. Politically, the film's story can never be fully disentangled from its disturbing connections to the Third Reich.

Metropolis premiered in Berlin in 1927, a collaboration between Fritz Lang (1890-1976) and his wife, Thea von Harbou (1888-1954). The screenplay was written by von Harbou, developed in tandem with a novel by the same name. Lang and von Harbou had been co-writing all of Lang's movies since the beginning of their partnership in 1921, and the collaboration had already proved creatively fruitful with popular hits, including a five-hour retelling of the folklore epic *Die Nibelungen* (taking place over two films). Adolf Hitler called the film his favorite, a more damning recommendation than it probably deserves.

But *Metropolis* was Lang and von Harbou's most ambitious collaboration yet. It was a big, expensive production–the most expensive in Germany at the time–encompassing hundreds of extras, extensive set design, and pioneering special effects. *Metropolis*, for

all its expense, was also a commercial flop. Its failure was the final straw for the already struggling film studio UFA, which declared bankruptcy. UFA was then purchased by Alfred Hugenberg, a powerful German nationalist and eventual Hitler supporter. As the Nazis came to power, UFA films became vehicles for Nazi propaganda. More on that later–but first, back to the film.

Metropolis's story centers on a futuristic city that's a frenzy of inequity; the capitalists frolic on the surface in opulence and luxury while the workers labor in a subterranean factory, serving a machine. The ruler's son Freder discovers the bleak slums below his pleasure gardens and is horrified; he volunteers for a stint with the machine, the better to relate to the common people. He falls in love with Maria, a saintly woman from below, who serves as the people's prophet, preaching patience and submission. Meanwhile Freder's father, the ruler of Metropolis, conspires with an evil scientist named Rotwang to replace Maria with a look-alike robot (presaging replicants, Cylons, and synths). According to her programming, robot Maria spurs the proles toward revolt–and chaos ensues. If this seems confusing to you, you're not alone.

In a contemporaneous review, H. G. Wells called it "unimaginative, incoherent, sentimentalizing, and make-believe." These

Fritz Lang and Thea von Harbou at work together in their Berlin apartment. This picture was taken in 1923 or 1924 for *Die Dame* magazine.

were far from his only unkind words for the film, which he also termed "immensely and strangely dull," "ignorant, old-fashioned balderdash," a "soupy whirlpool," "with a sort of malignant stupidity." It was a long review.

Never especially airtight to begin with, the film's plot was rendered even more incoherent by aggressive editing within months of its release. The Berlin original premiered at 153 minutes. The version U.S. audiences saw was only 115 minutes–with a whole new script created by American distributors for American audiences. In 1936, an even shorter ninety-one-minute version was released. Then Fritz Lang's original cut was lost–and with it, a full hour of footage.

For eighty years, *Metropolis* fans lamented the loss; for a time, almost no one alive had even seen the original cut, only the badly mutilated version often played at silent film festivals. As journalist Larry Rohter wrote in the *New York Times*, "For fans and scholars of the silent-film era, the search for a copy of the original version of Fritz Lang's 'Metropolis' has become a sort of holy grail."

The story of how the missing footage was eventually located is a fascinating piece of history in and of itself. It was discovered by Fernando Peña, an Argentine film archivist, in the archives of Buenos Aires's Museo del Cine. He did not stumble upon it by accident; in fact, he'd heard rumors of its existence for twenty years, but his attempts to unearth it were ever thwarted by bureaucracy. In 2008, when his ex-wife and fellow film archivist Paula Félix-Didier became director of the Museo del Cine, she invited him over to have a look. They got to searching and discovered the full-length cut. Some of it was damaged beyond repair, but plenty was salvageable, adding another twenty-six minutes to the film. (How did a German film end up in an Argentinian archive? Sheer coincidence. It was purchased soon after the premiere by Argentine film distributor Adolfo Wilson, who just happened to be visiting Berlin. He brought the 35mm reels back home with him. Eventually it became part of a private collection and then a government archive.)

The newly discovered material helps clarify the story considerably, making it a little easier to offer a plot summary. But the power of *Metropolis* has never been its story; it's always been the visuals. In a review for Tor.com, science fiction author Kage Baker wrote, "Yes, the visuals are brilliant . . . It's a seminal film. Certain images are unforgettable. You should certainly watch it if you get the chance. It still stinks." Kinder words than H. G. Wells might have used, certainly, but her conclusions were much the same: as a work of science fiction, it is extremely bad.

As an aesthetic, though? *Metropolis* really is stunning, in its rendering of a city somehow both decadent and drab, a double-edged future both luxurious and nightmarish. "Even if you've never seen *Metropolis*, you've seen a film, a dress, a building, or a pop video that was inspired by it," wrote journalist and film critic Pamela Hutchinson in the *Guardian*. "The film's look–the teetering architecture, the lever-and-dial mechanisms, the round-shouldered workers marching in unison, and of course, the robot . . . This silent film fires the imagination of everyone who sees it."

"Even if you've never seen Metropolis, you've seen a film, a dress, a building, or a pop video that was inspired by it," wrote Pamela Hutchinson. "This silent film fires the imagination of everyone who sees it."

The gold robot that graces the Metropolis poster might seem especially familiar. Legendary *Star Wars* artist and concept designer Ralph McQuarrie later based his vision of C-3PO on *Metropolis*'s robot, before she's transformed into the Maria look-alike. (See page 101 for more on McQuarrie.) And the story itself, in which a ruler father and a socially conscious son butt heads, might also have served as a *Star Wars* influence.

Roger Ebert also noted the film's vast influence on the genre, listing many other science fiction classics: *Dark City, Blade Runner, The Fifth Element, Alphaville, Escape from L.A., Gattaca*, and even Batman's Gotham City. Ebert also mentioned that "the laboratory of its evil genius, Rotwang, created the visual look of mad scientists for decades to come, especially after it was so closely mirrored in *Bride of Frankenstein*." Those decades continue; in its artfully self-aware depiction of Dr. Frankenstein's laboratory, the recent television show *Penny Dreadful* (2014-2016) casts its mad scientist in surroundings that bear a striking similarity to Rotwang's, and remain as recognizable to us as ever.

Though the film was a commercial failure in Germany, it did find some unwelcome supporters: Hitler and his minister of propaganda, Joseph Goebbels. In 1933, Goebbels invited Lang to his office and offered him a position as head producer of Nazi propaganda films for the now state-controlled UFA. According to Lang's account, Goebbels told him, "The Führer and I have seen your films, and the Führer made clear that 'this is the man who will give us the national socialist film.'" In Lang's telling, he immediately went home, packed his bags, and fled to Paris, leaving with such haste that he was unable to even stop at the bank. The story is probably apocryphal–a bit of self-mythologizing on Lang's part–as the evidence suggests he left Berlin within a few months, not a few hours. He also divorced von Harbou.

While Lang chose to leave Germany, von Harbou did not. Instead, she joined the Nazis and worked on propaganda films. The extent of von Harbou's own commitment to Nazi ideology remains an open question, although not a particularly relevant one. Whatever her personal beliefs, her role in the party's PR wing is simply indefensible. Perhaps von Harbou's Nazi affiliation is why her contributions to Lang's films from that period have been minimized. Perhaps, in the tradition of co-creator husbands and wives, they would have been minimized regardless; it's hard to say. Surfacing the contributions of unsung creators can also unearth some secret histories we'd prefer to forget. ✦

THX 1138:
A Decidedly Un-Lucas-Like Production

Long before George Lucas forever revolutionized science-fiction cinema with *Star Wars*, he wrote and directed a slow-burning, visually arresting film titled *THX 1138*. Though certainly not as commercially successful as Lucas's later endeavors, *THX 1138* is a dystopian classic, massively influential on the genre. In fact, it's one of those works that actually suffers from its own impact; you've probably already seen a dozen later

George Lucas paid tribute to his debut film with numerous references hidden in the Star Wars saga, particularly the number "1138," which is linked to cell blocks, battle droids, and more.

films that drew on this one as inspiration, making the original feel oddly derivative. (To be fair, the plot is pretty derivative itself, drawing on classics of mid-century dystopian literature such as George Orwell's *1984* and Aldous Huxley's *Brave New World*. But the film's coldly oppressive atmosphere and stunningly bleak visuals have influenced many later visions of a high-tech dystopia.)

THX 1138 began as a student film for George Lucas. He later reshot it as a feature film under the mentorship of Francis Ford Coppola, who had pitched it to Warner Bros.–with a tiny though bizarrely specific budget of $777,777.77. (Perhaps you can guess at Coppola's lucky number.) Meanwhile, Lucas was paid only $15,000 to write and direct the film. Not much, but also not bad for a twenty-three-year-old.

The film is set in a repressive underground society where technology reigns supreme, sex has been eliminated, and the drug-sedated populace labors emotionlessly to increase production. Constant surveillance and impassive robot-policemen enforce the law. The titular character, THX 1138 (played by Robert Duvall), falls in love with his female roommate. They stop taking their drugs and begin a sexual relationship, falling afoul of the law. Though not without its share of action sequences, the film suggests that freedom from oppression must first be found in the mind.

"*THX* was perceived as a bleak, depressing film upon its release," writes film professor and producer Dale Pollock in *Skywalking: The Life and Films of George Lucas*. "Even its admirers consider the movie to be austere and unemotional."

Honestly, it's difficult to imagine how this film could have come from the same director as an action-filled, big-hearted adventure like the *Star Wars* saga. Pollock suggests that audience reactions to *THX 1138* may have altered Lucas's perspective. "Lucas learned from the critical and popular reaction to *THX* that if he wanted to change the world, showing how stupid and awful society could be was not the way to proceed. It was a mistake he wouldn't repeat."

Instead, Lucas decided to make feel-good films with an aspirational vision. In *Star Wars*, rebels still risk everything to fight oppression–but good can triumph over evil. And unlike the bleak vision of *THX 1138*, which offers no alternate way of living for its characters, the *Star Wars* rebels are very clear on the world they want to build: a kinder galaxy where diversity is celebrated, life is cherished, and all planets deserve a right to self-determination. In the (much later) words of one Rose Tico: "Not fighting what we hate, but saving what we love." ✦

The Enduring Creations of Ralph McQuarrie

Y ou don't often hear his name spoken with the same reverence as George Lucas, but in his own way, Ralph McQuarrie (1929-2012) was equally instrumental in the making of *Star Wars*. The concept artist was the first person Lucas recruited to his design team–and his exacting, vibrant illustrations were crucial to obtaining funding for the film. With the paintings on hand, 20th Century Fox executives could really picture what Lucas was going for with *Star Wars*–and how groundbreaking it would be. McQuarrie continued to hold this pivotal role as visual designer of the *Star Wars* universe. In a tribute to McQuarrie's contributions–and their role in motivating and

Doug Chiang, who served as design director on Star Wars Episodes I and II, concept artist for *The Force Awakens*, and production designer for *Rogue One*, paid tribute to Ralph McQuarrie's immense influence on his own work and the look of Star Wars overall. Chiang stated, "Since I didn't go to art school, I learned to paint and draw through Ralph's work. The *Art of Star Wars* books and McQuarrie portfolios became my textbooks."

inspiring the whole *Star Wars* cast and crew–Lucas said, "When words could not convey my ideas, I could always point to one of Ralph's fabulous illustrations and say 'Do it like this.'"

Elsewhere, Lucas wrote, "His imaginary lands had history and his weirder inventions looked plausible." Indeed, like the best science-fiction artists, every one of McQuarrie's paintings was imbued with a sense of narrative, an inherent drama hinting at a story you'd like to know. McQuarrie envisioned Tatooine, the dusty desert planet of Luke Skywalker's childhood. He also designed our beloved characters: Darth Vader, Chewbacca, R2-D2, C-3PO. Darth Vader's infamous and character-defining mask, for instance, was McQuarrie's idea: "In the script, Vader had to jump from one ship to another and, in order to survive the vacuum of space, I felt he needed some sort of breathing mask," McQuarrie told the *Daily Telegraph* in one of his last interviews. He added a samurai helmet to complement Vader's flowing black robes, and the iconic character was born.

McQuarrie found the ubiquity of his famous character quite satisfying. (Even people who haven't seen *Star Wars*–yes, such people exist–can identify Darth Vader. Vader is even recognizable in flat silhouette!) "It's interesting to have done something out in the world that everyone looks at all the time," he said. "You become part of the public happening."

He also played a significant role in the creation of everyone's favorite anxious android, C-3PO. His design drew liberal amounts of inspiration from Fritz Lang's *Metropolis* and the art deco aesthetic, and this early painting was one of the first that Fox executives saw. It also inspired Anthony Daniels, the actor who voiced C-3PO. According to Daniels, he'd been intending to turn down the role, but the evocative painting changed his mind: "He had painted a face and a figure that had a very wistful, rather yearning, rather bereft quality, which I found very appealing."

In a charming tribute to McQuarrie's influential role, he was given a cameo in *The Empire Strikes Back*–briefly portraying Rebel General Pharl McQuarrie. He was uncredited and had no dialogue, but in 2007, Hasbro issued an action figure in General Pharl's image . . . a must-have for any true McQuarrie fan.

His work continues to inspire and influence the makers of today's *Star Wars*. The settings and environments he created–places that lived and breathed their own alien history–still serve as the background to the galaxy, shaping the look of the recent blockbusters *The Force Awakens*, *Rogue One*, and *The Last Jedi*. For instance, his original concept art helped shape the look of the farm where we encounter a very young Jyn Erso in the opening sequence of *Rogue One*.

Though he is best known for his *Star Wars* work, McQuarrie created concept art for many beloved science fiction properties. He worked on the 1978 *Battlestar Galactica* series; he worked with Steven Spielberg to design the alien ships in *Close Encounters of the Third Kind* and *E.T.*; and in 1985 he won an Academy Award for visual effects for his work on *Cocoon*. ✦

The Death Star's Architect: Concept Artist John Berkey

Though far from a household name, John Berkey (1932-2008) conceptualized one of science fiction's best-known symbols, familiar to just about anyone with even a passing interest in pop culture: the Death Star of *Star Wars* fame.

His role in developing the visuals of *Star Wars* was an early one, as he was one of the first artists to influence George Lucas. Lucas commissioned several paintings from Berkey during the stage where he was still trying to get studio funding to make *Star Wars*, and Berkey's conceptualizations of futuristic spacecraft helped Lucas bring his science fantasy to life. Berkey laid the visual groundwork for spacecraft such as the B-wings, Imperial Shuttles, and Mon Calamari ships.

"One of Berkey's illustrations–a rocket-plane diving down from space toward a gigantic metal world–seems to have especially caught and held the director's eye," says designer Michael Heilemann in an essay titled "John Berkey & The Mechanical Planet." "It would, in fact, be echoed in his film's climax as squadrons of Rebel X-wing fighters attack the Imperial Death Star."

Later, Ralph McQuarrie took over the concept art for *Star Wars*, contributing the lion's share of the arresting visuals that turned the franchise into a genre-defining hit. But there's no question that Berkey's ideas also played a role.

Like McQuarrie, Berkey also worked on *Battlestar Galactica* (1977). (Certain similarities between *Star Wars* and *Battlestar Galactica* then led to a lawsuit, but that's another story– see pages 105-107.) Berkey's passion for envisioning high-tech and futuristic space vessels has shaped the genre indelibly, deeply influencing our entire conception of space warfare.

SFF art expert and critic Jane Frank describes Berkey's style as "the perfect balance between painterly impressionism and hard-edged realism." In *The Art of John Berkey,* Frank collected more than one hundred of his illustrations and provides a nice overview of his contributions to the genre.

Ironically, Berkey never even saw *Star Wars*, the site of his best-known work. In 2005, he opined, "I suppose I should see it one of these days." ✦

[FOLLOWING PAGE] *Untitled* (1971) by John Berkey, often referred to as "Mechanical Planet" or "Tin Planet." Tempera, 14" x 14". The painting was purchased by George Lucas as inspiration.

Star Wars vs. *Battlestar Galactica*: The Legal Battle Over Space Opera's Look

W hen *Star Wars* hit the scene in 1977, it revolutionized science fiction forever. In the wake of the movie's smashing success, TV and film producers at every studio sought their own swashbuckling space opera. On television, the most successful of these was *Battlestar Galactica* (1978-1979), the original series created by Glen A. Larson.

Though not many present-day fans have seen the original *Battlestar Galactica*, the basic story will be familiar to anyone who saw (or absorbed by osmosis) the more recent twenty-first-century remake by SyFy–after a lengthy battle with the Cylons, the ragtag survivors of humanity flee the Twelve Colonies of Mankind in a massive warship, the "battlestar" *Galactica*. They journey through space searching for a long-lost thirteenth colony while being relentlessly pursued by the Cylons at every turn. Unlike in the SyFy remake, throughout which the Cylons' human appearances proved a major plot element, the original Cylons were metallic, humanoid robots–their sleek, bulky exteriors and awkwardly heavy strides not unlike the stormtroopers of *Star Wars*.

With a 148-minute run time and a $7 million budget, the pilot's production values rivaled that of a feature film. Narratively and visually, the show's early episodes delivered similar pleasures to that of *Star Wars*–and therein lay the problem, as some viewers believed them to be *too* similar. This camp included George Lucas and 20th Century Fox, who together launched a lawsuit against Universal, months before the show even premiered, based on the courtesy script Universal provided (provocatively titled *Galactica: Saga of a Star World*).

In its lawsuit, Fox pointed to "34 similarities" between the two properties. Some are eye-rollingly broad, seeming to implicate dozens–if not hundreds–of works in the science fiction genre, particularly in the decades since *Star Wars* cast its long shadow. Consider "The central conflict of each story is a war between the galaxy's democratic and totalitarian forces" or "The heroine is imprisoned by the totalitarian forces." Others are a little more specific, and perhaps damning: "Space vehicles, although futuristic, are made to look used and old, contrary to the stereotypical sleek, new appearance of space age equipment" or "There is a scene in a cantina (*Star Wars*) or casino (*Battlestar*), in which musical entertainment

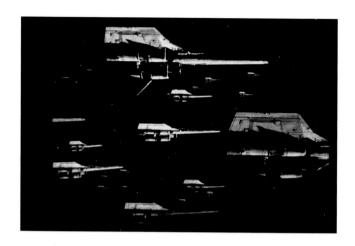

is offered by bizarre, non-human creatures." (Though, to be fair, fans of the French comic series *Valérian* might argue that the cantina scene wasn't original to *Star Wars*, either—see pages 236-238.)

Key characters also bore some resemblance to each other. Starbuck, a male character in the 1978 version, is a fighter pilot whose masculine charm and swagger rival that of Han Solo's. His more straitlaced friend, the handsome young Captain Apollo, carries a heavy family legacy as the son of military legend Commander Adama; his mother was tragically killed by Cylons. In earlier drafts of the script, Captain Apollo was named Skyler, telegraphing his connection to Luke Skywalker a bit too strongly.

But the resemblance that most strongly struck the average viewer were the visuals. "There's no escaping how much the original version of *Battlestar Galactica* looks like *Star Wars*," essayist and genre critic Ryan Britt writes for Tor.com. "From the red stripe painted on the fuselage of the Vipers, to the rag-tag worn-out look of the spaceships, to the feathery haircuts of Starbuck and Apollo, a small child or elderly parent in 1978 could have easily squinted at the television and believed this was *Star Wars: The TV Show*." It turns out there was a very good reason for these visual similarities. Two key creators lent their considerable talents to both projects, in fact going directly from the set of *Star Wars* to working for Glen Larson on *Battlestar Galactica*. Those artists were Ralph McQuarrie and John Dykstra.

Ralph McQuarrie, of course, was the concept artist who created many of the most iconic characters and landscapes in the entire *Star Wars* saga (see pages 101-102); his paintings, drawings, and sketches continue to massively influence the franchise. John Dykstra is a lighting and special effects virtuoso whose company Industrial Light & Magic (ILM) used a new motion-controlled camera that enabled some of *Star Wars*'s most groundbreaking special effects. For their work on *Star Wars*, Dykstra's team won Academy Awards for best special effects and special technical achievement.

Despite the accolades Dykstra would receive, George Lucas wasn't entirely happy with his work, and ended the contract early—perhaps making Dykstra's move to *Battlestar Galactica* all the more contentious. With his new company Apogee (which

Ralph McQuarrie designed concepts for the human fighter spacecraft Vipers, the Cylon Raiders and Basestar, and the Battlestar *Galactica* itself. The *Galactica* housed a fleet of about 150 Vipers.

included several employees from ILM), Dykstra created the visuals and special effects for the *Battlestar Galactica* pilot, which continued to be used throughout the series.

For his part, McQuarrie developed concept art and paintings for *Battlestar Galactica* that would set the look of the series—including the *Galactica,* the Cylon ships, and the vaguely Stormtrooper-esque Cylons themselves.

When the *Battlestar Galactica* pilot finally aired, the lawsuit was still ongoing. It had also grown more complex, since Universal had promptly countersued Fox, claiming that Fox had in fact stolen *Star Wars* from *them,* by plagiarizing a Buck Rogers serial from 1939 as well as *Silent Running* (1972).

As the lengthy pilot premiered, lines were drawn among viewers and fans: Was *Battlestar* a rip-off? SF master Isaac Asimov said yes: "*Battlestar Galactica* was *Star Wars* all over again," he wrote in a syndicated newspaper column in September 1978. "I couldn't enjoy it without amnesia." The ever-obstreperous Harlan Ellison was also #TeamRipOff, saddling the show's creator Glen Larson with the nickname "Glen Larceny." Others found the comparisons superficial, especially as the show progressed, giving it more opportunity to flesh out its characters and expand its plot lines, inevitably treading new territory.

The lawsuit was thrown out in 1980 (by a court that also found the resemblances superficial)—then appealed. Universal eventually settled with Fox for $225,000.

Battlestar Galactica itself only ran for a single season—outlived at the time by the lawsuit that followed it. While initially its ratings were strong, they dropped over the season, leading to its early cancellation. After a massive fan outcry—including a suicide—the show returned briefly as *Galactica 1980*. This iteration lacked most of the original cast, and was not good.

In 2003, the franchise returned on SyFy, first as a three-hour miniseries and then as a series that ran from 2004-2009, produced by Ronald D. Moore and David Eick. (Plus a handful of spin-offs such as *The Plan* (2009) and *Caprica* (2010-2011).) This grittier, sexier reboot staked out a territory far removed from its "Space Western" beginnings; now, comparisons to *Star Wars* would seem absurd. Yet both properties remain a lasting testament to the conceptual artistry of Ralph McQuarrie, who created the iconic visuals that so thoroughly define each story. ✦

McQuarrie provided early artwork and concepting for the metal-attired Cylon centurions, rudely nicknamed "toasters" in the 21st century remake.

"The Spice Must Flow": Iterations of *Dune*

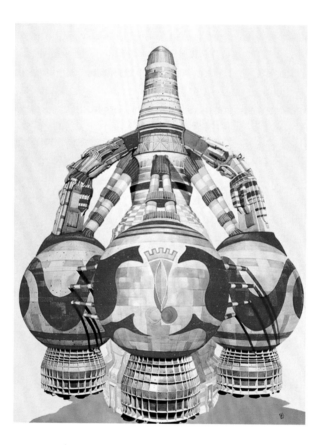

I n Frank Pavich's award-winning documentary *Jodorowsky's Dune* (2013), the famed director himself relays an odd and hilarious story about David Carradine, the actor tapped to play Duke Leto (a lead character). Alejandro Jodorowsky (b. 1929) invited Carradine to meet him in his hotel room. When Carradine walked in, he saw a jumbo-sized jar of vitamin E, which

Harkonnen's Flagship, concept art by Chris Foss for Jodorowsky's *Dune*.

Jodorowsky had purchased "to take one pill every day, in order to have the strength." As soon as Carradine crossed the threshold and laid his eyes on this delightful prize, he exclaimed, "Oh, vitamin E!" . . . and proceeded to swallow the entire bottle. Here, Jodorowsky does an impression of Carradine's insatiable vitamin E-gobbling: head tossed back, the imaginary jar pouring its contents straight into his gargling throat. "It was like a monstrosity!" Jodorowsky concludes.

This bizarre, unrestrained act signified to Jodorowsky that Carradine could pull off the ambitious role, and he told him, "You are the person I am searching for."

Jodorowsky is a charismatic, charming figure, and this story, like many of his recollections, is relayed with a fierce vitality that makes it quite enjoyable to watch. It's very funny. But as he moves on to other topics, some practical questions remain–who in the world, no matter how eccentric, would swallow a hundred vitamin E pills in one sitting? Wouldn't Carradine need a bit of beverage to wash them down? Did he . . . *chew* them? How long did this take? What were Jodorowsky and colleagues doing as the situation unfolded?

But no further explanations are forthcoming. This is the story; it is what it is. And this is the spirit in which it's best to encounter the documentary as a whole, and the larger-than-life legend of the greatest movie never made. It's a rousing vision, and a fantastic story. Would it have been an equally fantastic film? We'll never really know.

In the early 1970s, Chilean film director Alejandro Jodorowsky was making major waves in art house and indie film circles. His psychedelic western *El Topo* (1971) was an early cult film, some say the first "midnight movie." *El Topo* was followed by Jodorowsky's surrealist fantasy film *The Holy Mountain* (1973), which the *New York Times* called "dazzling, rambling, often incoherent satire on consumerism, militarism, and exploitation." So it makes sense that he was tapped to direct the film adaptation of Frank Herbert's *Dune* (1965), a groundbreaking novel to which many of the above descriptions apply. *Dune* (the novel) is a massive epic of the far future, where the corrupt, decadent villains of the galaxy execute complex political maneuvers in order to control the backwater planet Arrakis (colloquially called Dune). Though a barren and hostile place, Dune is home to an extremely rare element called "spice," an addictive substance and energy source that's essential to the function of the entire galactic order–essentially, what fossil fuels were to civilization in the 1970s, combined with a tinge of LSD.

Writing for the *Guardian* in 2015, novelist and journalist Hari Kunzru said, "Every fantasy reflects the place and time that produced it. . . . *Dune* is the paradigmatic fantasy of the Age of Aquarius. Its concerns–environmental stress, human potential, altered states of consciousness, and the developing countries' revolution against imperialism–are blended together into an era-defining vision of personal and cosmic transformation." Fueled by this timely vision, *Dune* became one of the bestselling science fiction novels of all time. It won the Hugo and the Nebula (the genre's biggest awards). As of 2003, it had sold twelve million copies.

A galaxy-spanning epic . . . a worldwide phenomenon . . . *Dune* was the perfect target

for Jodorowsky's almost limitless vision and ambition. In a 1985 essay on the subject, Jodorowsky wrote, "There is an artist, only one in the medium of a million other artists, which only once in his life, by a species of divine grace, receives an immortal topic, a MYTH." For him, *Dune* was that once-in-a-lifetime project. "I had received a version of *Dune* and I wanted to transmit it," he writes. "The Myth was to give up the literary form and to become Image . . ."

In Pavich's documentary, Jodorowsky articulates similar thoughts: "For *Dune*, I wanted to create a prophet. *Dune* will be the coming of a God."

For such a visionary project, there could be no ordinary cast and crew. Jodorowsky began assembling a team of "spiritual warriors," each individual painstakingly selected and tirelessly persuaded. Jodorowsky understood exactly the talents he required, and there could be no substitutions, no alternates.

In this way he assembled a truly remarkable creative team: legendary concept artists Jean Giraud (who went by Moebius for his sci-fi work), H. R. Giger, Chris Foss, and artist/writer Dan O'Bannon, all of whom later did outstanding, genre-defining work on Ridley Scott's *Alien*. Jodorowsky asked each of these three very different artists to work individually on specific aspects of the set design. This smart move ensured unique aesthetics for galactic actors separated by gulfs of space and time. The Swiss surrealist H. R. Giger, for instance, created the look

Terming it "easily the geekiest and most obsessive documentary I saw all year," *Entertainment Weekly*'s Chris Nashawaty declared *Jodorowsky's Dune* one of the ten best movies of 2014.

and feel of the degenerate, depraved world of House Harkonnen, poisoned by their own greed and perversion.

Jodorowsky also recruited Mick Jagger, Salvador Dali, and Orson Welles as actors. His own twelve-year-old son Brontis trained in fighting techniques for six hours a day for two years straight, in preparation for the lead role of young Paul Atreides. Together with avant-garde band Magma, Pink Floyd would create the soundtrack–a work that could have become an unforgettable SF classic in its own right.

Much of Pavich's documentary is devoted to Jodorowsky describing the bold strategies employed to convert these figures to his cause–and enumerating the various coincidences and serendipities that brought them together. Orson Welles, a legendary foodie, refused his pleas to play Baron Harkonnen until Jodorowsky promised to hire his favorite chef to cook for him every day on set. Salvador Dali invited Jodorowsky to join him at a table filled with Dali's friends and admirers, then posed a surreal riddle, claiming that he's often discovered clocks in the sand–has Jodorowsky ever found one? Jodorowsky is momentarily stumped, wanting to seem neither too bereft of clocks nor too boastful, until he hits on the perfect answer . . . he's never found a clock, but he's lost plenty. Dali is impressed and agrees to play the emperor. And so on.

Leading his design team with messianic fervor, Jodorowsky would give them a speech each morning: "You are on a mission to save humanity." As the documentary makes clear, his passion for the project inspired and motivated them, eliciting their very best work. "It was a phenomenally creative period," said Chris Foss in *Skeleton Crew* magazine. "Goaded by the guru-like Alejandro, I produced some of my most original work. We were literally a gang of three working under the master to create a multi-million-dollar movie."

For two years the team worked on sketches, scripts, concept art. Moebius storyboarded out the entire film with Jodorowsky's direction. All those materials now form a massive–as in unbelievably gigantic–book; allegedly only two of these books exist. We get a glimpse of this book in the documentary, rifling through the pages. Its rarity feels like a bit of a waste. Though it would no doubt cost a fortune to reproduce, it would make a hell of a coffee table book.

Everything was ready to begin filming, but it was not to be. By 1976, Jodorowsky had already spent $2 million in preproduction, and the film as imagined would need a great deal more funding to realize the vision. Not to mention it was intended to be a fourteen-hour-long experience akin to an acid trip. The film's financial backers got cold feet and pulled the funding, and just like that, the project was over. It was a devastating blow.

A few years later, the rights were acquired by Dino De Laurentiis. De Laurentiis first hired Ridley Scott–who'd recently directed *Alien*, working with some of the key creative talents involved in Jodorowsky's *Dune*. But a family tragedy compelled Scott to exit the project. Next De Laurentiis recruited David Lynch, still a relatively young and inexperienced director.

[FOLLOWING SPREAD] HR Giger: *Dune V*, 1976, 70 x 100 cm, acrylic on paper. Courtesy of the HR Giger Museum, Gruyeres, Switzerland.

H.R. GIGER 76
JODOROWSKY'S

Lynch's version of *Dune* is still plenty bonkers. It stars his frequent muse Kyle MacLachlan and the musician Sting. The band Toto took a break from blessing the rains down in Africa to create the soundtrack.

The film is undeniably awful–a fact that cheered the heartbroken Jodorowsky immensely. (As an admirer of Lynch, a kindred creative spirit, Jodorowsky blamed not the director but the short-sighted producers who'd done them both wrong.) Lynch's *Dune* cost $45 million to make and only grossed $31 million, a financial disaster. A TV adaptation called *Frank Herbert's Dune* premiered on Syfy December 3, 2000; the three-part miniseries was one of the channel's highest-rated programs and won Emmys for cinematography and visual effects. Writing for Tor.com, Emily Asher-Perrin pronounced it "the Most Okay Adaptation of the Book to Date," which is, well, something.

Jodorowsky wrote, "There is an artist, only one in the medium of a million other artists, which only once in his life, by a species of divine grace, receives an immortal topic, a MYTH." For him, *Dune* was that once-in-a-lifetime project.

In an odd twist, Frank Pavich's documentary–the best look we've ever gotten at Jodorowsky's *Dune*–was a hit at Cannes and a classic for fans, winning acclaim and awards.

Now, another adaptation is (hopefully) headed for the big screen. In 2017, Legendary Films hired director Denis Villeneuve to take a shot at it. Villeneuve directed *Arrival* (2016), a gorgeous, heartrending masterpiece of a film based on a brilliant short story by Ted Chiang. *Arrival* wowed genre and mainstream audiences alike, winning the Hugo Award for Best Dramatic Presentation and receiving Oscar nominations for best picture, best director, and best adapted screenplay (among others). Perhaps Villeneuve is the director to finally conquer this seemingly unconquerable story. +

"The Tourist": The Alien Sex Film Noir We Deserve

I magine this: *Men in Black*, but darker, stranger, sexier. *Star Wars*' Mos Eisley Cantina, but designed by H. R. Giger of *Alien* fame. A New Wave noir starring an enigmatic bombshell blonde, authored by a female screenwriter. That was "The Tourist": a 1980 screenplay by Clair Noto that never made it to the screen. If it had been made, it would have been the first film noir science fiction movie,

HR Giger: *The Tourist II, Biomechanic Bird Robot in His Room*, 1982, 70 x 100 cm, acrylic on paper. Courtesy of the HR Giger Museum, Gruyeres, Switzerland.

groundbreaking for the innovation that Ridley Scott's *Blade Runner* claimed instead. Some have termed "The Tourist" a masterpiece, and it frequently makes appearances on lists of the greatest sci-fi movies never made. But will it ever be more than a dream?

Noto's previous writing credits included a stint working on Marvel Comics' Red Sonja. One of her inspirations was the 1951 sci-fi classic *The Day the Earth Stood Still*, in which an alien walks among us disguised as a human. Another inspiration was the work of H. R. Giger, whose darkly erotic illustrations she followed in the pages of *Heavy Metal* magazine—making the artist the perfect candidate to render concept art for "The Tourist."

The script follows Grace Ripley, a gorgeous blonde, a corporate executive, and a secret alien exiled on Planet Earth. An encounter with another disguised alien draws Grace into Manhattan's seedy underbelly, where alien refugees congregate in a hidden place called The Corridor. The Corridor is home to a variety of extraterrestrials from many worlds; those who aren't disguised must spend their lives hiding away in this cramped underground slum. The Corridor is part internment camp, part sex club, where aliens get up to the type of kinky shenanigans you'd expect from higher beings stranded on a really boring planet a zillion light years from home. Noto said, "I wanted to portray sexual agony and ecstasy in a way I'd never seen before, and science fiction seemed like the arena."

HR Giger: *The Tourist VI, Alien Heads*, 1982, 70×100 cm, acrylic on paper, Courtesy of the HR Giger Museum, Gruyeres, Switzerland.

Grace navigates this weird secret world in search of a person who is rumored to have a way to leave Earth. The journey brings her face to face with her alien nemesis in a no-holds-barred confrontation.

Influenced by directors Federico Fellini and Michelangelo Antonioni, and inspired by the aesthetic of the New Wave, Noto's screenplay used an unconventional structure. It was a uniquely compelling and highly original work, which immediately captured the attention of directors and producers. In 1980 it was optioned by Universal. Director Brian Gibson, who would soon go on to direct *Poltergeist II* (1986) oversaw the script development. H. R. Giger, who had just played a major role in the creative design of the highly successful film *Alien* (1979), began envisioning the alien denizens of the Corridor.

In an interview with film critic David Hughes, Gibson said of "The Tourist," "What struck me as being totally original was the idea of a rather gloomy, existentialist *film noir*, with the premise of Earth being a dumping ground for monsters from various galaxies, which was very resonant with a depressed view of the human condition. It made it a movie with art-house appeal, but with a premise that had a much wider potential audience."

Unfortunately, it was the potential for a bigger audience that sunk the project. The studio wanted to revise Noto's unconventional script structure into something more appealing to mainstream audiences, as the large special effects budget for this visually lush movie would demand a big investment—in need of a big return. Script doctors struggled to mesh their edits with Noto's idiosyncratic voice. Creative differences and personality clashes stalled the project.

The screenwriter herself was candid about the script's structural challenges. "There are certain projects that have a form and a structure to them that any good writer can really come in and deal with," she told Fred Szebin for *Cinefantastique*. "This doesn't have that. It's all over the place; definitely a can of worms." But she was content with that approach, drawing as she had on New Wave influences. On this particular script I didn't give a damn to try to make a mainstream script," she added. Her characters were also inspired by figures from her own life, a source of creative fodder that future script doctors would not understand.

Noto regained the rights and took the script to Francis Ford Coppola's American Zoetrope. With the wild success of *The Godfather* and *Apocalypse Now*, Coppola was already legendary. But Zoetrope was a financial failure. The studio shut down in 1984, and Noto's script went back to Universal Studios. It spent the following years bouncing back and forth between creative teams, stranded in development purgatory.

Today, almost forty years since Noto first wrote the script, "The Tourist" still has its enthusiastic fans, many of whom would still love to see the screenplay become the film it deserves . . . or even a TV show. With its weird and unsettling atmosphere; its story about xenophobia and alienation, desire and isolation; and its strong female lead, perhaps the time for "The Tourist" has finally come. In the age of all-you-can-watch streaming originals, "The Tourist" might even be the making of Netflix, Hulu, or Amazon's next big hit. ✦

The Unicorn-Like Creations of Moebius, Concept Artist

From the *Alien* quadrilogy to *TRON* to 1980s Marvel, the direct and indirect influence of French artist and illustrator Moebius/Jean Giraud (1938-2012) is widespread and unmistakable. After getting his start in Western-themed comic books as a young artist, Moebius developed a gritty, dark style of realism that caught the eye of film directors who were looking to capture the Spaghetti Western aesthetic, including surrealist Alejandro Jodorowsky for his doomed adaptation of *Dune* (see pages 108-114). Despite that grand

film never getting made, the collaboration between Jodorowsky and Moebius led to the creation of a dark surrealist graphic novel (*Les yeux du chat*) that brought Moebius further into the worlds of science fiction and

Jean Giraud in conversation with journalists at the 26th Edition of the International Comic Show in Barcelona, April 2008. Photo credit: Alberto Estevez/ EPA/ Shutterstock.

fantasy. Later, the two would collaborate on another–and better-known–French graphic novel series, *The Incal*, first published from 1980 to 1988 in the French science fiction/horror comics magazine *Métal Hurlant*. Written by Jodorowsky and illustrated by Giraud, *The Incal* is a baroque and expansive space opera that centers on the adventures of an archetypal "everyman" character named John DiFool. After a move to California, Moebius made art for well-known DC and Marvel titles, including Batman, Iron Man, Static, and a Silver Surfer miniseries written by Stan Lee that won the Eisner Award for limited series in 1989. Moebius's style had a subtle influence at both houses, incorporating a grittier, more heavily textured technique than most of the illustrators of the decade.

The artist enjoyed a long run of successful projects in Hollywood after having made a name for himself in the United States. Moebius contributed character design and storyboard art for such blockbusters as *Alien*, *TRON*, *The Abyss*, and *The Fifth Element*. His style is as visible and as commonly imitated in 1990s science fiction as his contemporary H. R. Giger, though the latter is more commonly cited as the visionary artist responsible for the terror of facehuggers and chest-bursters. Moebius's work did not emphasize body horror, but it was just as instrumental in visual worldbuilding.

Not only a visual artist, Moebius wrote the story and created the conceptual art for Yutaka Fujioka's 1989 animated film *Little Nemo: Adventures in Slumberland,* and wrote a graphic novel series for the same story five years later with artist Bruno Marchand.

The artists and directors who claim Moebius as a major influence on their work reads like a who's who of the twentieth century. George Lucas tried to get Moebius to work with him on *Willow*, only to lose him to other projects and regret the loss for years afterward. He has been cited as an inspiration by Neil Gaiman, Federico Fellini, Paulo Coelho, Mike Mignola, and Hayao Miyazaki. Ridley Scott counted himself lucky for having had Moebius's input on the *Alien* franchise, and continued to cite his importance through *Blade Runner* and the whole genre of science fiction in film.

Moebius was eulogized by the French minister of culture at his 2012 funeral, described as a double loss to the French arts: both as Giraud and as Moebius. The artist is interred at Paris's elite Montparnasse Cemetery, where many of the greatest figures in the country's history are laid to rest.

But an artist never truly dies, so long as their work and the works that they touched live on. In his own words, Moebius admitted that he had become something legendary and uncatchable in a much-quoted moment of self-description acknowledging the effect he has had on the many different worlds in the art realm:

"They said that I changed their life. 'You changed my life. Your work is why I became an artist.' Oh, it makes me happy. But you know, at same time I have an internal broom to clean it all up. It can be dangerous to believe it. Someone wrote, 'Moebius is a legendary artist.' That puts a frame around me. A legend–now I am like a unicorn."

Moebius *is* a unicorn. You may not know what you saw, but you know you saw it. You never forget. ✦

How *WarGames*
Changed American Military Policy

Remember *WarGames*?

In this 1983 movie, a computer-savvy teen, played by the always lovably dopey Matthew Broderick, accidentally hacks into a computer at the North American Aerospace Defense Command (NORAD) while searching for fun new games to play. The computer challenges him to a game of "Global Thermonuclear War." Enthusiastically, Broderick agrees, and unintentionally sets off a nuclear crisis that could launch World War III.

"As a premise for a thriller, this is a masterstroke," the late, great film critic Roger

WarGames got a 21st century follow-up with the 2009 sequel, *WarGames: The Dead Code*. The movie went straight to DVD and, with a 25% rating on Rotten Tomatoes, was not a hit.

Ebert wrote in his review. Even today the film is a fun watch, even if such a thing could certainly never have happened. The very premise is patently ridiculous . . .

Or is it?

President Ronald Reagan wondered the same thing. And the terrifying answer changed the future of cybersecurity.

As a former film star himself, Reagan loved watching movies. He saw the film soon after it came out during some relaxation at Camp David. When he returned to the White House, he was scheduled to meet with national security advisors and senior members of Congress. The meeting agenda focused on forthcoming nuclear arms talks with Russia.

But Reagan was still thinking about *WarGames*. He interrupted the talk of Russia to ask his assembled national security advisors what they thought of the film. No one else had seen it yet, so he gave them the play-by-play, describing the film in detail while his audience listened in confusion.

In a retelling of the event, cybersecurity expert Fred Kaplan writes, "Some of the lawmakers looked around the room with suppressed smiles or raised eyebrows. Three months earlier, Reagan had delivered his 'Star Wars' speech, imploring scientists to build laser weapons that could shoot down Soviet missiles in outer space. The idea was widely dismissed as nutty. What was the old man up to now?"

Undeterred, Reagan asked his chairman of the Joint Chiefs of Staff, General John W. Vessey Jr. to investigate a key question: "Could something like this really happen?"

Vessey did. And his findings were . . . concerning. "Mr. President," he's reported as saying, "The problem is much worse than you think."

As it happens, the movie's shocking premise didn't just emerge from the fevered mind of a screenwriter. When Lawrence Lasker and Walter Parkes were writing the screenplay, they interviewed one of the world's foremost experts on computer security–an engineer named Willis Ware.

Ware had actually helped design the NORAD computer's software (so he knew exactly what Broderick was getting into). He'd written a paper on the system's vulnerabilities way back in 1967. Like Cassandra, he'd been warning fruitlessly about a life-and-death hacking scenario for decades. But when the story was brought to life by *WarGames*, the threat finally captured America's attention . . . as well the president's.

Fifteen months later Reagan signed a classified national security decision directive, the "National Policy on Telecommunications and Automated Information Systems Security." And cybersecurity was born.

WarGames did pretty well, too, earning $80 million at the box office, not bad for a film that only cost $12 million to make. It even got three Oscar nominations, including one for Lasker and Parkes's original screenplay.

WarGames' concluding line, "A strange game. The only winning move is not to play," tapped into America's Cold War-weary zeitgeist. But the film's lasting legacy is intimately connected with the cybersecurity concerns of today. ✦

The *Alien III(s)*
That Might Have Been

In James Cameron's *Aliens* (1986), Sigourney Weaver reprised her role as Ellen Ripley, reliving her greatest trauma as she joins a mission to the planet where the aliens were discovered–and now, it seems, are wreaking havoc. There, she discovers a small, terrified girl, the settlement's last survivor. Like Ripley, Newt has suffered unimaginable horrors through her encounters with the aliens; like Ripley at the end of *Alien* (1979), she's the only one left. Their relationship offers a powerful narrative thread as Ripley, the marines, and an android named Bishop take on one nasty beast after another.

The movie was a smashing success, receiving accolades from viewers and critics alike. It was nominated for seven Academy Awards and won two. (And Sigourney Weaver was nominated as best actress for her role, rare recognition for a science fiction film.) Despite the fact that it was made for only $18 million, it brought in $180 million worldwide, an impressive return on investment.

Unfortunately, *Alien 3*, the second follow-up from 1992, did not garner such praise. Though it wasn't a complete flop, reviews were mixed, and it did not enjoy the same commercial success. Its director, David Fincher, has since disowned it.

But, as journalist Abraham Riesman phrases it mournfully in *Vulture*, "there's an alternate universe where the series' propulsive momentum only increased . . . the alternate universe where legendary science-fiction writer William Gibson's *Alien III* (that's "III," not "3") screenplay was realized. It is, perhaps, a better world than ours."

When *Aliens* came to theaters in 1986, novelist William Gibson was a hot young talent and rising star; his first novel, *Neuromancer*, had been published in 1984 to wide appreciation. Unknown to the makers of *Alien*, the "dirty spaceship aesthetic" of the first movie had already found its way into his fiction, shaping the gritty world of *Neuromancer's* Sprawl. In 1992, speaking of the original *Alien* movie, Gibson told *Cinefantastique*, "I thought there were germs of stories implicit in the art direction. I always wanted to know more about those guys. Why were they wearing dirty sneakers in this funky spaceship? I think it influenced my prose SF writing because it was the first funked up, dirty kitchen-sink space ship and it made a big impression on me."

This latent influence spawned an ironic but charming loop. As Douglas Perry described it in *Cinescape* in 1995, "[David] Giler had read Gibson's award-winning novel *Neuromancer* and realized with a jolt that the futuristic Earth the novelist envisioned jibed perfectly with the exhausted techno-society represented by the *Nostromo* and its crew in Dan O'Bannon's original story." Giler and his fellow producer Walter Hill offered Gibson a chance to write the screenplay, and he accepted.

There was a catch, however. Sigourney Weaver would not be able to appear in this film; contractual disputes may have played a role, as she did eventually return as Ripley in the real-world version of *Alien 3*. Ripley was such a powerful protagonist in the first two films, and it would be a challenge to reinvent the narrative without her. Instead, Gibson chose to focus on his second-favorite character from *Aliens*; the android, Bishop. Giler and Hill gave Gibson a basic treatment for the story and sent him off to work.

In a way, Gibson seems an odd choice for a screenwriter. What is most brilliant and striking about his body of work is his talent for evoking a world through language. He has a talent for description that cascades in glittering onslaughts of synesthesia that cut like a diamond. You see and feel and taste his worlds, even the indefinable and ambiguous space of virtual reality (or as it's termed in his Sprawl trilogy, "the matrix"). The opening sentence to *Neuromancer* is one of the most famous in science fiction: "The sky above the port was the color of a television, tuned to a dead channel." For a virtuoso of description like Gibson, the screenplay format seems like a waste of his talents.

In a way, Gibson seems an odd choice for a screenwriter. What is most brilliant and striking about his body of work is his talent for evoking a world through language... You see and feel and taste his worlds, even the indefinable and ambiguous space of virtual reality.

Nevertheless, *Alien III* is a very solid story. Though his script was never translated to the big screen, the visual moments it evokes come through powerfully enough that your imagination fills in the gaps; there are scenes that one can picture so completely that it's as if you really watched them. The description that follows is based on Gibson's first draft, which can be read in its entirety online, offering it a kind of lasting narrative life of its own.

The script picks up where *Aliens* left off. In the closing minutes of that movie, only a few have survived the carnage on the planet where the xenomorphs were first discovered. The last characters standing are Ripley, a marine named Hicks, the loyal android Bishop, and a little girl named Newt. This small band of survivors has made it to their ship, the *Sulaco*, ready to get the hell out of this place. But the Xenomorph Queen has stowed away for one last major battle. Her massive stinger rips apart Bishop, separating his torso from his legs. Despite the severe damage, his upper body continues to function. Ripley and the Queen go head-to-head in a major showdown, as Ripley risks everything to save Newt, her surrogate daughter. The Alien Queen is ejected into space and the team survives. They go into hypersleep and head back toward Earth.

Gibson's *Alien III* opens on the *Sulaco* drifting in space. Ripley, Hicks, Newt, and the wounded Bishop are unconscious in their hypersleep capsules, oblivious to the navigation error that sends their ship into a disputed sector of space, claimed by the Union of Progressive Peoples (U.P.P.)—a Communist coalition that serves as an obvious stand-in for the 1980s Soviet Union and its satellite states.

A passing U.P.P. ship stumbles on the *Sulaco* and sends a small boarding party to check it out; an eerie, voyeuristic moment ensues, as the slumbering *Sulaco* crew has no idea they're being boarded and observed by enemy soldiers. "Commandos move down the line, guns poised," reads the script. "They peer in at Newt, Ripley, and Hicks, but the lid of Bishop's capsule is pearl-white." They open the capsule to discover an Alien egg rooted in Bishop's wounded torso. Seconds later, a feisty, well-rested face-hugger ejects itself and attaches to their Leader's head. His soldiers manage to shoot it without killing him but the alien's acidic body fluids spew everywhere and burn through his helmet. The commandos grab Bishop's torso and scramble back to their own ship.

The next sequence opens on a space station called Anchorpoint, "the size of a small moon, and growing"; "a vast, irregular structure, the result of the shifting goals of successive administrations." The *Sulaco* has just docked, with the team still in hypersleep. Tissue culture lab tech Tully is called in the middle of the night to come take samples and basically figure out what the deal is. Mysteriously, a couple of high-ranking people from "Millisci, Weapons Division" have also arrived . . . and the plot thickens.

Accompanied by a couple marines, Tully heads onto the *Sulaco* to collect atmosphere samples. Of course, just as they arrive in the hypersleep chamber, some unwelcome visitors arrive. Alien stowaways attack the marines, who barely manage to escape, hosing down the entire chamber with liquid fire from their flamethrowers. (In Gibson's second draft, this scene is omitted entirely, which is probably for the best as it's not entirely clear why or how the full-sized xenomorphs were roaming around the ship.)

In Anchorpoint's medical clinic, Hicks and Newt meet lab tech Spence, Tully's girlfriend; she will be one of the key players in this story. In accordance with Gibson's parameters, Ripley remains in a coma, stuck in the interminable nightmare of Alien carnage.

This leads to one of the story's most poignant moments. Newt stands beside the bed of the unconscious Ripley, "monitored by assorted white consoles. Her forehead is taped with half a dozen small electrodes."

"She's sleeping," Spence tells Newt. "Sometimes people need to sleep . . . To get over things . . ."

"Is Ripley dreaming?" Newt asks.

"I don't know, honey."

"It's better not to."

William Gibson's Alien 3 #3, written by William Gibson and Johnnie Christmas, illustrated by Johnnie Christmas. Published by Dark Horse Comics in 2019.

This short exchange encapsulates so much of what's gone before; the unspeakable trauma of survival, the cosmic dread the aliens represent, and the unshakeable bond formed between Ripley and Newt, who've each lost all except each other.

It also exposes the script's fundamental weakness. This early moment touches on deeper emotion than anything that follows. Newt gets shipped back to her grandparents on Earth, Ripley never wakes up, and the emotional stakes that remain are ambiguous. Every other character may as well be cannon fodder; as it turns out, the vast majority of them are.

Back on the U.P.P.'s *Rodina*, the Commies are mining Bishop's torso for data, learning all about the aliens. Meanwhile, in a clever cut shot, technicians on Anchorpoint are extracting similar biological information from Bishop's legs. Something unexpected is happening, and here, Gibson introduces an idea that in the real-life history of the franchise wouldn't emerge until 2012, in the prequel *Prometheus*. Gibson imagines the Alien Queen as a biological weapon, leaving behind an instinctually hungry residue that's as fiercely desperate for survival as its eggs. (The "black goo" in *Prometheus* is not alien residue, but the concept is similar; a biological substance that bends and mutates other living matter to its will and remakes it in its own image.)

The scary Millisci folks who've arrived on Anchorpoint are interested in exactly that. They inform Colonel Rosetti, Anchorpoint's head of military operations, that scientific testing will continue on the aliens' bizarre genetic material. ("The alien genetic material looks like a cubist's vision of an art deco staircase, its asymmetrical segments glowing Day-glo green and purple," Gibson writes.) Rosetti protests that such testing is in violation of weapons treaties. In a wink-wink manner, the Millisci people tell him the experiments are for cancer research. "We'll nourish the cells in stasis tubes, under constant observation," one says. Back on the U.P.P. *Rodina*, they're doing the same thing.

The Millisci command also insists that Tully, the marines who originally boarded the *Sulaco*, and anyone else who knows about alien shenanigans be forced to sign a rigorous nondisclosure agreement.

But silence breeds death. A number of people have already been exposed to the alien DNA. As Rodina and Anchorpoint play politics over the safe return of Bishop, and insiders and outsiders on Anchorpoint jockey for power, the infection is spreading beneath the surface. And it bursts forth in a spectacular fashion at a meeting of Anchorpoint's top brass, when one of the Millisci bad guys, a woman named Welles, is interrupted mid-evil-monologue to transform into something horrifying. This ain't a chest-burster; it's more like a whole-other-being-burster.

"Segmented biomechanoid tendons squirm beneath the skin of her arms. Her hands claw at one another, tearing redundant flesh from alien talons. . . . She straightens up. And rips her face apart in a single movement, the glistening claws coming away with skin, eyes, muscle, teeth, and splinters of bone . . . The New Beast sheds its human skin in a single sinuous, bloody ripple, molting on fast forward."

This point occurs about halfway into the script, and from that point forward, it's pretty

> There are bloody, acid-bathed battles, claustrophobic tunnel sequences, and people getting skewered by alien stingers at the most dramatically ironic moments; all the things we know and love from *Alien* and *Aliens.*

much nonstop carnage, with people molting into New Beasts left and right, and the loose New Beasts doing plenty of damage themselves. The same thing is occurring over on the *Rodina*, which calls for help from its comrades, who come quickly–to obliterate the entire ship with a nuclear missile. An effective containment strategy, no doubt. Only one female commando escapes in the small shuttle first used to board the *Sulaco*.

On the Anchorpoint, Tully goes down, leaving Spence, Hicks, and the recently returned and fully repaired Bishop to lead a band of soldiers and crew on a perilous journey through the station to reach the lifeboat bay. The remaining sequences are pure action, as New Beasts pick them off one by one and the brave crew dwindles to nothing. Meanwhile, Bishop departs on a secret solo mission to hack the fusion reactors on the station to blow the whole thing, leaving just enough time for their escape. There are bloody, acid-bathed battles, claustrophobic tunnel sequences, and people getting skewered by alien stingers at the most dramatically ironic moments; all the things we know and love from *Alien* and *Aliens*. On the big screen, this would no doubt be fast-paced, heart-pounding, and exquisitely satisfying, but on the page it can be a bit hard to follow.

There are implications that the alien DNA isn't just colonizing the people, but the ship itself. As in a side trip through a hydroponic farm, where "two of the Styrofoam structures have been overgrown with a grayish parody of vegetation, glistening vine-like structures and bulbous sacs that echo the Alien biomech motif. Patches of thick black mold spread to the Styrofoam and the white deck."

Another compelling scene sees Spence revisiting the Anchorpoint's eco-module, described in earlier scenes as "an experimental pocket Eden . . . lush rainforest, sun-dappled miniature meadows, patches of African cactus." Once an idyllic refuge, the eco-module is now poisoned by the aliens, too. The primates are cocooned, poised to hatch. The lemur has become an alien itself, screaming and pouncing from the trees above. As it represents the Anchorpoint's downfall, this arc also foreshadows the unthinkable, which has remained a source of ultimate dread throughout the franchise: What if the aliens make it to Earth?

In the story's tense final moments, the U.P.P. commando arrives at the rescue. Hicks, Spence, and Bishop are the only survivors who make it onto her shuttle. (The still-unconscious Ripley was previously launched to safety in a lifeboat.) As Hicks and Spence try to comfort the commando, who is dying from radiation poisoning, Bishop observes, "You're a species again, Hicks. United against a common enemy . . ."

But this particular version of *Alien III* would never be made (at least not into a film). Perhaps the producers had hoped for something more strikingly cyberpunk; perhaps they didn't know exactly what they were hoping for, but this wasn't it. David Giler told *Cinefantastique*, "We got the opposite of what we expected. We figured we'd get a script that was all over the place, but with good ideas we could mine. It turned out to be a competently written screenplay but not as inventive as we wanted it to be. That was probably our fault, though, because it was our story."

Gibson's script was followed by about thirty others. In the end, *Alien 3* was based on a script by independent filmmaker Vincent Ward, although some significant changes were made to his story. This is a secret history all its own, as Ward's original concept is also a famous unmade version–perhaps more famous, as it came much closer to being fully realized.

In Ward's treatment, the penal colony where Ripley crash-lands in *Alien 3* was originally meant to be, in Gibson's words, "a wooden space station inhabited by deranged monks." It's also a fascinating take on the franchise. As pop culture critic Ryan Lambie describes it on *Den of Geek*, "when Ripley lands on the planet in an escape vessel, the horrors she brings with her are, from the monks' perspective, straight from the depths of hell: the chestburster erupts from its victims like a demon. The full-grown alien is regarded as a dragon, or perhaps even the Devil himself." Concept art was created by artist Mike Worrall and architectural designer Lebbeus Woods; the wooden sets were even built. Then the film's release date was moved up and the producers decided to scrap the baroque weirdness and go with the more conservative setting of a prison planet. The frustrated Ward, who'd aspired to do something more ambitious with the story, then exited the production.

In 2018, it was announced that Gibson's *Alien III* would be getting a second life. Dark Horse Comics is creating a five-part comic series based on the script, adapted by talented writer/artist Johnnie Christmas. "When your first contracted screenplay (or screenplay of any kind, in my case) isn't produced, but the film is eventually made with a different screenplay, retaining nothing of yours but a barcode tattoo on the back of a character's neck, the last thing you ever expect is to see yours beautifully adapted and realized, decades later, in a different medium, by an artist of Johnnie Christmas's caliber," William Gibson told CBR. "It's a wonderful experience, and I have no doubt that Johnnie's version, which adheres almost entirely to the script, delivers more of my material to the audience than any feature film would have been likely to do." Christmas's past work includes the critically acclaimed *Sheltered* (Image Comics) and a collaboration with legendary writer Margaret Atwood on a graphic novel series *Angel Catbird*. It will be a pleasure to see his interpretation of Gibson's script. ✦

PAUL TREMBLAY

Behold, the Science-Fiction Cosmic Horror of *Phase IV*!

*P*hase IV (1974) could've been another schlocky, nature-run-amok B movie. Instead, it's a strange, daring film full of big ideas and stunning imagery that informs speculative film/fiction four decades later.

The movie's director, Saul Bass, was a legendary graphic designer and artist, credited as the founder of modern title design. A short list of his iconic title sequences include: *The Night of the Hunter* (1954), *Vertigo* (1958), *West Side Story* (1961), *Goodfellas* (1990), and both Alfred Hitchcock's *Psycho* (1960) and Gus Van Sant's curious (to be kind) remake (1999). In the original *Psycho*, Bass's credits also included "pictorial consultant." If you're looking to make a deep Internet dive, go read about Bass claiming he directed the infamous Janet Leigh shower scene, offering his detailed storyboards as proof. Bass

For a movie about killer ants, *Phase IV* was surprisingly heavy on the arthouse aesthetic, with surreal montages and inventively artsy shots.

also won an Oscar for directing a short documentary film in 1969. *Phase IV* (1974), however, was the only feature length film he directed, as it bombed at the box office and initially received tepid critical response.

The film opens with a deep space vista, replete with glowing galaxies, organ music to make the band Iron Butterfly jealous, groovy morphing colors, and an eclipse. The bright sun contrasted by its negative, which appears to be a black hole in space and time, is a visual motif that is repeated throughout the film. Via voiceover narration, Michael Murphy's character Dr. Lesko (a code-breaking mathematician-cum-biocommunicator, able to translate whale calls and whistles) speaks of a mysterious cosmic event, one we were able to observe and one many feared would result in worldwide catastrophes. All was quiet on earth until, well, ants. Yes, the nameless,

unknowable cosmic event wakes not the usual monstrous candidates (Lovecraftian squids and cephalopods), but jumpstarts global consciousness within the ants. The twitching trillions begin interspecies communication and cooperation. The resulting uber-hivemind is as alien as it is a formidable hyper-intelligence.

For the first nine minutes of the film, Dr. Lesko's voiceover is the only human on or offscreen. We get an ant-only extended jam (way more organ music) as we watch them swarm and crawl through their labyrinthine nests, antennae and legs twitching. We eventually find the queen's royal chamber, her head adorned in nature's version of a crown, and as the camera pans down the length of her body, we see her laying eggs from a grotesquely large, translucent sac. (Flash-forward twelve years to when Sigourney Weaver's Ripley first sees the queen alien in James Cameron's *Aliens* (1986), and that scene plays like a shot-by-shot repurposing of *Phase IV*'s hail to the queen.) Otherworldly and hypnotic, Bass's direction shows us these earthbound aliens interacting and planning, and he creates an ineffable sense of their culture without ever anthropomorphizing the creatures. It's an unsettling and thrilling trick, managing to propel the first-act narrative through the ants while demonstrating the alien-ness of their group intelligence.

At the behest of the United States government, Dr. Lesko joins the maniacal Dr. Hubbs in a chunk of ravaged Arizona desert where ants have run amuck (that's an entomological term). The two scientists hole-up in a white geodesic dome, stationed near a chorus of obelisk-like ant hives. The scientists attempt contact with the ants and when that doesn't work, Dr. Hubbs provokes aggression by destroying the hives. Science fiction horror ensues, including a truly disturbing scene in which the scientists press the "yellow" button and accidentally poison a family of farmers who did not evacuate in time. Kendra, the farmer's doe-eyed granddaughter, survives and becomes a third tenant of the dome.

The ants remain more than a few steps ahead as the humans succumb to the desert heat, paranoia, fear, and moral philosophizing. Dr. Hubbs (imagine a British, hirsute Jack Nicholson) loses what little he has left of his mind, and Dr. Lesko manages rudimentary communication with the ants using really old computers, audio wavelengths, and basic geometric shapes and concepts. It's not quite an *Arrival* (2016) level of linguistic theory in play here, but for the purposes of this essay, it's close enough.

Both endings of the film are wonderfully bonkers. Before release, the studio cut over four minutes of Bass's psychedelic freakout that is Kubrick's *2001: A Space Odyssey* meets a Jodorowsky film. The original ending of *Phase IV* was not restored until 2012. The ending that moviegoers saw gives us the CliffsNotes version of the freakout and a brief voiceover narration making sure that we (mostly) get what just happened. Dr. Locks and Kendra aren't going to be consumed but are instead being welcomed or initiated into the hivemind's super-intelligence. Got all that?

The movie was probably the unwitting introduction to what we so lovingly now call Lovecraftian or cosmic horror for many young minds who saw the film on TV in the 1980s and it's hard not to think of work from authors Nathan Ballingrud, Livia Llewellyn, S. P. Miskowski, John Langan, and in particular, the work of Laird Barron, which often evokes a naturalistic cosmic horror vibe.

They Remain (2018), directed by Philip Gelatt, is a wonderfully creepy and trippy adaptation of Barron's novelette -30-. Two scientists are hired by a mysterious corporation to study a remote area (the short story is set in the high desert, the film in a northeastern U.S. wooded area) where a death cult had encamped and done some death-cult-y terrible things. The scientists' home base–a white, segmented/paneled structure–is most certainly a nod to *Phase IV*'s desert dome. The characters slowly succumb to madness and a cosmic awareness, a disturbing connectivity between the cult members and perhaps even with the flora and fauna of the location itself.

Bass's vision and the imagery with which he presented his ants remains as mesmerizing today as it did when it first premiered. *Phase IV* will continue to echo within our genre memory because the film taps into a primal, ecstatic fascination with ancient, alien or otherworldly, and unknowable intelligence, one that is indifferent if not downright inimical to our existence.

Cue the organ music. ✦

A Boy and His Goblin:
E.T.'s Creepy Origin Story

One evening in 1955, a remote farmhouse in Christian County, Kentucky, received an unsettling visit from a gang of otherworldly creatures. The arrival of these child-sized goblins was heralded by strange lights flashing in the sky–observed by a number of local residents and even the police. But the goblins chose only one particular family to terrorize, the Suttons. They lurked in the bushes around the Suttons's farmhouse, jumping out from shadows, swarming around the house, emerging in windows. The family became so frightened they tried to chase the creatures off with shotguns. Named "the Kelly-Hopkinsville Encounter" after the names of the two nearest towns, the story is a famous one among alien hunters and UFO enthusiasts.

THE ZODIACAL LIGHT.

Steven Spielberg learned about the case while he was conducting research for *Close Encounters of the Third Kind* (1977), one of the most beloved of alien-contact movies. The story stuck with him, and as he began to formulate his ideas for a sequel to *Close Encounters*, he returned to it for inspiration. *Close Encounters* concludes on a note of wonder and connection; this next movie would explore the unsettling and occasionally terrifying side of visitors from other planets.

Perhaps having enjoyed enough attention for one lifetime–both terrestrial and extra–the Sutton family would not grant permission for their story to be made into a movie. So Spielberg and his collaborator,

The Zodiacal Light, 1882. One of approximately 7,000 illustrations created by the French artist and astronomer Étienne Léopold Trouvelot.

a production designer named Ron Cobb, hired a young screenwriter to create a script that drew some inspiration from the Kelly-Hopkinsville Encounter while fictionalizing the details as much as possible.

The resulting screenplay by John Sayles was titled "Night Skies." Ryan Lambie on *Den of Geek* describes the script as "grisly yet sometimes quirkily funny." The family is visited by five bug-eyed, short-statured aliens: "Hoodoo, who appears to have hypnotic powers. A pair of mischievous creatures named Klud and Squirt, a young, wide-eyed alien named Buddee, and the scariest member of their group, Skar, who can mutilate with a touch of his long, bony fingers." The story centers on the family's children, a teenage girl and two younger brothers.

With the "Night Skies" script in hand, Spielberg and Cobb began storyboarding it.

In 2014, Rick Baker revealed an amazing series of behind-the-scenes images from his work on the "Night Skies" alien crew. "I was so excited to be working on this project, to be able to design different alien characters of the same race," Baker wrote. The characters he created all bear a strong resemblance to one another (and to the future E.T.), while simultaneously expressing a range of personalities, from the cute, friendly Buddee to the sinister Skar.

Close Encounters concludes on a note of wonder and connection; this next movie would explore the unsettling and occasionally terrifying side of visitors from other planets.

They worked well together—Cobb was gratified to see that Spielberg appreciated his ideas, and together they built on Sayle's script. Then Cobb got an unexpected offer: Spielberg asked him to direct it.

Cobb told the *Los Angeles Times*: "Everyone in Hollywood is waiting for the phone call that will change his life. How many people does that happen to?" It seemed like he'd just gotten it.

Meanwhile, Rick Baker, the world-famous designer of special effects, started working on the bug-eyed, goblinesque aliens. His preliminary budget for a Skar prototype was $70,000.

But then . . . things got complicated. The next part of the story depends on pure serendipity. Spielberg was in the process of filming *Raiders of the Lost Ark* (1981), starring Harrison Ford. Ford's girlfriend at the time, screenwriter Melissa Mathison, was spending a lot of time on the North Africa-located set. Spielberg shared some of the script with her. Mathison's feedback cut to the emotional core of the story: the scenes that brought together the childlike alien Buddee and the family's youngest son. Perhaps . . . that should have been the real story all along.

Spielberg agreed. The final scene in "Night Skies" leaves Buddee stranded on earth, abandoned by his fellow aliens. Mathison intuitively understood this wasn't the end–this was the beginning. She started writing a script. Eight weeks later, she had a script of the movie that would become *E.T.* Spielberg loved the story so much he decided he wanted to make it instead of "Night Skies," and direct it himself.

Columbia Pictures, having already invested around $1 million into "Night Skies," wasn't exactly enthusiastic about scrapping it entirely. But Spielberg prevailed. This new film he'd envisioned ended up being made by Universal Pictures, who paid off Columbia for their initial investment. *E.T. The Extra-Terrestrial* was an instant and overwhelming success, becoming the highest-grossing film of the decade.

The "Night Skies" script never became a movie, but bits and pieces of it ended up in several other famous films, including *Poltergeist* and *Gremlins*.

Ron Cobb, who missed his opportunity to direct "Night Skies," was not a fan of the E.T. movie. However, there was a silver lining. His screenwriter wife took a closer look at his contract and found that his kill fee entitled him to one percent of *E.T.*'s massive profits. *E.T.* is still making money . . . so that phone call actually did change his life.

Baker, who developed the alien for "Night Skies," did not make out as well. There were disputes about compensation; Spielberg wanted Baker to make a cuter, cuddlier alien, but Baker had already spent a lot of time on the creepy one, and requested more budget before starting over. The conflict turned acrimonious and Baker was locked out of the project, a lasting source of bitterness for him.

In 2014, Baker shared some images of his original model, with the moniker "E.T.'s dad." "They turned around and took my stuff, altered it slightly, and made one of the most incredible movies in history," said Baker in *The Greatest Sci-Fi Movies Never Made* by David Hughes. It's quite easy to see how his original design influenced the alien we would all come to know and love as E.T., and though we'll always be happy to have E.T., it's a pity we never got to see his horrifying ancestor on the big screen. ✦

The Overlooked Genius of
Space Island One

—◇—

Very few people remember *Space Island One*, but for those of us who watched all twenty-six episodes, this hard-SF show about people living on a space station left a profound impression. Where other science fiction shows offer explosions and fight scenes, *Space Island One* is packed with complex characters, grounded scientific dilemmas, and a powerful message about the dangers of capitalism.

Space Island One was a 1998 British-German co-production that originally aired on the British channel Sky One. The show was created by Andrew Maclear (who's best known as the photographer who took several iconic pictures of John Lennon and Yoko Ono). It follows the intrepid crew of the Space Station Unity, an advanced scientific installation owned by a faceless corporation known only as "the Company."

This show gets a bad rap as a snoozefest—and it's true that a handful of episodes, including the pilot, feel seriously clunky. But at the same time, this show features some

Space Island One's regular cast was made up of Judy Lee, Angus Macinnes, Bruno Eyron, Julia Bremermann, Kourosh Asad, and Indra Ové.

of the strongest writing I've ever seen on television, including scripts by beloved novelists Stephen Baxter and Diane Duane. (And the second season is notably better than the first.)

And even at its worst, this show takes great pains to depict plausible science, and to keep the focus on developing its characters, decisions that pay off massively. One long-running storyline on the show, for example, involves veteran NASA astronaut Walter Shannon (Angus MacInnes) dealing with bone density loss as a result of too much time spent in space—a situation that has no easy answers.

Speaking of Shannon, he's a great example of how this show builds its characters over time. At first, the lone American among the crew, and the oldest crewmember, comes across as a buffoon, and another major storyline involves Shannon secretly wasting the space station's resources on calling phone-sex lines back on Earth, a huge and hideously expensive waste of bandwidth. But over time, Shannon develops so many layers, and shows so much unexpected warmth and valor, he grows into one of the show's most lovable MVPs.

But almost every character on *Space Island One* gets a challenging storyline. Scientist Harry Eschenbach (Julia Bremermann) inadvertently becomes pregnant, and winds up having the first baby born in space, which becomes a media circus. Her fellow scientist, Lyle Campbell (William Oliver) appears to be one of those cute, awkward nerds who populate television shows everywhere—until Lyle gets into a relationship with another scientist, and things take a dark, startling turn.

Actually, two out of the three main scientists we meet on *Space Island One* are female, and they're always shown to be good at their jobs. Likewise, the station's commander, Kathryn MacTiernan, handles an endless series of impossible situations with firm authority and sly creativity. Commander MacTiernan is the kind of leader who almost never raises her voice, but if you screw with her, she will put you down.

And then there's the show's underlying conflict: The station is owned by a for-profit company, which is constantly cutting corners and trying to find more ways to make money off it. The clash between scientific inquiry and capitalist profiteering keeps coming up as a theme throughout the show, until it slowly emerges as Space Station Unity's defining, insoluble problem.

When *Space Island One* appeared briefly on PBS in the United States, at first I saw it as "that weird show that's on before classic *Doctor Who*." The talky drama and long scenes where the characters discuss retracting umbilicals and correcting station attitude seemed way too low-key compared to other TV science fiction. But I kept getting sucked into the show's twisty drama, and its characters kept surprising me. By the time *Space Island One* reached its shocking conclusion, I had become obsessed. And I'd come to realize that I was lucky enough to see something really special.

Alas, *Space Island One* isn't available on DVD, or anywhere else. But you can find all the episodes online, if you search hard enough. And it's well worth the effort. ✦

EMILY ASHER-PERRIN

The (Very) Secret Adventures of Jules Verne

Steampunk, as a genre, has arguably existed for well over a century. It didn't have that name at the beginning, of course, and it didn't have conventions and rock bands and fashion shows dedicated to its retrofuturistic storytelling flair. In the beginning, it was a peculiar aspect of science fiction and fantasy that imagined an alternate nineteenth century, powered by miraculous steam-based contraptions. It showed up periodically, in the works of H. G. Wells and K. W. Jeter and Michael Moorcock. It reared its head in 1970s *Doctor Who* serials and *The Wild Wild West*, in Miyazaki's *Castle in the Sky*, and the very end of *Back to the Future Part III*. Steampunk was all over the place, but outside of literature it was often relegated to an embellishment. It made for pretty props, set pieces, and gadgets . . . and that was about it.

Until the year 2000, when a strange little show popped up on the Sci-Fi Channel called *The Secret Adventures of Jules Verne*.

SAJV—as it was termed by its small but avid fan base—lasted just one season before ghosting us without much fanfare. Creator Gavin Scott came by the concept when he learned that Jules Verne initially wrote *Twenty Thousand Leagues Under the Sea* out of anger over the Russian invasion of Poland, but was asked by his publisher to change Captain Nemo's background (from Polish nobleman to the son of an Indian raja) because the Russian Empire was an ally of France. Scott posited that perhaps all of Verne's "fictional" plots and characters were based on real events, and several different versions of a screenplay emerged. They all failed to find backers, but an early draft sent to George Lucas got Scott a job writing a few episodes of *The Young Indiana Jones Chronicles*. After Indy, and some work on Hollywood screenplays (*The Borrowers*, *Small Soldiers*), he came back to Verne and cobbled together a group of disparate investors to make what would now be a television series.

The show told the tale of a young, hungry Jules, desperate to make it as a writer and full of strange proposals for steampunk instruments and engines. Verne runs into trouble quickly, however. It turns out that his daydream inventions are the result of this quirky

ability he has *to see into the future*, resulting in a host of nasty customers tracking Verne down to tap his brain for schematics to war machines and other means to dominate a planet. He gets protection in the form of a few new friends, the *real* Phileas Fogg and Passepartout (of *Around the World in Eighty Days* fame), and Fogg's super-spy cousin Rebecca. Essentially, the plot of *SAJV* gives us a different reason behind Verne's aborted or heavily altered works; it's not that he was too young to publish *Paris in the 20th Century*, as his editor suggested. Rather, if he were to publish it, he would probably attract more attention from any number of living or undead megalomaniacal villains, who would kidnap and maybe torture him for information in order to bring about global domination, or destruction, or doom, or other bad words beginning with *d*. (Devastation! Drama?)

The show had a lofty pedigree for something shot largely on a single soundstage. It was full of well-known talent: John Rhys-Davies popped in as Alexandre Dumas, père; Patrick Duffy lent his talents to the role of a handsome vampire; Margot Kidder showed up to perform a séance. Phileas himself was played to rigid perfection by Michael Praed, known by many children of the 1980s as the painfully pretty lead outlaw on *Robin of Sherwood*.

The Secret Adventures of Jules Verne was ambitious to a fault–in its one and

A Jules Férat illustration from the Hetzel edition of Jules Verne's *The Mysterious Island*, first published in 1874.

only season the characters found themselves time traveling to alternate realities to meet the real Three Musketeers, battling a golem, stopping an assassination attempt against Queen Victoria, accidentally getting involved in both the American Civil War *and* the Russian Emancipation Reform of 1861, and frequently coming to blows with Count Gregory, a steampunk cyborg in charge of the aptly-named League of Darkness, who desperately wanted to get his hands on Jules Verne's brain. There was no aspect of science fiction, fantasy, or horror that the show was afraid to tackle, no brand of humor or melodrama that it shied away from.

It was not to be, and largely because the show was similar to Verne himself–ahead of its time. *The Secret Adventures of Jules Verne* was the first hour-long series to be shot entirely in HDTV format, but none of the networks airing the show had the ability to broadcast in high definition yet. As a result, the series had to be converted down to film, making the episodes over-dark and cheap-looking. The CGI, costumes, and design that the show had poured all its money into emerged on-screen in blurry shades of muted gray.

All that work, lost to the very audience *SAJV* needed to impress.

But if you looked close enough, all of those flourishes remained. Phileas's iconic traveling balloon became a decked-out dirigible named the *Aurora*, a flying Victorian house paneled in rich wood and accented everywhere with brass, full of crystal decanters and patterned china teacups and a workshop for testing various aparatuses. Fogg and his cousin were always lavishly clothed as befitting their station and wealth, and Rebecca's job as a government agent meant that underneath her clothes, she was always wearing her "practical" leather catsuit–think *The Avengers'* Mrs. Peel, but with a corset and Batman's utility belt. Verne's inventions and Passepartout's odd experiments were meticulously rendered and delightful to behold. Even the obvious reuse of that single soundstage and its redressed sets couldn't dim the show's dynamism, or its earnestness.

That six-month blip of *SAJV*'s existence was a heady and exhilarating time for its fans, and it was taken from us far too soon. Due to the large number of investors in the show, the odds of getting the rights to put it on DVD and Blu-ray, or bring it to streaming, are slim. But there are copies out there–recorded off the TV and burned onto discs, passed from one enthusiast to another. I have my own precious set, and from time to time, I slip a disc into my DVD player and revisit the odd steampunk adventures of twentysomething Jules Verne and his highly unlikely set of friends. ✦

James Cameron's Explorations of the Watery Depths On-Screen and in Real Life

Most people know James Cameron (b. 1954) as the blockbuster director who gave us the beloved science fiction films *The Terminator* (1984), *Aliens* (1986), *The Abyss* (1989), and *Avatar* (2009), along with the slightly popular *Titanic* (1997). *Avatar*'s many innovations in 3-D technology and special effects, combining live action and CGI, made it a landmark film in cinema history–and as of this writing, it remains the highest-grossing film of all time in its earnings at the box office ($2.8 billion). The second highest? *Titanic*. Cameron broke his own record, which has to be a record in and of itself.

Of course, none of this is particularly obscure. But Cameron's record-busting extends beyond the box office. On March 26, 2012, Cameron made science history. He became the first person to ever make a solo descent to the bottom of the Mariana

From 1899 through 1910, Jean-Marc Côté and a variety of other French artists imagined the futuristic environs of the year 2000 in a series of postcards. *A Monster of the Abyss* was one of Côté's contributions. Never distributed at the time, it was discovered and published by Isaac Asimov in 1986.

Trench, the deepest point in the ocean–35,787 feet below the surface. Cameron was also the first person to capture this incredible experience on film, and only the third person to ever make the journey.

The first two were Don Walsh and Jacques Piccard, who headed down there in a submersible in 1960. They stuck around for twenty minutes, just long enough to get their bearings, unload some ballast, and munch on some candy bars, before returning to the surface. They assumed someone else would break their record within a couple years, spending more time and gathering more scientific data. Instead, no one ever went back– until Cameron decided to give it a go more than forty years later.

The feat might remind you a bit of the plot of *The Abyss*, in which a dive team makes a perilous journey to the ocean floor to recover a missing submarine. It's a fun movie, and the visual imagery is sublime, an early indication of Cameron's passionate fascination with the oceanic depths. In fact, *The Abyss* played a big role in piquing Cameron's interest in ocean exploration. As he worked on the movie, he turned to real-life deep-sea-diving experts for research and consultation–including Don Walsh.

Then, of course, there was *Titanic*, and while the movie itself takes place on the surface, the reference material is now situated on the ocean floor, two and a half miles deep. As he worked on *Titanic*, Cameron made a dozen submersible dives down to the site of the wreck. Later, he returned to the same location for twenty more dives, as his team explored the haunting, waterlogged wreckage of the unsinkable ship. This voyage became the 3-D IMAX movie *Ghosts of the Abyss* (2003). Necessity being the mother of invention, the project also spurred Cameron to advance the technology for underwater filming, which came in handy down there in the black depths of the Mariana Trench. (While discussing Cameron's history of aquatic-associated films,

The film *James Cameron's Deepsea Challenge* tells the full story behind the expedition. It depicts Cameron's journey to the bottom of the ocean, focusing primarily on the human interest aspects of the endeavor.

La descente commença à 1 h. 25 (Page 171.)

it would be remiss not to mention one of his lesser-known films, *Piranha II: The Spawning* (1981). This campy horror tale of piranhas gone wild was also the legendary director's theatrical debut. But Cameron doesn't really claim it as such, because conflicts in production left him with no control over the final product. In fact, Cameron says he asked them to remove his name from the movie before its release. Apparently no one else was eager to take credit for the flying piranha movie either, and the studio refused. Later, in an interview with *60 Minutes*, Cameron called it "the greatest flying piranha movie ever made.")

Back to the science. Cameron's descent to the Mariana Trench was termed the Deepsea Challenge expedition. The journey took years of preparation. "The only way to make my dream a reality was to build a new vehicle unlike any in current existence," Cameron told *National Geographic*. "Our success during seven prior expeditions building and operating our own deep-ocean vehicles, cameras, and lighting systems gave me confidence that such a vehicle could be built, and not just with the vast resources of government programs, but also with a small entrepreneurial team."

It took them seven years to build the vehicle: a twenty-four-foot-long submersible craft (the *Deepsea Challenger*), made from steel encased in specially developed glass foam, equipped with cameras for filming and robotic arms for grabbing up scientific samples. Analysis revealed these samples contained at least one hundred new microorganisms. Test dives also netted some interesting finds, including some shrimp-like creatures called amphipods and a new species of sea cucumber.

Cameron documented the journey in a film titled *James Cameron's Deepsea Challenge 3D*, profiling the team, the technology, and the quest to break a record–along with those terrifying but exhilarating moments in the hadal depths. The *Deepsea Challenger* is now at the Woods Hole Oceanographic Institution (WHOI), helping to advance further ocean research.

"I've always dreamed of diving to the deepest place in the oceans," Cameron said. "For me it went from a boyhood fantasy to a real quest, like climbing Everest, as I learned more about deep-ocean exploration and became an explorer myself in real life. This quest was not driven by the need to set records, but by the same force that drives all science and exploration . . . curiosity." ✦

One of Émile-Antoine Bayard's illustrations for *Around the Moon* (1870) by Jules Verne.

ARCH— ITEC —TURE

SOME OF THE MOST INFLUENTIAL FIGURES IN SCIENCE FICTION are not, in fact, writers or moviemakers, but the architects who imagined the city of the future and the house of tomorrow. They envisioned different ways of living. They wrote about the way our society influences our surroundings, and the way our surroundings influence us. These visions have inspired generations of writers and influenced set designs for SFF television and film.

In a way, architects are storytellers, too—and while their contributions were often made from behind the scenes, they unquestionably shape the genre. In this chapter, we explore the contributions of architects, theorists, and draftspeople . . . and the ways that genre storytellers have been inspired by their works.

A housing interior from Arcosanti, the "urban laboratory" in the Arizona desert. Photo by Joshua Lieberman.

Hugh Ferriss: Draftsman, Theorist, Gotham Visionary

Hugh Ferriss (1889-1962) was a draftsman and architectural theorist of the art deco era who, despite never working in comics, is often referred to as the "Father of Gotham City." Born in St. Louis, Missouri, Ferriss studied architecture at Washington University in his hometown, but quickly shifted his focus to rendering sketches of potential buildings for other architects. His trademark style of illustration became highly recognizable; he often depicted buildings against a dark night sky, lit by spotlights and surrounded by shadow.

As an architect, Ferriss only oversaw a few actual buildings throughout his entire career, none of them particularly well-known. But Ferriss's reputation does not rest on his physical structures. Instead, he is celebrated for his drawings and theories that influenced generations of architects as well as film designers. Along with Batman's Gotham City, Ferriss's work has inspired striking and breathtaking fictional cities like *Blade Runner's* 2019 Los Angeles and *The Fifth Element's* twenty-third century New York City.

In his book *The Metropolis of Tomorrow,* Ferriss collected his architectural philosophy and illustration, claiming modestly in the foreword (and speaking of himself in the third person), "these studies are not entirely random shots in the dark . . . his foreshadowings and interpretations spring from something at least more trustworthy than personal phantasy."

The book contains written analysis of urban planning and policy and its implications for city living, coupled with detailed and evocative illustrations of the city both as it is and could be. In fact, it's divided into three sections: "Cities of Today," "Projected Trends," and "An Imaginary Metropolis." In that second section, he examines the consequences of New York City's rapid urbanization and fast-sprouting skyscrapers, and "A visualization is presented of the cities which would come into existence were these trends, or these propositions, carried forward." The third embodies his vision for a well-planned city.

This exploration presents visions of not just one possible city but many, providing a veritable grab bag of inspiration for many futurists to come. As he worked through the implications of urban planning proposals on society and everyday life, Ferriss occupied himself with precisely the topics that occupy many science-fiction writers and storytellers: What makes a dystopia? What makes a utopia? How does the way we live affect who we are? Where will this path take us? Is there an alternate and better way of living?

There are dystopian cities where skyscrapers tower among the clouds, vast and unrestrained; urban pyramids dot the landscape, massive as cities themselves; and the human scale is made minuscule juxtaposed with these megalithic structures. It's easy to look at these shadowed and looming cityscapes and instantly envision a person lost in the crush of future humanity, adrift in a city grown so massive it's devouring itself.

Indeed, these works were part of the inspiration for *Blade Runner*. As historian and urban theorist Carl Abbott writes in *CityLab*, "The iconic science fiction film *Blade Runner* opens with a nightmare scene of future Los Angeles. Aircars maneuver through darkness lit by fire and explosion among monolithic office towers. These commercial ziggurats . . . rise like vast pyramids over the shadowed streets."

But it's not all a dystopian vision. In Ferriss's brighter renderings it's easy to view the orderly rows of skyscrapers and imagine a utopian future where people are capable of coming together to build something bright, beautiful, and vast, a high-tech habitat for millions of humans to live together in peace and prosperity. His description of this city, and the structures that fill it, presents a future where science and the arts are valued as thoroughly as business, where religious diversity is celebrated . . . a city that Ferriss hoped could "serve in actualizing whatever may be man's potentialities of emotional and mental well-being." ✦

Hugh Ferriss architectural drawing, 1889–1962, Avery Architectural & Fine Arts Library, Columbia University.

Dreams in the Desert:
The Utopian Vision of Paolo Soleri

By the year 2050, the world population is projected to reach almost ten billion, and the majority of these people will live in cities. Paolo Soleri (1919-2013) anticipated this future. His solution: the *arcology*, a term he coined. Arcology is a portmanteau of "architecture" and "ecology," reflecting Soleri's belief that a city should function as living system, perfectly integrating people and nature.

An arcology is a self-sufficient, self-contained city that moves upward, not outward. It's the megastructure you've probably seen in countless science fiction books, movies, and video games, where people spend their whole lives in one vast building that contains all the life support systems they need. Like a generation spaceship, but on earth. Arcologies are found in *The World Inside* by Robert Silverberg, *The Water Knife* by Paolo Bacigalupi, *High-Rise* by J. G. Ballard, and others.

In *Arcology: The City in the Image of Man* (1969), Soleri collected his draw-

Concrete walls, domed rooftops, and a village in the desert: the design of Tatooine, Luke Skywalker's home planet, was said to be inspired by a visit George Lucas paid to Arcosanti. The actual scenes were shot in Tunisian deserts, where some film set relics still remain. Image from *Star Wars Episode IV: A New Hope* (1977). Photo credit: Lucasfilm / Fox / Kobal / Shutterstock.

ings and sketches of imaginary cities like Novanoah and Babelnoah, invented to explore his concepts. But Soleri didn't stop there. In 1970, Soleri and his supporters began building an actual arcology in the Arizona desert, a physical prototype and a testing ground for his philosophy. They called this "urban laboratory" Arcosanti.

Attempting to build your own city from scratch in the high desert of Arizona might seem like a slightly over-the-top move. Though a professor at Arizona State University and a relatively well-known architect, Soleri was disgruntled by society's unwillingness to embrace his ideas–and he wanted to prove an arcology would work. By many accounts, Soleri was a controlling megalomaniac. Despite his narcissism–or perhaps because of it–he attracted a passionate group of followers, who supported his creative endeavors but also enabled his destructive behaviors. In 2017, Soleri's daughter Daniela publicly revealed that her father had sexually abused her as a teen, a trauma that continued to haunt her even as she continued to support his work.

Of course, these revelations do cast a pall on the architect's legacy. In an essay reflecting on her father's complicated life, Daniela wrote, "That work will have to stand on its own, and not be seen as an inseparable part of Soleri as a person, including his best and worst behaviors. For me that work deserves recognition and use, but its value will never negate his faults, or obscure the larger lessons."

Though Soleri passed away in 2013, Arcosanti is still under construction. Only a small part of Soleri's original planned city has been built. Arcosanti's primary purpose is as a hands-on learning experience for enthusiasts of eco-friendly urban planning. The site hosts more than 30,000 visitors a year. Workshop participants roll up their sleeves, get their hands dirty, and help build. An onsite metal foundry enables attendees to practice the trade of metalworking and the sales from the foundry help support the project.

"Despite its compactness, Arcosanti contains all the necessities of village life: a café, a bakery, an art gallery, apartments and dorms for residents and guests, gardens and greenhouses, a foundry, woodwork and ceramic studios, an amphitheater and a swimming pool, which overlooks a static tide of sand and rocks," wrote the *Washington Post*'s Andrea Sachs in 2008, after a field trip to the desert.

One of the site's best-known visitors was George Lucas, who was said to be inspired by the aesthetics of Arcosanti as he envisioned *Star Wars*' Tatooine, the desert planet of Luke Skywalker's origin.

As a young architect, long before he began his work on Arcosanti, Soleri studied under the great Frank Lloyd Wright, arguably the most acclaimed American architect of the twentieth century. Wright's influence can be seen in Soleri's dedication to integrating his buildings with their natural surroundings. But while Wright's work feels inextricably connected to mid-century modern, Soleri's vision of the future seems to belong to another century altogether.

Writer and artist James McGirk spent five weeks at Arcosanti in 1998, past its heyday in the seventies and eighties. Writing for *Wired* in 2013, he looked back on the experience as

compelling, enchanting, but ultimately disappointing–this idealistic community, built by flawed and ordinary humans, could never fully live up to the utopian future it promised. Still, there were moments of bliss. McGirk writes about an evening when a massive thunderstorm swept across the Arizona desert as the residents blasted classical music. "At that moment," McGirk writes, "if you let your eyes glaze over just a bit, you could imagine yourself in a toga, a thousand years in the future, when Arcosanti was just a tiny outpost, and the entire world was tucked into an arcology. Looking back, I sometimes still suspect that Soleri's time will come." ✦

ARCOSANTI. Southern exposure.

The Arcosanti site is located about 60 miles north of Phoenix, taking Interstate-17 to Exit 262 at Cordes Junction. Since 1970 thousands of students and professionals have come to Arcosanti to participate in seminars, conferences and workshops conducted by Paolo Soleri and his staff. Photo Credit: Ken Howie.

MATTHEW KRESSEL

Reality Ahead of Schedule: The Designs of Syd Mead

F ew individuals have had more of an influence on our vision of the future than concept artist Syd Mead (b. 1933). From his design of automobiles, hotels, and luxury aircraft to his concept art for such groundbreaking films as *Aliens, Blade Runner, Star Trek: The Motion Picture,* and *TRON,* Mead's visionary eye almost single-handedly defined the science-fiction aesthetic for a generation.

Mead trained as an industrial designer at the Art Center School in Los Angeles, and immediately after his graduation in 1959 he began working for the Ford Motor Company's Advanced Styling Studio. His renown as a concept artist quickly grew, and after just two years Mead left Ford to illustrate books and catalogs for major corporate clients, including U.S. Steel. In 1970, Mead formed his own company: Syd Mead, Inc. Mead's most notable client during this formative period was Philips Electronics, for which he created inspiring

Syd Mead created the look of *Blade Runner*'s (1982) intimidating skyline. Photo credit: Ladd Company/ Warner Bros/ Kobal/ Shutterstock.

visualizations of the future: living rooms with wall-sized TVs (a very science-fictional concept at the time), hospitals with self-help kiosks, high-tech gadget-filled kitchens, and futuristic learning centers that anticipated our Internet-connected classrooms today.

Yet for all his breathtaking industrial work, Mead is probably best known for his concept art for many of the seminal science-fiction films of the eighties. He began working with Hollywood in 1979, designing the hyper-evolved sentient space probe *V'Ger* for *Star Trek: The Motion Picture.* The following year, Mead was hired as a "visual futurist" by Ridley Scott to design the electrified parking meters, utilitarian vehicles, flying cars, and oppressive skyline in the smog-choked, neon-lit streets of *Blade Runner.* Mead went on to work on *TRON*, for which he designed many of the most memorable elements in that groundbreaking CGI film, including the sleek and aerodynamic light-cycles, the glowing light suits, and the distinctive "recognizer" ships. For the classic film *Aliens*, Mead designed the deep-

space USCMC ship the *Sulaco,* the drop-ship and ground vehicles, and the famous power loader in which Ripley fights the Alien Queen. Mead also worked on the films *Short Circuit, Timecop, Johnny Mnemonic,* and *Mission: Impossible III.*

Mead's concept designs work so well because he uses his background in industrial design to envision not only how such things might look, but how they would function.

Mead once quipped, "I've called science fiction 'reality ahead of schedule.'" ✦

The full title of this concept art by Syd Mead is *Reaching for Aquarius: A Designer Looks Ahead—Party Scene.* It was published in 1969 for *Automobile Quarterly,* accompanied by the following description from Mead: "Holographic projection offers unlimited environmental excitement by means of computer generation as shown in the background. Electronic body suits maintain muscle tone, hallucinogenic vapors from goblets provide refreshment, and electronic helmets receive, store and retrieve communications!" © Syd Mead Inc. www.sydmead.com.

ART—AND —DESIGN

THE AUTHOR'S NAME IS ALWAYS RIGHT UP FRONT—SPLASHED across the cover of the magazine, or typeset in bold down the spine of the book. The illustrator's name, meanwhile, is often relegated to the fine print, buried deep in the credits. Accordingly, visual artists are seldom as celebrated or treasured by fans, and their names are much sooner forgotten.

And yet, SFF's artists and illustrators have made immeasurable contributions to the genre. Consider the pulp artists who churned out vision after vision of the high-tech future, the lurking monsters, and the alien bizarre; the cover artists whose iconic imagery on novels is forever intertwined with our memories of those stories; the fine art painters whose dreamy visions manage to evoke a place we could never describe in words—and inspire the next generation of storytellers who are determined, at least, to try.

Fortress on the Rocks (1988) by Paul Lehr. Acrylic painting, 24" x 20".

In this chapter, we explore the contributions of a few of SFF's many highly original and accomplished visual artists, and the roles they played in setting our imaginations alight.

Weird Tales Regular, Pulp Illustrator Virgil Finlay

One of the greatest illustrators in the history of speculative fiction is Virgil Finlay (1914-1971). Finlay had a unique and highly detailed pen-and-ink technique, and was extraordinary productive–he completed around 2,600 drawings and paintings throughout his thirty-five-year career. Nevertheless, as the pulp era his work dominated has faded in memory, so has Finlay's reputation and name. Though today's illustrators remain inspired by his techniques, fans may have forgotten the man who invented them.

Finlay's artistic legacy is inextricably bound up with the big pulp magazines of his day, particularly one of the most influential of all time: *Weird Tales*. He sold his first illustration to *Weird Tales* in 1935 when he was only twenty-one years old. He would eventually contribute around twenty cover illustrations and 220 interior illustrations for the legendary publication.

Of course, his appearances were not limited to *Weird Tales*. Eventually he would be published in just about every major genre magazine, including *Famous Fantastic Mysteries*, *Amazing Stories*, *Fantastic Story Quarterly*, *Galaxy*, and many others. His subject matter reflected the typical preoccupations of pulp magazines: bug-eyed aliens; eldritch monsters; weird landscapes; and spaceships, space farers, and space maidens.

He also appeared in *The American Weekly*, a tabloid-esque Sunday newspaper supplement,

Weird Tales, March 1939. Cover art by Virgil Finlay.

Robert Weinberg writes: "Finlay wasn't merely great. He was the greatest. His heroines were the most beautiful; his heroes were the most heroic; and his monsters and villains were the most frightening."

which employed him as both a staff artist and a freelancer between 1938 and 1951. Early in his career, he was even commissioned by *Weird Tales* editor Farnsworth Wright to complete twenty-five illustrations for a chapbook edition of Shakespeare's *A Midsummer Night's Dream*—a little side project. Sad to say, this venture was not commercially successful at the time. Today, it is a collector's item.

Finlay artworks remain highly recognizable due to the unusual illustrative approach he developed. He did his drawings on scratchboard, which has a dark coating that can be scratched and scraped away in fine lines with a sharp blade. This allowed him to place white lines and areas against a dark background. Then, using a super fine-point lithographic pen, he'd apply dark lines, cross-hatching, and stippling to the light areas. Stippling is quite time-consuming; it involves applying many, many tiny dots to create delicate shading. To maintain an even and consistent look, Finlay would clean the tip of his pen after applying each dot.

This combination of techniques enabled him to create incredibly detailed drawings, which set an astonishing new visual standard for the coarse-papered pulps of the era. In his introduction to *The Collectors' Book of Virgil Finlay*, editor, critic, and art collector Robert Weinberg writes: "Finlay wasn't merely great. He was the greatest. His heroines were the most beautiful; his heroes were the most heroic; and his monsters and villains were the most frightening."

In time, Finlay expanded into other styles, also using gouache, oils, and even watercolor to create full color paintings and illustrations. But he remains best known for the pioneering visions of his black-and-white work in pen-and-ink. ✦

Untitled, original interior magazine illustration by Virgil Finlay. Ink on paper, 15.5" x 12.5".

STEPHEN SONNEVELD

The Surrealist Stylings of Richard M. Powers

As is the plight of many artists, commercial work was a necessary evil in the career of Richard M. Powers (1921-1996), whose true aspiration was to have his pieces recognized in art galleries. Powers would achieve that goal, with return showings at New York's Rehn Gallery, and works now in the permanent collection of the Museum of Modern Art. Yet it was the images he produced for widely-circulated SF novels that would see Powers recognized as one of the most influential artists of the era.

It was a sign of the times in which Powers lived that SF was not considered a respected genre. Reportedly, the artist himself was no fan. Ironically, his artwork, which graced the covers of texts by Arthur C. Clarke, Kurt Vonnegut, and Philip K. Dick, was part of the collective moment that brought SF to age, and to recognition.

Like his surrealist influences, Powers was trained in classical styles at schools in his home-town of Chicago, and later, New York. His early work on mysteries, westerns, and SF books reflected that competence. When Ian Ballantine founded his imprint in 1955 to push SF beyond its pulp roots, Powers was brought on to create covers. He soon became the de facto art director as well. Powers unleashed his imagination onto the canvas, evolving his work from the standard representation of robots, spaceships, alien goddesses, etc., into surreal landscapes and abstract compositions that reflected the emotion and themes of the books. Powers even hand drew the lettering when needed, experimented with collage and mixed media, and sometimes changed the orientation from portrait to landscape if he felt that layout engaged the audience better. Not only was this surrealism-over-representation style aped by other SF artists and publishing houses (many of which hired Powers directly), the trend influenced other aspects of commercial art throughout the era, from album covers to advertising.

In a way, Powers's career is similar to an SF story: a man caught between two worlds–the one he desires, and the one that sustains him. In the final chapter, his bold contributions helped secure SF's reputation as a respected art form in the twentieth century. ✦

Richard M. Powers cover art for the 1977 Fawcett Gold Medal edition of John D. MacDonald's 1951 novel *Wine of the Dreamers.*

The Dreamy Atmospheres of Painter Paul Lehr

Paul Lehr (1930-1998) was one of the most prolific SFF illustrators of the 1950s-1970s, creating cover art for hundreds of books. His art also appeared in *Time, Fortune, Playboy, Reader's Digest, OMNI,* and *Analog*. Working with oils, acrylics, and gouache on masonite or wood panel, Lehr developed a highly recognizable style: dreamy, surreal, and atmospheric. Drawing on a vividly saturated color palette, Lehr often depicted vast landscapes marked by massive, mysterious objects.

In *Science Fiction and Fantasy Artists of the Twentieth Century: A Biographical Dictionary,* Jane Frank describes Lehr as "one of the very few artists who are able to evoke the science fiction genre without depicting the specific scenes from the books they illustrate." Lehr's paintings often feel like a dreamscape; hinting at deeper mysteries, evoking the uncanny and the sublime. "It's that amazing storytelling aspect of his work that has made Lehr a legend in the sci-fi community," writes Riley Reese for *Futurism*. "Lehr's unique spin on dreamy, surreal, and often somewhat mystical takes on alien worlds became almost synonymous with Bantam Books in the mid-to-late 1960s."

Lehr himself advocated a naturalist perspective for the SFF illustrator, suggesting that aspiring artists study the strange beauty of our own often uncanny planet in their quests to capture the alien in others. "We have the imagery of science fiction all around us in our own world . . ." he wrote. "With the kitchen light on during a summer evening, look out through the screened window . . . myriads of insects of all shapes, sizes, and colors, with designs undreamed of–creatures that boggle the imagination. Trees and stumps, forming strange and mysterious shapes. Reflections in water–stones and cratered rocks–it is all there. If we are to become successful in projecting images of other worlds, alien creatures, and the concept of time, we must study our own surroundings first."

One of Lehr's paintings now belongs to the permanent collection of the National Air and Space Museum in the Smithsonian Institution. This painting, which first appeared in the *Saturday Evening Post* in 1959, depicted the first Moon landing–ten years before it happened. ✦

Cosmic Assembly (circa 1990s) by Paul Lehr.
Acrylic painting, 27.5" x 34".

Space and Science-Fiction Artist David A. Hardy

As of 2018, David Hardy (b. 1936) is the oldest living science fiction artist, with a career spanning an astonishing sixty-four years–he illustrated his first book in 1954, a nonfiction work by Patrick Moore titled *Suns, Myths and Men*. Hardy got his start as a space artist, creating technically skilled depictions of space exploration and astronomical marvels. In 1970, he began producing science fiction work as well, introducing fictional and fantastical elements. But, he cautions, it's very important to distinguish between space art and SFF art. "Sci-fi art is based in the imagination," he explained to the *Guardian*. "With space art, you need knowledge of chemistry, physics, astronomy, and volcanology."

Along with hundreds of SF book and magazine covers, Hardy has worked for science magazines such as *Astronomy*, *Sky & Telescope*, *Astronomy Now*, and *Popular Astronomy*– and books by Arthur C. Clarke and Carl Sagan. He also edited an illustrated history of space art titled *Visions of Space: Artists Journey Through the Cosmos* (1989).

One of Hardy's trademark elements is a green alien named Behn, aka "Space Gumby," whom he first developed in his work for *The Magazine of Fantasy and Science Fiction*. A frequent visitor to Hardy's space-scapes, Behn brings an element of playful, tongue-in-cheek humor to the grandeur of outer space.

Hardy's fans include legendary rock star Brian May, former guitarist for Queen–and an accomplished astronomer in his own right, completing his PhD in 2007. (His thesis was titled "A Survey of Radial Velocities in the Zodiacal Dust Cloud.") May said of Hardy: "He creates his own special kind of virtual reality–through his astounding vision and technique we glimpse landscapes in worlds where man has never set foot."

Hardy is a recipient of the Sir Arthur Clarke Award (2005) and the Frederick Ordway Award (2015). He's even had an asteroid named after him: david hardy (1989 SB). ✦

Hardy launched the Bhen series with a 1975 cover for *F&SF* that depicted the friendly green alien encountering the *Viking 1* soon after its landing on Mars. Forty years later, this 2015 *F&SF* cover shows Bhen making his mark near the European Space Agency's ExoMars rover, projected to land in 2020.

Psychedelic Master Bob Pepper

Bob Pepper (b. 1938) is largely responsible for New Wave science fiction's embrace of an aesthetic described as "1960s Technicolor"–stylized and psychedelic, an ice cream acid trip. One of his best-known works is not actually in the science fiction genre, but an iconic and influential album cover straight out of the Summer of Love: *Forever Changes* (1967) from the band Love.

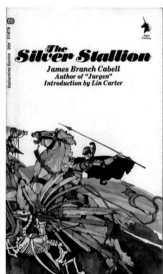

On the fantasy side, Pepper was a highly prolific illustrator of books from Ballantine, working on a popular series of fantasy reprints for noted editor Lin Carter. Carter chose underrated gems, popular classics, and personal favorites to revive in this series that ran from 1969 to 1974. Many of these editions remain highly sought after–perhaps in part because of their outstanding cover art.

Pepper brought this same aesthetic to science fiction, creating a number of highly distinctive covers for DAW editions of Philip K. Dick's novels, including *A Scanner Darkly*, *Ubik*, and *Do Androids Dream of Electric Sheep?*.

In the 1980s, he also illustrated two popular fantasy tabletop games: *Dragonmaster* and *The Dark Tower*. *Dragonmaster* featured a deck of playing cards similar to the tarot, and these cards remain popular collectibles. ✦

Bob Pepper provided the striking cover art for this 1969 Ballantine Books edition of *The Silver Stallion* by James Branch Cabell, which was first published in 1926. *The Silver Stallion* is a classic of the sword-and-sorcery tradition, blending fantasy, history, humor, and magic as French nobles vie for power. It's currently out of print.

A New Realism: Contemporary Cover Artist Michael Whelan

Michael Whelan (b. 1950) was the first living artist to be inducted into *The Science Fiction Hall of Fame,* who termed him "one of the most important contemporary science fiction and fantasy artists." They cited his influential role in establishing a new realism for cover illustrations, in contrast to the surrealist style that dominated in the 1950s and 1960s. "His art, though, is far more intricate and naturalistic–despite the otherworldly subjects–than that of his pulp era predecessors," they wrote. His style is often referred to as imaginative realism.

Some of Whelan's best known paintings include cover art for Anne McCaffrey's Dragonriders of Pern series (Del Rey), particularly *The White Dragon* (1978), Michael Moorcock's Elric books (DAW), Robert Heinlein's *The Cat Who Walks Through Walls,* and Stephen King's *The Dark Tower.* To date, he's won fifteen Hugo Awards, three World Fantasy Awards, and twelve Chesley Awards. ✦

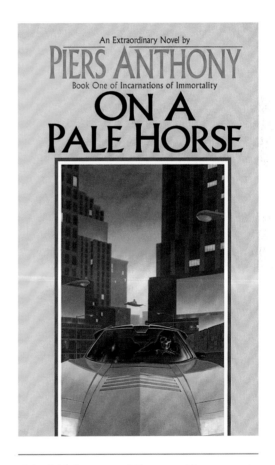

Michael Whelan created the memorable cover art for Piers Anthony's *On a Pale Horse* (1983), the first installment in his Incarnations of Immortality series. This edition was published by Del Rey Books.

On Fantasy Maps

I n 1665, a German Jesuit and polymath named Athanasius Kircher published an eclectic scientific treatise called *Mundus Subterraneus*. It included, along with a natural history of dragons and a diagram of the Earth's many unknown interior chambers, a convincingly detailed map of "Insulae Atlantidis"–the island of Atlantis.

What strikes you about it most is the confidence. There's nothing vague or sketchy about Kircher's Atlantis, it's highly specific. Situated square in the middle of the Atlantic, and colored a creamy yellow, it's shaped like an upside-down Africa, with six wiggly rivers and two east-west mountain ranges. It's like Kircher's been there personally–this isn't terra incognita, it's thoroughly cognita. However firmly one grasps the fact of Atlantis's nonexistence, Kircher's map still triggers an instinctive longing, an invitation *au voyage* that whispers: Quit your job, throw it all over, and go to Atlantis right now!

It's a magic trick of sorts: maps look like evidence. They imply the existence of the terrain they represent. (Though the practical traveler should note that Kircher put south at the top of his map. In fact many medieval cartographers put east at the top, because Jesus.)

Some books are published with maps; some books cast a spell so strong that they demand to be mapped after the fact. A hundred years after Dante published his *Divine Comedy* people were already drawing maps of the Inferno. The England of the *Canterbury Tales* and *Pride and Prejudice* and the Mississippi of *Huckleberry Finn* have all been mapped.

> It's a magic trick of sorts: maps look like evidence. They imply the existence of the terrain they represent.

It didn't matter that these places didn't exist, what mattered was how much people wanted them to. Fictional maps are a visual trace of the ridiculous, undignified passion that we pour into worlds that we know aren't real. They seem to confirm the ridiculous faith we place in novels–to see one is to say, silently and only to yourself, *See? I knew it was real!*

It's hard to say for sure how fully aware Kircher was that his map of Atlantis was fictional, but it's fair to say that Jonathan Swift knew that Lilliput and its implacable enemy Blefuscu didn't exist when, sixty years later, he inserted a map of them into the first edition of *Gulliver's Travels*. It's a typical Swiftian joke: The novel in English had only just been invented, and fiction and nonfiction weren't completely disentangled yet (there was significant debate only a few years earlier as to whether *Robinson Crusoe* really happened or not). Swift was offering a practical demonstration of how easily the tools of realism can be used to create something unreal.

But the modern fantasy map really came into its own with the work of J.R.R. Tolkien. Maps like the one of the Hundred Acre Wood in *Winnie-the-Pooh* were drawn to look like the work of a child, but Tolkien's maps claimed the full authority of serious cartography. They were a testament to a new kind of worldbuilding, in which fictional settings aspired to the same kind of solidity and self-consistency that we were used to associating with reality. At first the maps were drawn by Christopher Tolkien, the author's son, but for *The Lord of the Rings* Tolkien doubled down and hired a professional: Pauline Baynes, who before she was a celebrated illustrator was in fact a trained cartographer–she cut her teeth drawing naval charts for the Admiralty during World War II.

Map of Hell (circa 1485) by Sandro Botticelli, from an illustrated manuscript of Dante's *Divine Comedy* commissioned by Lorenzo di Pierfrancesco de' Medici.

Not all fantasy novels are mappable. Novels are, after all, made of words, and therefore largely exempt from the strict observation of the laws of time and space in a way that maps aren't. Thomas Malory's *Morte d'Arthur*, for example, has no inherent geographical logic whatsoever. The knights just light out into the forest, questing or hunting, and the landscape stretches and distorts, or maybe shifts itself tectonically, to get them where the plot needs them, bang on time. The same is true of *Charlie and the Chocolate Factory*. To be mapped is to be trapped and flattened, dried out and fixed on the page. Some books won't put up with it.

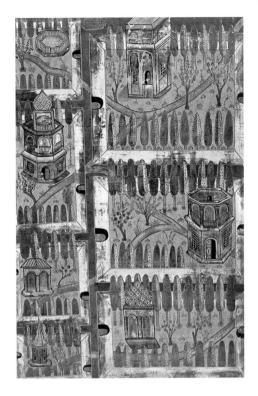

But maps aren't just window dressing, they're fundamentally a part of fantasy as a genre. Before it's about anything else, fantasy is about landscape: green fields, green hills, a place to which the characters and the reader feel connected in a way that's no longer possible in our alienated postindustrial age. Fantasy is about longing, about the yearning to be not here but elsewhere. Maps are about the same thing. A map is not an idle exercise: It's a plan to go somewhere.

Though it's not always easy for fantasy novelists to live up to their maps. One reason George R. R. Martin took so long to deliver *A Dance with Dragons* was the difficulty he had calculating and reconciling all the distances and travel times—it was, he wrote on his blog, "a bitch and a half." It was something Tolkien himself struggled with: "If you're going to have a complicated story you must work to a map," he wrote, "otherwise you'll never make a map of it afterwards."

It's a problem new to the cartographic age of fantasy: The map now actually precedes the territory. If you've ever wondered why the Beor Mountains in Alagaësia are ten miles high, it's because when he was making the map Christopher Paolini accidentally drew them out of scale. He was going to fix it—but then he decided he liked them better that way. ✦

Bosnian scholar Matrakçı Nasuh (1480–1564) wrote extensively on mathematics and history. He also created a series of maps of sixteenth century Persia.

MUSIC

BEHIND THE SCENES, MUSIC IS MORE OFTEN THAN NOT THE storyteller's fuel. Consider Stephen King's affection for heavy metal—and the way he's woven some of his favorite lyrics and images into his classic works.

On the other hand, musicians have equally been inspired by SFF storytelling of a more textual—or visual—nature, and often sought to tell science fiction stories of their own. This chapter explores landmark concept albums that from the 1960s onward, turned music into a bona fide genre of SFF storytelling . . . as well as some of the ambitious (maybe *too* ambitious) science fiction and fantasy albums that never made it to shelves.

Steven Wilson is founder of the alternative rock band Porcupine Tree, discussed in more detail on pages 196-197. An extraordinarily versatile and talented musician, Wilson's most recent project is a solo album titled *To The Bone* (2017). Photo credit: Lasse Hoile.

Science-Fiction Storytelling in the 1960s and '70s, Set to Music

Just as the 1960s welcomed a New Wave in science fiction literature (see pages 39-42), it also marked the beginning of an SFF musical renaissance that lasted well into the 1970s. Pop culture was alight with the excitement of the Space Age. The generation's brilliant minds were reading Tolkien and T. H. White, Asimov and Heinlein, and the iconography of both ancient epics and futuristic galaxies filtered into their own creative efforts. The free-flowing LSD inspired plenty of weird and trippy work as well.

One of the era's most ambitious concept albums was *In The Court of the Crimson King* (1969), the debut album from British prog-rock band King Crimson. This highly influential album is an anti-war polemic that cloaked its criticisms in the allegory of good and evil, blending soaring drama and psychedelic sound. It also inspired Stephen King, who took the name "the Crimson King" for his epic fantasy series *The Dark Tower*.

In 1972, David Bowie delivered what is possibly the greatest SF concept album of all time: *The Rise and Fall of Ziggy Stardust and the Spiders from Mars*. This ambitious glam-rock opera tells the story of Ziggy Stardust, a supernatural bisexual rockstar with a magnetic charisma and an alien connection.

Writing for the *Guardian* on the 2009 release of a 40th anniversary re-mastered version (with surround sound mixed by Steven Wilson), Graham Fuller called *In the Court of the Crimson King* "the masterpiece that essentially launched progressive rock." The band, and the album, have inspired other groups discussed in these pages, such as the Mars Volta. In 2019, the hyper-influential album will celebrate its 50th anniversary.

Ziggy Stardust is the messiah sent by aliens to deliver the human race from selfishness, violence, and greed. Bowie was a fan of William Burroughs and Stanley Kubrick, both inventive and experimental science fiction storytellers in their own medium, and was inspired by their work. In his book *Strange Stars*, Jason Heller describes how Burroughs's use of collage and deconstruction techniques inspired Bowie's work: "A pioneer of postmodern sci-fi pastiche as well as the literary cut-up technique, in which snippets of text were randomly rearranged to form a new syntax, Burroughs straddled both pulp sci-fi and the avant-garde, exactly the same liminal space Bowie now occupied."

Burroughs and Bowie met for a discussion published in *Rolling Stone*—a sort of mutual interview between two great minds. During this conversation, Bowie sketched out his own interpretation of Ziggy Stardust: "The time is five years to go before the end of the Earth. It has been announced that the world will end because of a lack of natural resources. Ziggy is in a position where all the kids have access to things that they thought they wanted. The older people have all lost touch with reality, and the kids are left on their own to plunder anything. Ziggy was in a rock 'n' roll band, and the kids no longer wanted to play rock 'n' roll. There's no electricity to play it."

It's an incredibly influential album, no less because as he took on the persona of Ziggy Stardust, David Bowie inspired a generation of queer and questioning kids who fell in love with his unapologetically androgynous, flamboyant, bisexual persona. He didn't just invent Ziggy through music—he lived him through fashion and style.

Soon after came Pink Floyd's *The Dark Side of the Moon* (1973), the height of prog rock, a hippie classic, and one of the bestselling albums of all time. It explores the cosmic concerns of space, time, and the human experience. If you were born in the seventies or eighties (or, let's face it, the nineties), there's a good chance this is the album your dad jammed to while getting high in the garage. It's not Pink Floyd's only sci-fi influenced work by any means—some of their other great songs include "Set the Controls for the Heart of the Sun" and "Interstellar Overdrive."

David Bowie's tragic passing from cancer in January 2016 prompted a global outpouring of mourning and commemoration, leading many to revisit the artist's greatest works from over the decades. Many of his albums re-entered the Billboard 200 chart, including *The Rise and Fall of Ziggy Stardust and the Spiders From Mars*, which peaked at No. 21, forty-four years after its initial release. *Blackstar*, his final album, released just two days before his death, debuted at No. 1.

In 1975, the universe welcomed Parliament's *Mothership Connection*. Beyond the long shadow it cast on the funk music genre, *Mothership Connection* marked a major milestone in science fiction storytelling by bringing Afrofuturism to a popular audience (as Nisi Shawl explores on pages 175-177). This mythology laid groundwork for new threads of Afrofuturist storytelling across genres—not just the music of twenty-first century innovators like Deltron 3030 and Janelle Monáe (see pages 194-195 and 198-201), but also some of the best speculative work emerging today in fiction, film, and comics.

In 1976, Rush released one of the final big concept albums of the era: *2112*. The story is told via the twenty-minute title track, which occupied one entire side of the band's breakthrough album. The grandiose sci-fi storytelling is underlined by deep cuts and conveyed via a high-charged wall of sound that's both dynamic and volatile, frequently changing pace to match the emotional highs and lows of the narrative.

Naturally, the story takes place in the year 2112, when the world is ruled by the oppressive Solar Federation. Art and music are regulated by priests—until a guy finds an old-ass guitar and discovers the pleasures of the forbidden. The priests of the Temples of Syrinx can't let that stand; they destroy it. This young martyr to the music kills himself in protest, provoking chaos . . . and the beginning of a new era. *Consequence of Sound* calls the story a "classic tale of the individual versus an oppressive, collectivist entity," comparing the world of 2112 to "Winston Smith's world in *1984* or that of John the Savage in *Brave New World*."

2112 is right up there with *Ziggy Stardust* and the *Crimson King* for greatest concept album in the universe. In future albums, Rush continued to explore science fiction themes, depicting an interstellar voyage through a black hole in the lengthy tracks "Cygnus X-1" and "Cygnus X-1 Book II," respectively found on *A Farewell to Kings* (1977) and *Hemispheres* (1978).

Just as the musicians who created these works were inspired by their favorite SF novels—often the tales they'd treasured as children—the vast mythologies hinted at in these albums went on to inspire a new generation of writers, who found in fragments of lyrics, and the feelings they evoked, the genesis of their own speculative stories. And the interchange and interplay between musicians and writers continues. ✦

With lyrics like "light years in time, ahead of our time, free your mind and come fly with me," *Mothership Connection* invited its listeners to embark on a journey toward a different future. It presented a mythology in which funk music is the key to building a better world, casting Black people as the heroes and heroines of an epic science fiction story.

Astro Black

The future looked black. More to the point, it *sounded* black. Back in the mid-1970s, pre-President Reagan, post-MLK, Parliament/Funkadelic gave up the intergalactic funk in honor of an awakened community of musically oriented science fiction fans. Or perhaps it's more accurate to describe them as SF-oriented music fans? At any rate, their semi-cargo-cultish audience eagerly absorbed the group's outlandish, nay, offearthish stylings. The 1976 Mothership Connection tour featured a smoke-shrouded pyramidal spaceship cajoled into landing onstage by a song; the show's star Afronauts wore silver lamé platform boots and swooping capes and collars, while the rest of the crew sported dangling furs, bobbing feathers, and bug eyes. Lyrics exhorting listeners to bathe in the healing energies broadcast by their radios and promising to expand their molecules, personae with names like Starchild and Dr. Funkenstein–all these deliberately chosen images and elements and a myriad more underscored P-Funk's science-fictional bent. Those predilections had their predecessors.

One of the most frequently cited of Parliament/Funkadelic's predecessors is Sun Ra (1914-1993), the highly theatrical jazz composer and perfomer, who many claim was Afrofuturism's Ur-musician. Long, long ago–In the thirties? Forties? Fifties? Accounts vary.–following a non-corporeal journey to a planet he believed was Saturn, Sun Ra began spreading the news that space was the place. From the fifties through the early nineties he played avant-garde jazz alongside an ever-changing lineup that at times included thirty musicians, singers, dancers, and fire-eaters. "It's after the end of the world, don't you know that yet?" he asked on the 1970 live album *It's After the End of the World*, making it clear that his forays into the speculative encompassed not just space but time.

Another influence, and a near contemporary: Jimi Hendrix (1942-1970). Guitarist Eddie Hazel was an obvious Hendrixite, and the psychedelic component of P-Funk's shows and recordings has often been linked to Hendrix. But what about that SF content I mentioned? Plenty of Hendrix songs–"Third Stone from the Sun" and "1983 . . . (A Merman I Should Turn to Be)" to name a couple–are solidly genre. His love of Flash Gordon movies and postapocalyptic novels is documented in books and articles. Did Messrs. Clinton and Hazel (as well as P-Funk mainstays Bernie Worrell and Bootsy Collins) neglect that aspect of Hendrix's pioneering work when taking inspiration from it? Doubtful.

Why, though, does Afrofuturism resonate so strongly in the echoing halls of musical knowledge? Perhaps, partly, for the same reason it's a force to be reckoned with on any curve of the Afrodiasporic sphere: alienation and cognitive dissonance, the mainstays of the SF experience, science fiction's hardcore jollies, are, for us, the default. As a child I tried to explain this to a white neighbor by sharing my theory that I came from Mars. Outsiders make myths of our exclusion. And then we play those myths, and sing them, and dance them, because we recognize that artistic expression of a truth makes it even more valid. Science fiction, as author Greg Bear says, is the modern mythos.

So the intersection of music and Afrofuturism is a regularly visited spot. Sun Ra, Jimi Hendrix, Parliament/Funkadelic to be sure–and P-Funk's contemporaries, too: Sly & the Family Stone, who accompanied the band on the Mothership Connection tour; Gil Scott-Heron, who predicted worldwide transformation in "The Revolution Will Not Be Televised"; Earth, Wind & Fire, whose neo-Egyptian symbolism and proselytizing for Cosmic Consciousness fit right in with the Afrofuturist tradition.

It's a living tradition. It can be found anywhere you look. Punk rock embodied Afrofuturism, if only briefly, in Poly Styrene, lead singer of X-Ray Spex. (Her songs "Germ

Saxophonist John Gilmore, a member of Sun Ra's Arkestra, in 1990. The Arkestra was a flexible, ever-evolving ensemble of dozens of musicians that Ra led for decades. The Arkestra often performed in fantastic costumes that blended influences from Egyptian myth and iconography and Space Age science fiction, creating an early aesthetic for Afrofuturism. Photo credit: Sefton Samuels / Shutterstock.

Free Adolescents" and "The Day the World Turned Day-Glo" come particularly to mind.) Disco and New Wave diva Grace Jones has always been presented as beautifully inhuman, erotically robotic, and shockingly unearthly through her hair, clothes, makeup, and mannerisms. Yet another quondam disco star, Michael Jackson, was known for "moonwalking," a dance move that seems to defy mundane causality. Jackson performed several Afrofuturistic numbers in the years following that early part of his solo career. His hit dance tune "Another Part of Me" first appeared in 1987 in the indubitably science-fictional short film *Captain EO*. "Remember the Time," released in 1992, foregrounds the familiar Afrofuturist Egyptian aesthetic; "Scream," released in 1995, originally accompanied a video in which MJ and his sister Janet sang and danced aboard an orbiting spacecraft.

Throughout the eighties and nineties, electronica and house–originally black musical forms–helped Afrofuturism keep on keepin' on. Some SF authors had begun by then to lament the growing difficulty of writing about a future that got closer and closer every day. They complained that fast-paced innovation overtook their storylines, but electronica started off inviting listeners to discover the future by living in it, and went on to celebrate what could be found there.

Something experiential and empirical in the nature of music blends nicely with African-based attitudes toward science, time, and technology. This may be why the flow goes both ways, into the aural realm *and* out of it. Not only does genre fiction inspire Afrofuturist music, the music's figures and numbers and other components inspire genre fiction–as when, for example, an avatar of P-Funk's Starchild appears in my 2008 story "Good Boy." Or when an anthology collecting that story is titled *Mothership*. Or sometimes when an Afrofuturist composer and performer such as DJ Gabriel Teodros writes the stuff himself. His 2015 story "Lalibela" appears in *Octavia's Brood: Science Fiction from Social Justice Movements* and is reprinted in Volume 1 of the *Sunspot Jungle* anthology.

Because of this ongoing back-and-forth, and with Beyoncé ("Single Ladies"), Kendrick Lamar ("Alright"), and Janelle Monáe (*The ArchAndroid*) constantly updating Afrofuturism's sound, scholars like Kinitra Jallow, Erik Steinskog, and DJ Lynnée Denise have endless sources of new material to examine in their studies of the subject. And those of us less studious have endless sources of material to which we can shake our multidimensional booties. ✦

Outsiders make myths of our exclusion. And then we play those myths, and sing them, and dance them, because we recognize that artistic expression of a truth makes it even more valid. Science fiction, as author Greg Bear says, is the modern mythos.

The Who's Lifelong Search for the "One Note"

After the massive critical and commercial success of *Tommy* (1969), a rock opera about an abused boy, the Who found themselves in search of an equally ambitious concept for their next album. For lead guitarist and songwriter Pete Townshend, that concept was *Lifehouse*–a science-fiction rock opera that would expand the potential of audience participation to dizzying new heights. The album would be supplemented with film and live performances, making it a full multimedia experience.

The *Lifehouse* storyline went through several iterations, but here's the general thrust of it: In the not-too-distant future, environmental degradation means most people are locked up inside their houses 24/7, where they encounter the world solely through their connection to an experience/entertainment network called "The Grid." (If you're thinking that sounds a little like the Internet, you're not alone.) Basically, the populace spends their lifetimes jacked into virtual reality, wearing haptic feedback suits to enhance the experience.

Of course, in 1970 there wasn't much popular terminology for virtual reality or haptic feedback suits; no one had even seen *The Matrix*. Perhaps this was *Lifehouse*'s downfall; as Pete Townshend tried to explain his brain-busting concept to his bandmates and manager, they were just like ". . . We don't get it."

Anyway, in this world governed by virtual reality, a hacker named Bobby discovers rock 'n' roll, which is outlawed by the Grid. Bobby lives outside the virtual reality network–you could say he's taken the red pill–and so from his position in a commune of fringe-people and farmers, he begins broadcasting classic rock to the helpless denizens of the Grid. The music will happen live in a concert hall called Lifehouse, played by none other than the Who. Like *Mothership* and Rush, this story would lean into its own medium by casting music as a powerful and mystical force and the key to freedom from oppression.

The *Lifehouse* narrative focuses on a family of humble turnip farmers, who also live outside the Grid, in the unpolluted wilderness of Scotland. Their teen daughter Mary runs away to go to the concert. This is where narratives diverge; in some iterations, the parents go after her together, in others it's just Ray. Anyway, Ray and sometimes Sally arrive at the rock festival just in time to find Bobby and the band hitting the One Note . . . that one

powerful and mystical sound, fully in tune with the vibrations of the universe, that unites all people and achieves world peace.

Perhaps even more complicated than the virtual reality stuff was Townshend's conception of music as a metaphysical force. The idea was that Bobby, on his path to the One Note, would create songs that uniquely represented individual audience members, connecting directly to their souls. More challengingly, Townshend imagined that in their role as the band, the Who would find a way to do the same thing. It's one thing to envision the supernatural; it's quite another thing to aspire to execute it. In 1978, Townshend admitted as much to *Trouser Press*: "What fell apart with it . . . was that I actually tried to make this fiction that I'd written happen in reality. That's where I went wrong, actually trying to make a perfect concept."

Their attempts to capture the sublime began and ended at the Young Vic, a theater in London where the band booked a months-long residency. The goal was to develop the concept through daily live performances in which the band's synergy with the audience would organically melt into total harmony. Instead, the confused audience heckled the new material and demanded to hear the hits.

Under pressure from the rest of the band, Townshend reluctantly gave up the *Lifehouse* concept. They narrowed the material down to the strongest songs, which became the basis for

The Who performing in Chicago in 1975. Left to right: Roger Daltrey, John Entwistle, Keith Moon, Pete Townshend. Photo credit: Jim Summaria.

a non-concept album, *Who's Next*—widely regarded as one of the best rock albums of the twentieth century. Those songs include "Baba O'Riley," "Won't Get Fooled Again," and "Behind Blue Eyes," some of the Who's biggest and most enduring hits.

But Pete Townshend remained fascinated by the SFF elements of *Lifehouse* and never abandoned his vision for it. He drew on it heavily for inspiration on his 1993 solo album *Psychoderelict*. In 1999, the BBC produced *Lifehouse* as a radio play. In 2000, Townshend released a six-disc boxed set called *Lifehouse Chronicles*.

Lifehouse Chronicles includes original 1971 demos of *Lifehouse* songs, live recordings, new studio recordings, orchestral arrangements for the radio play, and the radio play itself. Unfortunately for *Lifehouse* fanatics, the full box set is out of print and hard to find; used copies go for $300 or more online. On the other hand, *Lifehouse Elements*—a one-disc sampler with eleven tracks—is widely available, and offers a rousing glimpse of the *Lifehouse* that could have been. ✦

JOHN CHU

Sweet Bye and Bye and Speculative Fiction in Musical Theatre

Scientists have located, "under the waters of Flushing Bay," the time capsule buried during the 1939 New York World's Fair. On the United States' tricentennial, scientists recover and open the capsule. They find among its contents a letter from a Solomon Bundy to his namesake in the future. He bequeaths his future namesake five shares of stock in the Futurosy Candy Corporation, which is now "the biggest candy cartel there is." These five shares from 137 years ago gives his namesake a controlling interest in the company and make him one of the wealthiest people in the world.

The Solomon Bundy of 2076 is a tree surgeon who thinks of himself as being "born too late." He is completely unprepared to be the president of the Futurosy Candy Corporation. This is, of course, precisely what he has just become.

This reads like the setup for a science fiction satire. And it is. But it's also the 1946 musical *Sweet Bye and Bye*, featuring robots and a partially drowned New York City, not to mention a second act where Solomon Bundy flees to Mars on a space liner. The pedigree of the creative team was also out of this world, with a book by S. J. Perelman, the revered *New Yorker* writer and humorist, and Al Hirschfeld, the legendary caricaturist, lyrics by Ogden Nash, the popular poet, and music by Vernon Duke, whose collaborators over his career included Ira Gershwin and Johnny Mercer. Sadly, despite all this talent, the original production failed before it reached Broadway. The score was thought lost for decades until it was rediscovered in a warehouse in Secaucus, N.J., in the mid-eighties, but happily, sixty-five years after the show opened, it was made into an audio recording in 2011.

Setting *Sweet Bye and Bye* in the future heightens what Tommy Krasker, the producer of the 2011 recording, identifies as the theme of the show: "How do you really find your way in a world of limitless possibilities?" Unfortunately, while this was the show Duke and Nash wrote, what Perelman and Hirschfeld wrote was a farcical revue. The show then had an exceptionally difficult out-of-town tryout. The original leading man couldn't sing. His replacement couldn't remember lines. The original leading lady had a nervous breakdown (but was replaced by Dolores Gray). The show closed in Philadelphia, canceling its Broadway run. As brilliant as the score was, the book didn't work, and fixing it left the score in tatters. There was never a version of the show to present both elements in their full genius. (Although one can listen to the 2011 recording and imagine the wonderful show that could have been.)

Despite the heavy hitter talent behind *Sweet Bye and Bye*, it is not a successful example of the subgenre, but there are a surprising number of shows that do work. Theater, from its various origins, has always included the fantastic. So works like Kurt Weill's *One Touch of Venus* (1943), where a statue becomes the literal goddess Venus, have never been out of bounds. Even in works that are essentially mimetic, like Rodgers and Hammerstein's *Carousel* (1945) and *Damn Yankees* (1955), Billy Bigelow tries to fight his way into heaven in the former, and Joe Boyd makes a pact with the Devil, kicking off the plot of the latter.

Musicals like Kurt Weill and Alan Jay Lerner's *Love Life* (1948), Leonard Bernstein's *1600 Pennsylvania Avenue* (1976), and *Heading East* (2001) play with time differently than *Sweet Bye and Bye*. They span multiple centuries while their characters age only years, if at all. This drives home that the struggles in marriage, American democracy, and Asian American immigration recur over the broad sweep of history. Speculative devices function for works meant to be performed in the same way they function for works meant to be read—they heighten those works in a way that would be more difficult, if not impossible, without them. ✦

Caricaturist Al Hirschfeld, who contributed to the book for *Sweet Bye and Bye*. Photo credit: Carl Van Vechten.

ANNALEE NEWITZ

X-Ray Spex, Poly Styrene, and Punk Rock Science Fiction

I n the mid-1970s, a young woman from Brixton named Marianne Elliott-Said had a profoundly transformative experience. She went to a Sex Pistols concert and was galvanized by the realization that punk meant expressing herself however she wanted. Shortly thereafter, she saw a fiery pink UFO hovering in the skies over Doncaster. By 1976, she'd taken the name Poly Styrene and formed a punk band called X-Ray Spex, whose singles "Oh Bondage Up Yours," "Identity," and "World Turned Day-Glo" rocketed up the charts. Though X-Ray Spex only released one album, *Germfree Adolescents* (1978), the band had a profound effect on punk rock, feminist fashion, and science fiction.

Proudly calling herself "artificial" and "a poseur," Poly sang about a future of genetically-engineered humans, consumer droids, environmental apocalypse, and mind-blowing explorations of outer space. Wearing retro fashion mixed with gilded junk, she belted out songs that combined elements of ska, punk rock, and new wave synth weirdness. In 1977, she told an Australian TV interviewer that her trippy sound and look weren't about LSD, but futuristic fantasy: "I wanted to write something using all kinds of plastic words and artificial things and sort of make a fantasy around it. It's about the modern world."

Germfree Adolescents should be read in the tradition of Samuel Delany, Octavia Butler, and Joanna Russ, with some sarcastic notes of Philip K. Dick thrown in for good measure. In the song "Genetic Engineering," she gives us a future ruled by biologists, where a "worker clone" is a "subordinated slave" ruled by "expertise proficiency." But in the song "Plastic Bag," she's become a clone herself, calling her mind a "plastic bag that corresponds to all those ads."

Poly's lyrics were often absurdist and surreal, almost as if she were channeling Delany's *Dhalgren*. But there was also no mistaking her rage. Like Russ and Butler, whose characters are often treated like aliens and monsters by the men around them, Poly wanted the world to know what it felt like to be a mixed-race woman in a scene dominated by white men.

Her song "Identity" tackles this head-on, asking, "Do you see yourself on the TV screen . . . When you see yourself does it make you scream?" Here she's grappling with

the problem of representation in the media. Like many punk and ska acts inspired by her, from the Specials to Bikini Kill, Poly loved to dress up in outfits that were arresting precisely because they defied gender norms. In the song "Highly Inflammable," she trills about a person who is both man and woman, who "wants to join the hermaphrodite clan."

Over a decade later, intersectional and queer feminists would explore this issue, highlighting how women of color in mass media are either demonized or rendered invisible. In her lyrics, Poly calls identity a "crisis you can't see."

Early in her career, Poly explained that her obsession with artificiality came from women's punk fashion, recalling that she started writing "Oh Bondage Up Yours" after a Sex Pistols show where she saw "two girls handcuffed together." Poly liked the way they were "drawing attention to the fact that they were in bondage as opposed to pretending they weren't." For Poly, bondage wasn't just a matter of identity. It was about a future ruled by consumerism. "Oh Bondage Up Yours" describes a fake consumerist utopia with wordplay: "Chain-store, chain-smoke . . . chain-gang, chain-mail!" She throws off her bondage by immersing herself in it completely. "I consume you all!" she screams in the chorus.

The science fiction of X-Ray Spex was ahead of its time. Poly was an intersectional feminist in an era when that concept had no name. And she was describing a cyberpunk future long before cyberpunk became popular. Her music gave voice to a generation for whom authenticity was artificiality, and futurism felt like a dead end.

Though she struggled with depression that often kept her out of the limelight, Poly continued writing genre-inspired songs until the end of her life. Her final album, *Generation Indigo*, was released in 2011 a month before she died at fifty-four of metastatic breast cancer. Like all of her work, it was eclectic; there's an electroclash satire of MySpace culture called "Virtual Boyfriend," and a dreamy post-punk song called "Ghoulish" about loving creatures who seem monstrous but are actually just nice guys.

In the video for "Ghoulish," we're given a final glimpse of the alternate future world that Poly made real for so many young people who never saw themselves on TV. We watch a surreal version of *American Idol* unfolding, as mixed-race kids and queers dance for judges who offer bizarro commentary. Finally, a Michael Jackson impersonator lights up the stage with amazing moves and magical glitter powers, the judges cheer, and we have our new idol. The room fills with dancers, many of them mixed-race and androgynous, and we zoom in on the winner. He looks up from beneath his white fedora . . . and we realize this Michael Jackson clone has been female all along. She turns to the camera, her face alight with mirth, and lip syncs to Poly Styrene singing, "I'm not so foolish to be scared."

This moment sums up what Poly Styrene has left in her wake. It's a narrative fusion of sharp social satire and playfulness that keeps the world's horrors at bay. But it's also a promise. Maybe one day, in a world without slave clones, we'll see ourselves on the mobile screens and it won't make us want to scream. ✦

X-Ray Spex in concert, September 14, 1991.
Photo credit: Ian Dickson / Shutterstock.

Weezer's *Songs from the Black Hole*

Weezer's first album, *Weezer* (aka *The Blue Album*), went triple platinum when it was released in 1994, and launched the band to sudden and stratospheric success. Lead singer Rivers Cuomo felt that he, too, had been launched into outer space . . . and for the band's sophomore effort, they set out to make a concept album exploring the experience. As Ryan Bassil put it in *Noisey,* "*Blue Album* had been released to critical acclaim and Rivers Cuomo, a maverick in despondency, had mixed feelings about its success."

The album would have been a musical space opera, titled *Songs from the Black Hole*. Cuomo envisioned *Songs from the Black Hole* in the tradition of Pink Floyd's *Dark Side of the Moon,* as one coherent, flowing musical narrative. The band wrote the songs and shared two track lists, but the album's concept was eventually rejected, and *Songs from the Black Hole* was never officially released. Many of its songs were eventually recorded

Weezer released their eleventh album in October of 2017. The band's creative inspiration for *Pacific Daydream* is "reveries from a beach at the end of the world," and includes the hit "Feels Like Summer."

and released in other forms. With the track lists and lyrics floating around on the Internet, plus some eventual versions of the songs, it's possible to piece together a vision of what might have been. But the full album in its bombastic and space-operatic glory was never truly realized, to the lasting disappointment of fans.

The album's story is reminiscent of the best YA SF drama, a "space opera" that's definitely heavier on the opera than it is on the space. A group of the top young graduates from the Star Corps academy are on a mission in space, which is to stop a planet called Nomis from getting "swallowed by its sun" . . . but their main focus seems to be on who's boinking whom. (And yes, "boink" is a direct quote.) "Basically, the concept was bat-shit crazy ridiculous," concludes *Vice*.

The lead character is Jonas, the moody, brooding ship's captain, jaded and depressed by the whole space travel experience, and caught in a love triangle between two shipmates, Laurel and Maria, an allegorical representation of Cuomo's own love troubles at the time. Meanwhile, Jonas's buds Wuan and Dondo—stand-ins for his bandmates—are eager and enthusiastic about the trip to space. The ship, *Betsy II*, is named after Weezer's tour bus, which they called *Betsy*.

Maria is a friend with benefits who wants something more, while Jonas keeps jerking her around. His friends talk shit about her. Dondo calls her a "cheap ho," and Jonas sets out to comfort her, telling her he hates Dondo . . . who "acts like he knows he's got a big dick." (Keep this in mind; it will be important later.) The long middle of the narrative is mostly Jonas angsting about various things, like how annoying it is that all his fans constantly want to have sex with him, and how getting what you want is never as amazing as you think it will be.

They finally prepare to land, to the great excitement of Wuan and Dondo and the typical pessimism of Jonas, who demands to know why they even bothered to yank him out of his pod. (Earlier in the album, Maria begs him to come to her pod, and they discuss the types of leisure activities they could enjoy within its privacy. Perhaps the fact that Jonas is now alone in his signifies some trouble in paradise.)

Then . . . SPOILER ALERT! . . . Maria gives birth to Jonas's kid, a baby girl. Awestruck and emotional to meet his offspring, Jonas is finally ready to commit. "She's Had a Girl" is a sweet, haunting song that might even make an OK lullaby. Jonas's backup girl Laurel dumps him, despite the fact that she still loves him; this song, "I Just Threw Out the Love of My Dreams" is one of the most compelling songs from the album, a catchy and affecting number sung by Rachel Haden.

But alas, Jonas should have put a ring on it, for his return to Maria reveals an unsettling discovery . . . a used condom. An extra-large used condom. Who could have left behind such an artifact? Well, none other than Dondo, his shipmate with the big dick.

The final song, titled "Longtime Sunshine," sees Jonas singing wistfully of purer and simpler times. He elects to stay behind on Nomis, perhaps to be devoured by the sun, which would explain the title. With all the relationship drama going on, it's not exactly clear what happened regarding the mission or the fate of the sun-doomed planet. "Longtime Sunshine" is a wistful and melancholy song that also pulses with energy and a catchy, driving beat.

As a work of science fiction, the story leaves a lot to be desired. But as music—as a raw, unfiltered taste of Weezer during their most inspired period—it's exhilarating and satisfying. It would be fantastic to hear the thing in its entirety, produced with full theatrics (heavy on the synthesizers). Along with the standout songs already mentioned, there's the opening number "Blast Off!," which Jason Crock describes as "a fleeting rush of distortion-driven joy." Writing for *Noisey* (*Vice*), Ryan Bassil proclaimed the album "better than almost everything they've released in the last fifteen years."

But it was not to be. Cuomo recorded some demos for the album during Christmas of 1994, using synthesizers he'd found at a pawnshop in Connecticut. The band continued to work on the album throughout the early months of 1995, but personal issues began to get in the way. In March, Cuomo underwent difficult and extensive surgery on his leg, followed by painful physical therapy. At the end of 1995, he enrolled at Harvard to study music. He found his time there lonely and isolating. He continued to suffer from chronic pain.

These difficult experiences pushed Cuomo's creative interests in a different direction. *Songs from the Black Hole* was always kind of a goofy, tongue-in-cheek concept, good-naturedly accepting of its own ridiculousness. The whimsical tone no longer worked for him. Instead, he went in a darker, more confessional direction. The result was Weezer's actual second album, *Pinkerton*. Cuomo called it "an exploration of my 'dark side'—all the parts of myself that I was either afraid or embarrassed to think about before."

Pinkerton was not treated kindly by critics, who'd expected something better, based on the success of the *Blue Album*—or at least something different. Cuomo himself eventually joined in on panning it, calling it a "hideous record" and a "hugely painful mistake." He regretted the intensely personal nature of the album, telling *Entertainment Weekly* in 2001 that the experience was like "getting really drunk at a party and spilling your guts in front of everyone and feeling incredibly great and cathartic about it, and then waking up the next morning and realizing what a complete fool you made of yourself."

Those scars took some time to heal, but they did. Eventually, Cuomo made his peace with the album. A retrospective look reveals its unmistakable impact on the world of rock 'n' roll. Still, it's tempting to imagine what might have been, and what direction a completed *Songs from the Black Hole* might have taken the band.

A few of the songs from *SFTBH*'s track list made it onto *Pinkerton*: "Tired of Sex," "Getchoo," and "No Other One." These songs were written before the *Black Hole* concept came to be, so it was easy to transition them. Indeed, they make more sense on a confessional album like *Pinkerton* than they did as the diary of an angst-ridden and oversexed astronaut.

Two more songs from *Black Hole* were later released as *Pinkerton* B sides: "I Just Threw Out the Love of My Dreams" and "Devotion." Five more songs made it into *Alone: The Home Recordings of Rivers Cuomo*, a demo compilation. Three more tracks made it onto *Alone II*, and six onto *Alone III*. Alternate versions recorded at shows also circulate on the Internet and among fans. With all this material to choose from, playlists approximating the imagined album can be found easily. So cue one up . . . and imagine. ✦

The album's story is reminiscent of the best YA SF drama, a "space opera" that's definitely heavier on the opera than it is on the space. "Basically, the concept was bat-shit crazy ridiculous," concludes *Vice*.

Speculative Music
of the New Millennium

The dawn of the new millennium heralded a particularly rich moment for SFF-inspired music, and the late nineties and early oughts brought us several lasting masterpieces of the genre. Radiohead delivered the heavy hitters: *OK Computer* (1997) and *Kid A* (2000). The Flaming Lips contributed the unforgettable *Yoshimi Battles the Pink Robots* (2002). And there were plenty of others: OutKast's *ATLiens* (1996), Air's *Moon Safari* (1998), Daft Punk's *Discovery* (2001), Goldfrapp's *Black Cherry* (2003), and The Mars Volta's *De-Loused in the Comatorium* (2003).

OK Computer regularly makes it onto lists of greatest albums of all time, so if you haven't listened to it yet, you probably never will. Still, if you haven't, you should. It's a masterpiece that perfectly blends its many disparate influences into something altogether new. The album utterly encapsulates a mood that pervaded science-fiction storytelling in the late nineties: trepidation about the unknown future blended with a weary ennui at the isolation and inau-

Goldfrapp live at the annual Summer Series at Somerset House in 2017. Photo credit: Sonic PR/Daniel Roberts.

thenticity of an artificial present. (Or as *Newsweek* puts it: "The terrifying and dehumanizing malaise of modern life and consumerist culture. Exhibit A: Every song on the album.")

Also, one the album's best-known songs is titled "Paranoid Android," inspired by Marvin the depressed robot in Douglas Adams's *Hitchhiker's Guide to the Galaxy*. Marvin also suffers from the galaxy's most severe case of ennui, spouting grim lines such as "Here I am, brain the size of a planet, and they tell me to take you up to the bridge. Call that job satisfaction? Cos I don't." Meanwhile, on the track "Subterranean Homesick Alien," "aliens hover making home movies for the folks back home," and like the overlooked women in James Tiptree Jr.'s classic story "The Women Men Don't See," the song's narrator only wants the aliens to take him with them.

While not exactly a concept album per se, *Yoshimi Battles the Pink Robots* delivers a coherent narrative across several songs, more in the tradition of prog rock's grand epics. Obviously, the heroine of this story is Yoshimi, a black belt and all-around badass, who along with an army of similarly badass girl warriors, is called to keep "the city" safe from the scourge of psychedelic robots with an evil plan for world domination. Her counterpoint is unit 3000-21, the robot who discovers in itself the seeds of humanity, "feeling a synthetic kind of love . . . one more robot learns to be something more than a machine." *Rolling Stone* calls the Flaming Lips' tenth album "a delightful iridescent bomb of buoyant electronics, imaginary Japanese anime and plaintive vocal surrender."

After *Southernplayalisticadillacmuzik* put OutKast on the map as a majorly talented rap duo to watch, *ATLiens* solidified that reputation with its delightfully funky and futuristic hip-hop. The influence of George Clinton and the Parliament/Funkadelic collective is evident. *ATLiens* speaks to the duo's feelings of alienation, and weaves a narrative of personal marginalization together with imagery from science fiction and folklore that expands the story into something much larger. The lyrics are both smart and catchy, and are underlined with addictive beats and spaced out sci-fi sound effects.

Air's *Moon Safari*, Daft Punk's *Discovery,* and Goldfrapp's *Black Cherry* each offer a unique take on synth-pop electronica, with abstract, minimal lyrics and lengthy instrumental interludes. The science-fiction appeal of these albums is primarily in their enchanting space-pop sound. *Moon Safari*, for instance, includes the track "Kelly Watch the Stars," whose lyrics consist of the one line "Kelly watch the stars" . . . repeated seventeen times. *Slant Magazine* writes of the album, "At the same

The iconic cover art for Air's debut album, *Moon Safari*, first released in 1998, with a tenth anniversary re-release from Virgin Records. *Rolling Stone* included it in a list of the best albums of the 1990s.

time that it's space-y and breathless, it's also organic and downbeat; at the same time that it's nostalgic, it's also clearly planted in the future." This is the music that plays in the passenger lobby of the space yacht while you wait for the hyperdrive to kick in.

Like Air, Daft Punk is a French electronica duo. *Discovery* is a more uptempo album, with a pulsing dance beat and lyrics that are almost hypnotically repetitive. (This album includes the world-conquering workout anthem "Harder Better Faster Stronger.") *Treble Zine* calls it "a record that truly sounds like an outer-space version of an '80s rock band." *Discovery* is primarily instrumental and doesn't listen like a concept album, but in a fairly unprecedented move, the duo turned it into one—by releasing an animated movie alongside it that wasn't widely seen.

Interstella 5555: The 5tory of the 5ecret 5tar 5ystem is a Japanese-French anime that tells a story solely through its visuals, using the entirety of *Discovery* as its soundtrack. *Interstella 5555* is about a blue-skinned alien techno band kidnapped by evil earthling music executives (and followed by space pilot Shep, who is in love with bass player Stella). The band's memories are reprogrammed and they are forced to perform as the Crescendolls (see *Discovery*, track five). Shep intervenes, and slowly the band overcomes their amnesia to piece together what happened and how they ended up here, so they can go back home. It's a pretty hallucinatory ride, but critics hailed the trippy film as a success, comparing its kaleidoscopic pleasures favorably to Disney's *Fantasia*. The film was created in a collaboration between Daft Punk, Leiji Matsumoto, Cédric Hervet, and Toei Animation, and reportedly cost $4 million to make.

De-Loused in the Comatorium (2003), the debut studio album from the Mars Volta, with album cover art by Storm Thorgerson. This weird concept album follows the metaphysical journey of Cerpin Taxt. From the accompanying storybook: "Faith vanishings, hence the litter passing by muttering underbreath, and waterlike, I thought someone might still be able to spot me . . . testator nomadic. Trailing a tail of trick mirrors, hyperventilating as I did past my own temple."

Goldfrapp's *Black Cherry* is slinky, seductive, and charged with sexual tension. It's the perfect album to accompany dark and erotic fairy tales for adults in the vein of Angela Carter, Tanith Lee, Helen Oyeyemi, or Catherynne M. Valente. Writing for *Bustle* on Alison Goldfrapp's "fantasist's dream" wardrobe, Freyia Lilian Porteous describes Goldfrapp's music as "sparkling with something akin to both fairy dust and the sheen of a futuristic spaceship." Perhaps not just a perfect accompaniment to Tanith Lee's fairy tales, but her equally luscious and uniquely feminine science fiction stories, such as *The Silver Metal Lover*, *Electric Forest*, and *Don't Bite the Sun*.

The Mars Volta's debut full-length studio album, *De-Loused in the Comatorium*, is about as far as you can get from Goldfrapp's chilled out pop . . . but prog rock has its virtues too, as well as a storied legacy in the halls of SFF.

The Mars Volta formed in 2001 from the same duo who previously performed as successful band At The Drive-In: Omar Rodriguez-Lopez and Cedric Bixler-Zavala. This voluntary reinvention speaks to the innovative impulses that motivated the duo's creativity–a desire to tread new territory. With *De-Loused in the Comatorium* they delivered that, and the album was both a critical and a commercial success. It pays tribute to their close friend Julio Venegas, an artist whose troubled life ended in suicide–after recovering from a drug overdose that left him in a lengthy coma. This tragic story is recreated in *De-Loused* as the fictional story of Cerpin Taxt, whose mind undertakes a series of nightmarish voyages as his body remains comatose following an overdose on morphine and rat poison.

Bixler-Zavala and Rodriguez-Lopez also wrote a storybook to be released alongside the album. This story weaves a more complex fictional narrative to accompany each song's lyrics, detailing the people and places that Taxt encounters on his otherworldly journey. Much of this story, like the album's lyrics, is a surreal and Burroughs-esque stream of consciousness whose chaotic litany of words evokes a vision through accretion rather than explanation. ✦

At The Drive-In live in concert in 1999 at 3B in Bellingham, Washington. Left: Omar Rodriguez-Lopez. Right: Cedric Bixler-Zavala on vocals. Photo credit: Jacob Covey.

The Timeless Brilliance of Deltron 3030

I t's been nearly two decades since the world was given the debut record from Deltron 3030–the hip-hop supergroup comprised of Del the Funky Homosapien, Dan the Automator, and Kid Koala–and yet *Deltron 3030* remains relevant, prescient, and exciting. It came out while I was in high school, right at a time where I was thirsting for more–for art that addressed the oppressive structures that dictated the difficulties in my life. For music that made me feel less alone. For the escapism of densely-constructed worlds. Del's lyrical complexity and vocal uniqueness–which I'd

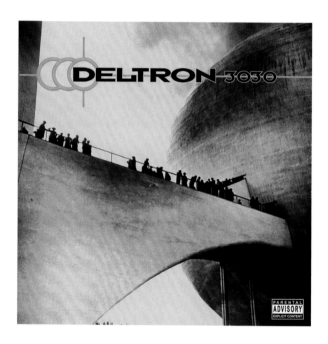

fallen in love with on his fourth album, *Both Sides of the Brain*–was present here. He's got a voice that is instantly recognizable, and even to this day, *no one* sounds like Del. But this voice was paired with a sweeping, operatic story set in the year 3030, where hip-hop is the last hope in a society ruined by a set of oppressive oligarchs.

I devoured it. Here was a world where I could easily imagine myself as the hero, even though I can't rhyme to save my life. Musically, both Dan the Automator and Kid Koala provided a soundtrack that managed to straddle the line between soulful throwbacks and futuristic intensity. Nothing in hip-hop sounded like this record!

Truly, the brilliance of *Deltron 3030* was multifaceted. The complex future that's spread over the album felt living, real, and frightening. Half the planet is an unlivable desert, populated by brain-eating cannibals. And the world that *is* tenable is controlled by a vicious military force, which is where the album's hero, Deltron Zero, rises to the occasion. While referencing *The Matrix*, *Ghost in the Shell*, *Metropolis*, and other popular science fiction narratives, Del's rhythmic lyrics portray the struggle between independence and fascism, violence and hope, self-determination and despair. And practically *all* of it works as a scathing indictment of the problems and issues that Del and his contemporaries were dealing with back in 1999 and 2000.

I don't know if it's sad that, eighteen years later, the album is just as politically and socially familiar. It seems fitting, though, because *Deltron 3030* is cyclical in nature. When "Memory Loss" hits and Deltron Zero loses his memory upon his return to Earth, we're

shown how the forces that hurt us repeat over and over, in large part because humans are so ignorant to the repetitive nature of history. Let *Deltron 3030* be your lesson then. Let the sultry grooves and beats take you over as you immerse yourself in the intoxicating and invigorating experience of one MC's fight against a dystopian world. It's an album that rewards multiple listens, and it remains one of the more underrated albums in the genre—well, *both* the genres of hip-hop and science fiction. Get into it. ✦

Deltron3030's Del the Funky Homosapien.
Photo credit: Elliothtz.

The Science-Fiction Soundscapes of Porcupine Tree

Composer, singer, and guitarist Steven Wilson (b. 1967) founded Porcupine Tree in the 1980s as a solo project, but as the music found its footing as postmodern psychedelic prog rock, Porcupine Tree evolved into a genuine band. Their music is often experimental and ambitious, changing significantly from album to album. Their discography is incredibly varied, making them one of the era's most difficult musical acts to classify. Writing for *Rolling Stone*, David Fricke called their music "an aggressively modern merger of Rush's arena art rock, U.K. prog rock classicism–especially Pink Floyd's eulogies to madness and King Crimson's angular majesty–and the postgrunge vengeance of Tool."

Despite the unpredictability of each new album from this innovative group, one clear uniting element is a preoccupation with outer space and the otherworldly, a thread running though their discography to date. These themes are perhaps most explicit on their first album, *On The Sunday of Life* (1991), when the band was still finding its footing, with over-the-top and occasionally parodic lyrics rife with lush and purple prose. The album includes acid-trip-ready tracks such as "Jupiter Island," which evokes "magenta forests on a crimson sea, the electric clouds are as vivid as can be," and "It Will Rain For A Million Years" ("I locked myself inside the capsule and watched the planet slowly turning blue . . ."). Perhaps the most over-the-top of all is the track "Space Transmission," which purports to convey a message from someone who has been trapped on Planet Earth in darkness ever since the sun exploded fourteen years ago.

Porcupine Tree's early albums also wear their Pink Floyd influence on their sleeves, paying homage to their prog rock progenitor through similar expansive soundscapes and psychedelic riffs. The SF *Encyclopedia* draws this comparison specifically with regard to *The Sky Moves Sideways* (1995), which "details a materially disintegrating world, but this apocalypse is so dreamily hallucinogenic as wholly to avoid the usual outré stylings of this manner of end-of-the-world music."

Lightbulb Sun (2000) includes the fantastic track "Last Chance to Evacuate Planet Earth Before It Is Recycled," which samples a recorded speech by the leader of the suicidal cult Heaven's Gate, whose members believed themselves to be representatives of another dimension. Explaining the cult's impending departure, its leader states, "Let me say that

our mission here at this time is about to come to a close . . . We came from distant space . . . We are about to return from whence we came."

Voyage 34: The Complete Trip (2000) also samples an existing recording, while continuing to riff on the concepts of inner and outer space. The found audio that serves as the backbone of this concept album reports on a young man's bad acid trip in the 1960s. "It was an anti-LSD propaganda album," Wilson said to Rolling Stone, "and it was perfect to form a narrative around which I could form this long, hypnotic, trippy piece of music." Though primarily instrumental, the album nevertheless transports its listener into psychedelic planes.

Perhaps the best way to enjoy Porcupine Tree's early, SFF-adjacent and influenced work is through their retrospective compilation album Stars Die, which collects some of the band's best work from 1991–when it was really just Steven Wilson and a synthesizer–to 1997. It includes the fantastic tracks "And The Swallows Dance Above the Sun," "Synesthesia," "Stars Die," "The Sky Moves Sideways," "Fuse the Sky," and "Dark Matter." It's the perfect soundtrack for an especially dark night watching the especially bright stars, dreaming of all the worlds that have long since died, even as on our own distant planet we continue to glimpse their long-lost light. ✦

Steven Wilson live on the *To The Bone* tour. Photo credit: Hajo Mueller.

Metropolis Meets Afrofuturism: The Genius of Janelle Monáe

A dark alley behind an apartment complex in Neon Valley Street. Two figures running hand in hand, one human, the other android. The buzz of chainsaws and the crackle of electro-daggers. This evocative image begins the tale of Cindi Mayweather, spun in lyrical form by Janelle Monáe: songstress, poet, dreamer, prophet, feminist, Afrofuturist.

To listen to Janelle Monáe is to immerse oneself into an audio-cinematic experience. From her debut EP *Metropolis* to her current album *Dirty Computer*, Monáe's songs sweep through genres with the ease of donning clothes: crooned ballads, punk rock screamfests, bubblegum pop, swelling orchestral arias, blistering rap. Through it all, science fiction wends like a pulsing heartbeat. Fritz Lang's *Metropolis* influences the cre-

Named by NPR as the top album of 2018, *Dirty Computer*—Janelle Monáe's third studio album—was showered with accolades by critics and fans alike. *Rolling Stone* called the accompanying 46-minute film ("emotion picture") "a timely new sci-fi masterpiece," exploring the way Monáe deploys classic science fiction tropes of enigmatic identity, fluid reality, and fascist dystopia in service of her own inventive mythology. Image credit: Atlantic Records.

ation of Neon Valley Street, with Monáe adopting its titular poster image for her album cover of *ArchAndroid*. There are references to electric sheep, time travel, and a prophecy about a cyborg messiah who will unite the whole world.

"I thought science fiction was a great way of talking about the future," Janelle Monáe told *Bust Magazine* in a 2013 interview. "It doesn't make people feel like you're talking about things that are happening right now, so they don't feel like you're talking down to them. It gives the listener a different perspective."

But Monáe doesn't just borrow science-fiction motifs. She rewrites them in Afrofuturistic terms that reflect her own experiences as a black, queer woman trying to survive in a world that sees little value in her. *Metropolis* and *ArchAndroid* particularly explore how androids are used as stand-ins for the marginalized and the oppressed. Monáe joins the ranks of other black music artists who have blended science fiction into their works: George Clinton/Parliament, Sun Ra, Missy Elliott. But Monáe stands out as having a single narrative span across several albums—that of Monáe's alter ego, Android 57821, otherwise known as Cindi Mayweather.

Cindi Mayweather is an android who has committed the sin of falling in love with a human. Monáe tells her story in fragments, in music lyrics, and music videos. Throughout *Metropolis*, Cindi runs from bounty hunters, gets captured, and languishes in cybertronic purgatory. In the video for the song "Many Moons," she is programmed to sing at an android auction, where she experiences a strange power that levitates her, then shorts her out. In *ArchAndroid*, she discovers that she may be the archangel who could save the world. In the video for "Tightrope," a tuxedo-clad Cindi causes an almost-successful rebellion in The Palace of the Dogs asylum. In *The Electric Lady*, considered a prequel to *ArchAndroid*, Cindi is still on the run, known as Our Favorite Fugitive.

The story is fragmented, and may in some cases contradict itself, but Monáe keeps it going by framing the narrative in suites numbered I through V (much like a science fiction series). She also fleshes out Cindi's story through music videos, liner notes, Websites, motion picture treatments (music video concepts in written form), and even short films and fan art put out by Monáe and her producers at Wondaland Records. All of this is woven into a cohesive narrative that not only works, but also gives glances into a richer world full of

"I thought science fiction was a great way of talking about the future," Janelle Monáe told *Bust* magazine in a 2013 interview. "It doesn't make people feel like you're talking about things that are happening right now, so they don't feel like you're talking down to them."

intrigue, drama, love, loss, and revolution.

Monáe's use of Cindi Mayweather brings to mind Ziggy Stardust, David Bowie's alter ego and subject of his fifth album, *The Rise and Fall of Ziggy Stardust and the Spiders from Mars*. His album features a bisexual, androgynous being who was sent as a messenger from extraterrestrials and is used by Bowie to explore sexual themes and social taboos. In Bowie's case, however, he did not want to be continually defined by Ziggy and dropped the persona. Janelle Monáe could have done this as well, but rather than fade Cindi Mayweather into obscurity, Monáe chose to continue the narrative of Android 57821 by taking a new direction–utilizing clones of herself.

Monáe's clones populate her album covers and videos: strutting at android auctions, serving as waitresses and newscasters, dancing in unison, causing small rebellions that fail. Some of these clones have names–the album cover of *Electric Lady* is depicted as a painting of Cindi Mayweather and her "sisters": Andromeda, Andy Pisces, Catalina, Morovia, and Polly Whynot. Monáe can then shift her narrative while remaining in keeping

Janelle Monáe's work reinvents the boundaries of identity performance with herself as the fictional and ever-evolving character at the story's center. (The comparisons to David Bowie are unavoidable.) In *The New Yorker*, Doreen St. Félix wrote in 2018 that the artist "has taken the concept album to complex heights."

with the android universe she's created. This is most prevalent in *Dirty Computer*, where we are introduced to Jane 57821, who shares the same number as Cindi Mayweather, but is older, less naïve, and more of a revolutionary than a messiah. This reflects Monáe's own change as she becomes more open about her pansexual identity, as well as responding to the #BlackLivesMatter and #MeToo movements. Even the music style shifts from the angelic crooning of Cindi Mayweather in *ArchAndroid* to the throatier rasp of Jane/Janelle in *Dirty Computer*.

It's a brilliant strategy. In having multiples selves, Monáe can expand upon the world-building of her narrative, told in multiple viewpoints but all originating from herself. She is not locked into a single narrative, but is able to explore all facets of her self-identity, from her queerness to her blackness to her religious faith. This makes Monáe not only an excellent musician, but also an amazing storyteller, one who is telling a science fiction story in real time.

In her SyFy Wire article "Octavia Butler and America as Only Black Women See It," Tari Ngangura wrote, "It is a rare writer who can use sci-fi not simply to chart an escape from reality, but as a pointed reflection of the most minute and magnified experiences that frame and determine the lives of those who live in black skin." Through her music, the story of Cindi Mayweather/Django Jane/Janelle Monáe is bringing people who have been in separate worlds–science fiction enthusiasts, the hip-hip community, queer folk–and uniting them in a shared universe just as diverse as her musical styles. ✦

FASHION

CAN A COSTUME TELL A STORY? CAN CLOTHES BE "SCIENCE fiction?" And what mark have textiles made in the grand tradition of SFF worldbuilding (aka the art of imagining the day-to-day details of life in other dimensions)? As a traditionally feminine craft, textile arts have been even more neglected within the pantheon of science fiction—and sometimes intentionally made secret—than have other crafts such as design and architecture. And yet, like every lost thread, the way we dress has plenty to say about the way we live, in our imagined futures and imaginary pasts.

In this chapter, we explore the contributions of forward-thinking fashion designers who defined the look of The Future. Though their art was showcased on the catwalk instead of cosplay conventions, their expansive visions nonetheless seeped into fiction, film, and television, seeding and crosspollinating with the work of costume designers (and sometimes they were one and the same).

In the vein of costume design, we take a closer look at a lost aspect of SFF worldbuilding: the mundane yet crucial question of what people wear, and where they get it. In some lands, the women have plenty of pockets. In others, they craft with magic threads. In our own dimension, contemporary fashion icons engage in uncanny creations, weaving images with apparel that are both savage and strange.

A model on the runway at Alexander McQueen's fall 2006 show at the Palais Omnisport de Paris Bercy. Photo credit: Giovanni Giannoni/ Penske Media/Shutterstock.

Plenty of Pockets:
Fashion in Feminist Utopian SFF

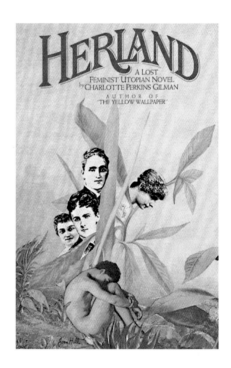

Compliment a woman on her outfit and she's likely to tell you three things: she'll thank you; she'll share where she got it from, and the deal she got if it was on sale; and, if it has pockets, she'll tell you about them. These three elements—pleasure in appearance, availability and sustainability of fashion, and functionality of design—are creatively and purposefully utilized in the feminist utopian visions of Charlotte Perkins Gilman's *Herland* (see pages 13-17) and Marge Piercy's *Woman on the Edge of Time*.

In Gilman's utopian novel, three male visitors are approaching the hidden community that they've named Herland, musing about the fashion they will find:

"Suppose there is a country of women only," Jeff had put it, over and over. "What'll they be like?" . . . We had expected them to be given over to what we called "feminine vanity"–"frills and furbelows."

Yet what they find overturns their preconceptions and ultimately pleases them. The women had "evolved a costume more perfect than the Chinese dress, richly beautiful when so desired, always useful, of unfailing dignity and good taste." The men begrudgingly admit that "[t]hey have worked out a mighty sensible dress." One of the things that make the dress "sensible," in addition to layers that change with temperature and task, is a stunning array of pockets:

"As to pockets, they left nothing to be desired. That . . . garment was fairly quilted with pockets. They were most ingeniously arranged, so as to be convenient to the hand and not inconvenient to the body, and were so placed as at once to strengthen the garment and add decorative lines of stitching."

Women's clothing in Gilman's time was characterized by restrictions. Their traditional dress–corsets, fanciful hats, layers, ruffles–meant a mincing step, and preoccupation with what men deemed the "frivolities" of fashion–was used as justification for dismissal. The implications of clothing, Gilman knows, are political and omnipresent. The garb in Gilman's utopian Herland has a functional, graceful simplicity, and especially emphasizes freedom of movement.

Gilman suggests that a society free from men for millennia would also be free from the patriarchal norms and limitations of masculinity and femininity; in their place is Gilman's nuanced reimagining of motherhood. As one of the visitors notes:

"These women, whose essential distinction of motherhood was the dominant note of their whole culture, were strikingly deficient in what we call 'femininity.' This led me very promptly to the conviction that those 'feminine charms' we are so fond of are not feminine at all, but mere reflected masculinity–developed to please us because they had to please us, and in no way essential to the real fulfillment of their great process."

This link between patriarchal pressure and toxic femininity in fashion is revelatory both to the outsiders and to Gilman's readership. Performative femininity results from patriarchal pressure; in the absence of a male gaze, women don't much care what they look like.

Fashion is also a means to display wealth, especially for the upper-class visitors. The visitors attempt to bribe the Herlanders with jewelry and expensive trinkets, but the Herlanders' instinct is to put the pieces in their museums for study, not on their bodies for display. There are no class divisions in their utopia, and that carries through their fashion. There are no cheap, ill-fitting garments, and no ornate ones, either.

If there is fashion in *Herland*, there is *a* fashion, with changes dictated more by functionality or efficiency than by changing tastes or personal preference. There is no profitable industry manipulated by capitalist and patriarchal interests. The only changes or variations to clothing are to improve it; the same way their ecosystems become more balanced, or their educational games become more sophisticated, so their clothing might become ever more comfortable and practical. "In [fashion], as in so many other points we had now to observe, there was shown the action of a practical intelligence, coupled with fine artistic feeling, and, apparently, untrammeled by any injurious influences." Gilman is finely attuned to functionality in fashion, and also pays attention to aesthetics. There is equal access to good clothing and, of course, *pockets*.

We find another critique of traditional women's fashion and the fashion industry in Marge Piercy's classic *Woman on the Edge of Time*. In Piercy we especially see the costs to disadvantaged women, centering the financial burden more than the physical discomfort of fashion. Unlike Gilman's single-sex community, Piercy's utopia, Mattapoisett, offers multiple options for individual expression irrespective of sex or gender.

Woman on the Edge of Time takes place partly in the present and partly in the future. At its center is Connie, a thirty-seven-year-old Hispanic woman living in 1970s New York, a quasi-dystopian reality that still exists today–especially for poor women of color. Connie, who struggles to get by on welfare, prizes her much-patched purse, single tube of lipstick, and precious plastic comb. She strives to be visually acceptable and appropriately feminine to her social worker, who holds Connie's fate in her hands, and to her well-off brother, who is another key to her freedom. The task can be overwhelming.

Connie's niece, Dolly, is a prostitute, and fashion places similar demands on her. In order to please her pimp and attract clients, she spends her hard-earned money on the clothes, shoes, makeup, and the plastic surgery needed to meet their standards.

Piercy, and Connie, are both explicitly and eloquently critical of prostitution. Geraldo, Dolly's pimp,

With a new introduction by the author

Woman on the Edge of Time

MARGE PIERCY

a novel

"This is one of those rare novels that leave us different people at the end than we were at the beginning. Whether you are reading Marge Piercy's great work again or for the first time, it will remind you that we are creating the future with every choice we make."—GLORIA STEINEM

"took away the money squeezed out of the pollution of Dolly's flesh to buy lizard boots and cocaine and other women." Geraldo's ostentatious if "elegant" display of wealth from questionable sources is meant to increase his power, and feeds an industry that exploits divisions of wealth. Here we see the struggles that poor women have in keeping up with the demands of fashion–demands laid out not only by the fashion industry but also by welfare workers and johns, and anyone else with power they have to please.

Connie stands up for Dolly, intervening in Geraldo's physical assault of her niece by striking him. Geraldo, seeing Connie as a threat to his control, commits her to a mental asylum. Women in the insane asylum long for their own clothing, makeup, and hair products, but such items are privileges often withheld. This dehumanizing means of control lays out with stark clarity how precious that self-sufficiency and self-expression is. "She had had too little of what her body needed and too little of what her soul could imagine."

It's from inside the dreary, unrelentingly gray walls of the asylum that Connie forms the mental link with Luciente, a "sender," and travels to the colorful future of Mattapoisett.

Piercy imagines—for us and for Connie—a utopia free from the constraints of class and sex roles dictated by the capitalist patriarchy.

Individual expression is found in everything from the style of someone's hair to the tattoos on their bodies. Importantly, everyone has access to what they need: "We all have warm coats and good rain gear. Work clothes that wear well."

The opportunities for fashion beyond function are limited only by imagination and responsible use of communal resources, and take the form of "flimsies" and costume pieces. As Luciente explains, "A flimsy is a once-garment for festivals. Made out of algae, natural dyes. We throw them in the compost afterward. Costumes you sign out of the library for once or for a month, then they go back for someone else." Flimsies can be sensual, theatrical, or fantastical—there is no fashion industry, yet every party could be another fashion show. "Part of the pleasure of festivals is designing flimsies—outrageous, silly, ones that disguise you, ones in which you will be absolutely gorgeous and desired by everybody in the township!" For Gilman, the absence of both men and the male gaze correlates with an absence of sensuality; Piercy imagines a sensuality for all genders that is still free from the oppressive male gaze.

There is also more variety of self-expression in Piercy; in one small village we see shaved heads and intricate braids, for example, as well as men in dresses. Luciente explains what fashion can mean for her: "Sometimes I want to dress up beautiful. Other times I want to be funny. Sometimes I want to body a fantasy, an idea, a dream. Sometimes I want to recall an ancestor, or express a truth about myself."

A common theme in Piercy and Gilman (and feminism overall) is sustainability. In Herland, resources are limited by their constrained geographical ecosystem, while in Mattapoisett people are still recovering from and making reparations for the damage caused by generations past. Sustainability comes through on all levels, in fashion as in food as in energy—everyday clothing is made to last, and everyone has enough; in Piercy, the flimsies are compostable and costumes are shared.

Fashion is more integral to feminist SFF than one might expect. Its minor role in *Herland* is as notable as is its vivid presence in Mattapoisett. Both *Herland* and *Woman on the Edge of Time* contain poignant critiques of contemporary femininity and the fashion industry that feeds it—and feeds on it. They come up with creative solutions to problems that continue to plague women—our pants are still not adjustable, our dresses still don't have pockets, and fast fashion takes precedence over sustainability. Gilman and Piercy designed better futures, and better fashion, for us to work toward. +

The Fashion Futurism of Elizabeth Hawes and Rudi Gernreich

Science fiction is a genre offering visions of potential futures, and it is apparent that pretty much every medium of artistic expression has produced some version of futurism, either as a purely esthetic conceit or a more deliberate extrapolation. It is somewhat surprising to see, however, that we rarely treat fashion as a legitimate form of futuristic exploration, especially of the latter kind.

The boundary between art and fashion is at least permeable and in many cases nonexistent, so it is perhaps not surprising that the imagination finds expression through fashion–be it the Steampunk costuming community, or the surreal creations of Elsa Schiaparelli and Alexander McQueen, or the phantasmagoria of Rei Kawakubo. And yet, when it comes to science fiction, there is a notable divergence between space-era inspirations of the likes of Paco Rabanne that seem to treat the futuristic stylings and materials as mostly esthetic, and the true futurism embraced by Elizabeth Hawes and her protégé Rudi Gernreich; that is, they did not merely embrace the futuristic trappings, but genuinely grappled with what the future of humanity will be, and what will we wear when it finally arrives. What especially sets them apart

Metallic dress designed by Paco Rabanne in the late 60s, from the collection of the Peloponnesian Folklore Foundation. Photo credit: Peloponnesian Folklore Foundation.

is their understanding of fashion as the ultimate convergence of the human body and its role in societal change, from the labor movement to the sexual revolution.

Elizabeth Hawes (1903-1971) was one of the greatest as well as one of the most thoroughly forgotten American fashion designers; she was a labor activist, a critic of the fashion industry, and a futurist, who could trace her fashionable roots to the Russian Constructivist movement (the esthetics of which are somewhat obscure now, but is recognizable in Bauhaus). She was a sharp-tongued and hilarious writer who criticized the fashion industry as well as the post-WWII attempt to push the female body back into domesticity, but she spoke mostly through clothes. She had designed some stunningly beautiful haute couture ensembles (a few of which, most famously her Pandora outfit, featured stylized labia), but later in her career she came out strongly in favor of agendered clothes, whose association with futurism started with Russian constructivists, such as Varvara Stepanova and Alexander Rodchenko, and was strongly aligned with the early Soviet concepts of a future society.

Constructivists saw clothing as strictly utilitarian, and believed that in the future it would be used to indicate professional affiliation rather than class or gender. It represented a move away from the past, where clothing denoted barriers and exclusion based on class. Hawes and her Russian antecedents envisioned a future where everyone was equal and where professional affiliation would be the only meaningful and visible divide. (Consider

that early Communists also advocated free love as well as doing away with the institution of marriage altogether. While their record on equality between sexes is a lot more spotty, the association between the socialist movement and suffrage, as well as the work of Clara Zetkin and others, assured that there was at least lip service paid to gender-based justice.) Hawes herself was known to dress in turtlenecks under a buttoned shirt, worn with suspenders and men's trousers, and flat shoes. And her commitment to functionality bore fruit when she designed the uniforms for the American Red Cross volunteers in 1942.

After World War II she took a long break from fashion to advocate for women's and workers' rights (socialism, suffrage, and labor movements were deeply intertwined still); was placed on the FBI watchlist (which later interfered with her attempts to relaunch her business by informing all her business contacts that she was a dangerous radical); moved to the U.S. Virgin Islands;

Tunic by Paco Rabanne, created from chain-linked aluminum plates and metal wire. This piece is held in the permanent collection of the National Museum of Scotland, Edinburgh.

knitted separates for her friends and herself; and traveled to California. Her effort to restart her fashion career there failed, but she met Rudi Gernreich, a protégé and a kindred soul.

Born in Vienna in 1922, Gernreich was among the Jewish refugees who arrived in the United States in 1938; his first job was at a morgue, where he washed bodies to prepare them for autopsies. (In the future, when a reporter asked if he ever studied anatomy–because his clothes were so body-conscious–he said, "You bet I studied anatomy.") He later studied art at the Los Angeles City College, and apprenticed for a clothing manufacturer. He also did costume design for Hollywood but did not enjoy it. His claim to notoriety came from his radical use of new materials (he was the first to incorporate vinyl and plastic into clothing design), as well as his views of the human body, liberal even for the sixties.

Gernreich's designs were conscious social commentary, as well as an attempt to create clothes for the "twentieth century and beyond." He especially was interested in desexualizing the human body and making nudity normalized, not a subject of puerile voyeurism or puritanical shame. His monokini (swimsuit that exposed breasts) was famously scandalous; but he also gave us thongs, which he intended as unisex swimwear once California banned nudist beaches. He designed soft-cup bras and swimwear without built-in bras, dresses with cutouts, and short skirts. He also pushed for unisex clothing, including skirts for men. He showed his collections interchangeably on male and female models, in a way embracing true androgyny.

Constructivist gender-neutral fashion tended to be neither feminine nor masculine but rather childlike: colorful jumpsuits, simply cut tunics and pants, and emblems indicating professional affiliation were devoid of the weight of gendered expectations and designed for the ease of movement. Gernreich delighted in exposing the body for that very purpose–he was a dancer, and saw nudity as a way of freeing the body to move without inhibition; and despite the radical differences in the silhouette, the shared desexualizion marks both.

In 1970, Gernreich returned to costume design–the lovers of obscure SF may remember the British series *Space: 1999* and its Moonbase Alpha uniforms designed by Gernreich. They are closer to what we normally associate with futuristic unisex clothing: matching sets and jumpsuits that conform closely to the wearer's body. They shy away from imposing a male or female shape upon the wearer, both fitting and subverting the familiar futuristic imagery we know from hundreds of sci-fi films and shows.

In 1967, the Fashion Institute of Technology mounted an exhibit called "Two Modern Artists of Dress: Elizabeth Hawes and Rudi Gernreich." The exhibit presented their work as a commentary on the evolution of fashion, and how quickly things like Hawes's bias-cut, soft dresses and Gernreich's trapezoidal shapes went from shocking to commonplace. But looking back at them fifty years later, we can appreciate that they still appear forward-looking, and we can recognize them as works of two visionaries who projected their social conscience directly onto the human shape. +

Model Peggy Moffitt wearing a chevron-print jacket and skirt suit with oversize metallic buttons from the spring/summer '68 collection by Rudi Gernreich. Photo credit: Sal Traina/Penske Media/Shutterstock.

David Bowie's
Queer Glam Futuristic Fashion

David Bowie was an artist in every sense of the word, but he was first and foremost an artist in the medium of self-image. There are few figures of the last century who are so commonly cited for their personal stylings and the effect they had on everything from trends in menswear to the look of science fiction/fantasy heroes and villains alike. And there are only a handful of others discussed with the same gravity when it comes to gender fluidity and the expression of identity through work and persona alike. In an era easily defined by toxic masculinity as a knee-jerk reaction to the sexual revolution, David Bowie remains a reminder that there is more than one way to be a man, and that fully automated luxury gay space communism can be ushered into the world purse-first.

Other writers will be happy to lead you through a gallery of Bowie's most iconic looks; the aggressive femininity of his Ziggy Stardust years followed by the queer space pirate oeuvre

David Bowie in concert in 1973 at the Hammersmith Odeon, London, Britain. Photo credit: Ilpo Musto/Shutterstock.

of his *Aladdin Sane* period. The eighties when he wore menswear like a power lesbian are breathlessly followed in pictorial essays by the nineties, when he acted as the ultimate accessory to his extraordinarily beautiful wife, model and actress Iman. But let us examine the work that Bowie's image did in the far-reaching influence of his futuristic fashion; let us define him through his legacy.

In the world of fashion itself, Bowie was both a direct and an indirect player. Hedi Slimane, former creative director of the formidable house of Yves Saint Laurent, dressed Bowie for multiple tours and brought that influence to the reigning trends in menswear, updating tired silhouettes to something slimmer and more daring than ever before, drawing on the inherent femininity of Bowie's persona and unabashed presentation. Likewise, the late Alexander McQueen worked with the glam rocker and came back to his own house infected with new ideas. Such is the versatility of Bowie's image as a medium that McQueen returned with the opposite direction from Slimane for designs based on the Grammy-winning artist: The wide and daringly masculine Union Jack vinyl coat that Bowie wears on the cover of his *Earthling* album was one of the notable results of their collaboration.

In an era easily defined by toxic masculinity as a knee-jerk reaction to the sexual revolution, David Bowie remains a reminder that there is more than one way to be a man.

In music, there are recording artists who took their cue from Bowie in crafting an image that shocked and transgressed the masses: KISS, Marilyn Manson, and Lady Gaga (particularly her early meat-dress days), to name a few. With Bowie as their patron saint and pioneer, these folks were able to follow in a series of high-heeled footsteps that allowed them to defy gender norms (men in makeup, prosthetic breasts, and corsets in the case of the first two) and engage in the reinvention of the artist as a brand. (Lady Gaga's trajectory from "Poker Face" to "Alejandro" is a master class in reinvention, with Professor Bowie advising her thesis.) Bowie's example comes from a time when a singer could blithely rename himself without obliterating his online brand-building. His spiritual descendants have a different level of commitment to a personal brand, but still cannot help but follow the Pied Piper of preening when it comes to visually rebooting their public image.

In science fiction, Bowie's influence is subtler and difficult to track, as it clearly runs two ways. Many of Bowie's songs are science-fictional in nature, including lyrics about astronauts and other spacemen ("Space Oddity," "Scary Monsters (And Super Creeps)," "Life on Mars"), while others engage with time travel and create speculative fiction ("Drive-in Saturday," "Cygnet Committee"). Bowie lists some of the greats of science fiction among his influences: Michael Moorcock, Stanley Kubrick, Anthony Burgess, and George Orwell, to name a few. In all of this cross-pollination, Bowie's queer aesthetic is at work in a genre that had been defined in the previous decades by a kind of cowboy masculinity; a James T. Kirk manliness that imagined all our future in space to be the purview of men in military uniforms

accompanied by the sour-faced geeks who make it all possible with math. While Samuel R. Delany and Joanna Russ were writing to queer the soul of science fiction, Bowie was queering its image. Costumes for Luc Besson's 1997 hit *The Fifth Element* bear the stamp of Bowie by way of designer Jean Paul Gaultier. Even his turn as Goblin King Jareth in Jim Henson's 1986 musical *Labyrinth,* Bowie contributed to the queering of the fantasy villain/sex symbol. Jareth wasn't just another evil fop turning coded queerness into menace; he played Jareth as a frighteningly sexual figure of magic and beguilement that led thousands of young LGBTQ viewers to begin to understand a hunger for which they had no name.

People throw around the word "iconic" an awful lot these days, but the thing that defines an icon is that it lasts. There are individual photos of some ragtag feather-trimmed leotards that David Bowie wore in 1974 as Ziggy Stardust that not only linger in the public consciousness, they continue to show up on runways and in science fiction costuming even now, forty-five years later. There is no other artist who can be said to have passed on a glamorous queer aesthetic to such disparate inheritors as NASA, Yves Saint Laurent, and Lady Gaga. No other singer can be credited with so substantially contributing to a popular American genre of fiction that its aesthetics are forever indissoluble from the image of their futuristic androgyny. No other person is an icon in the way that David Bowie will always be. His self-construction is his greatest, most enduring work of art. ✦

David Bowie as the Goblin King made a magical and captivating villain in *Labyrinth* (1986). Photo credit: Jim Henson Productions.

Textile Arts Are Worldbuilding, Too

Y ou've almost certainly read this scene before: female main character declares embroidery, sewing, or other needlecraft dull and glares enviously at her brothers who get to pick up a sword. She is going to be a hero.

Instead of a mundane and necessary part of survival in the Medieval Era-influenced fantasy landscape, much like hoeing turnips or tending to horses, needlework becomes a symbol for all that is beautiful but needless in traditional femininity–something to be rejected by the heroine in her path to glory.

This rejection of the traditionally feminine craft of needlework as boring and, more importantly, useless is at the heart of many a heroine origin story. They mark her as different from the rest of the giggling girls who have nothing more on their mind than pretty things and boys. From Terry Pratchett's Magrat declaring that being queen is "all tapestry and walking around in unsuitable dresses" to Patricia Wrede's Cimorene trying to escape "endless rounds of dancing and embroidery lessons," heroines have been running away from frivolous feminine needlework for quite some time.

Often the rejection of needlework is overt, like that of the titular heroine of Margaret Peterson Haddix's *Just Ella* spitting out, "Why not just stay locked in the castle, doing needlepoint forever?" But in other stories, such as Juliet Marillier's *Daughter of the Forest*, the heroine is simply oblivious to the fact that "other girls of twelve were learning to do fine embroidery, and to plait one another's hair into intricate coronets," as she reads book after priceless book.

Despite being such a huge part of medieval life, the textile arts are rarely given the spotlight in the fantasy genre that takes so many of its cues from the Middle Ages (or at least, the Pre-Raphaelite conception of it). Even when pedants are picking apart the lack of farms in Middle-earth or the Seven Kingdoms, very few ask where is the army of women who spin and weave and embroider all those beautiful clothes and banners. It is rare that the embroidered surcoat is given as much elaborate description as the armor it would be worn under.

These feminine crafts can take on this symbolic value because their practical applications have faded from our cultural consciousness due to our modern economy and manufac-

turing methods. With machines taking over the spinning and weaving and sewing, as well as the labor being hidden in factories, clothes have become for many of us inexpensive, even disposable. As such, the act of crafting has become a hobby and a luxury rather than a necessity.

It is thus sometimes difficult to remember that every brightly colored scrap of bunting at a medieval tournament has to be made by hand. We do not always see how tournaments demonstrate power and wealth: that it is worn upon the body of the knight as much as it is the body of the knight.

But in rare cases, fantasy worldbuilders do find ways to give the textile arts their due. Though embroidery is dismissed by the antagonist monarch of Brandon Sanderson's *Elantris* as merely something that entertains and occupies women, its heroine finds allies in the queen's sewing circle. It is those women who support her and that she leads into her reformation of the monarchy. It is also those same women who join her in practicing fencing, which she claims as feminine sport.

Brave appears at first to be a story treading old ground with a princess, Merida, who rejects the traditional trappings of femininity, preferring archery to tapestry and needlepoint. But the narrative twists to dwell on the importance of a queen's oratory skills and how she keeps the peace among her people. The Anglo-Saxon idea that women are "peaceweavers" is echoed here, the imagery evident in her grand act of sewing together her mother's tapestry to break the curse.

Jen Wang's *The Prince and the Dressmaker* stands out as an exception as it builds an intricate world of dresses and pageantry around its central relationship of prince and dressmaker with the plot culminating at a glorious fashion show. It positions beautiful clothes not as an epitome of femininity to be rejected but instead it is to be embraced and celebrated. Department store off-the-rack clothing becomes a leveling force in society as the king asks, "In a world where department stores exist, where do kings and princes even fit anymore?"

Textile arts have an astonishing history from the smuggling of silk worms out of ancient China to the "knitted" code of the computer that went to the Moon. Half of England's wealth was on the backs of sheep. But little of this makes its way into our fantastical worlds. Ever since Tolkien edited out the Lothlórien elves embroidering and spinning mist into rope in the early drafts of *The Lord of the Rings*, textile arts have become a part of fantasy's hidden history. ✦

Original illustration by fantasy artist
and illustrator Olivia Rose, 2018.

Savage Beauty: Alexander McQueen

"I find beauty in the grotesque, like most artists. I have to force people to look at things."

Traditionally, an evening or bridal gown closes a runway show—one last remarkable look not to be forgotten. In Alexander McQueen's (1969-2010) fall 1998 show, inspired by Joan of Arc, the final look was a bodysuit dripping with red beads. The model's face is completely hooded, and she stands, head thrown back, hands held stiffly palm-out, within a ring of fire. The evening gown is martyrdom. The bride's flesh is melting.

Theatricality (and the Gothic morbidity that often accompanied it) became McQueen's calling card, and much of his work was influenced by fairy tales, movies, and contemporary art. He designed collections inspired by *The Birds*, *The Hunger*, *Picnic at Hanging Rock*, *The Island of Dr. Moreau*, vampires, and fairy stories. But his sensibility went beyond homage or spectacle, and these shows moved into the realm of storytelling in their own right. They reflected—and became—the speculative. Some beats were clearly science fiction—a model in a white dress spray-painted on the runway by robot arms, or

Alexander McQueen Collection at London Fashion Week, February 28, 1997. Photo credit: Ken Towner/ Evening Standard/ Shutterstock.

a hologram of Kate Moss in a fluttery gown, hovering above the stage. Others suggested an uncanny connection between the human and the animal; in his "Widows of Culloden" show, a bride sported antlers that plowed through her veil. But the varied methods reflected the same story: all things are beautiful; all things are strange; all things are doomed.

This slightly fantastical sensibility is the designer's legacy, a sense of story that gave cultural weight to the tailoring. (We appreciate a lovely dress; we remember a dress with a story.) And his embrace of the Gothic monstrous explored the industry's own preconceptions of acceptable beauty, which collided frequently with his passion for the uncanny. At the end of his spring 2001 show, glass walls dropped to reveal writer Michelle Olley, naked save for a gas mask, amid a cloud of live butterflies and moths in an homage to photographer Joel-Peter Witkin's "Sanitorium." During "They Shoot Horses, Don't They?," which recreated a Depression-era dance contest, the final model 'died' on the dance floor, and stayed there until after the bows (when McQueen helped carry her offstage). For his Spring 2007 collection, he sent a gown of real flowers down the runway, which fell apart as the model walked; fashion, nature, youth, and other fleeting things.

McQueen, in the exploration of these stories, designed his share of unwearable garments; among the finely-tailored blazers and carefully-draped dresses were challenging, restrictive pieces that required a body as a sacrifice as much as for a model. (This is a man who interpreted vampires via a transparent bustier filled with worms, and commissioned a metal spine-and-ribcage corset as a couture exoskeleton.) But as his runway shows garnered attention and his gowns became red-carpet staples, the more his Gothic-couture aesthetic was accepted by the mainstream.

Even if you think you haven't seen a McQueen, you may well have. Works from McQueen's latter collections were so aligned with current ideas about fantastic fashion–a sensibility he helped craft with a decade of conceptual shows–that his pieces sparked several onscreen homages. Look no further than Fleur's wedding dress in *Harry Potter and the Deathly Hallows: Part One* (a near-direct copy of a piece from the Fall 2008 collection) and Queen Ravenna's cape in *The Huntsman: Winter's War* (inspired by a gold feather coat from the Fall 2010 collection–the last he designed).

McQueen wasn't free of controversy; a designer who tried so deliberately to provoke was occasionally bound to do it. (In his spring 1997 show, he sent Black model Debra Shaw down the runway in a square shackle that hemmed in her elbows and knees; he insisted it was commentary on constrained bodies, but for obvious reasons, debate raged.) But his darkly-fantastic speculative collections, and the shows that accompanied them, are his most visible and enduring legacy. He died in 2010; the last collection he completed was "Plato's Atlantis" (featuring the 'armadillo boots' Lady Gaga made infamous). The concept itself was science fiction: climate change so severe it prompts a new era of human evolution–into sea creatures. "When the waters rise," he noted, "humanity will go back to the place from whence it came." It was beautifully doomed–with McQueen, what else would it be? ✛

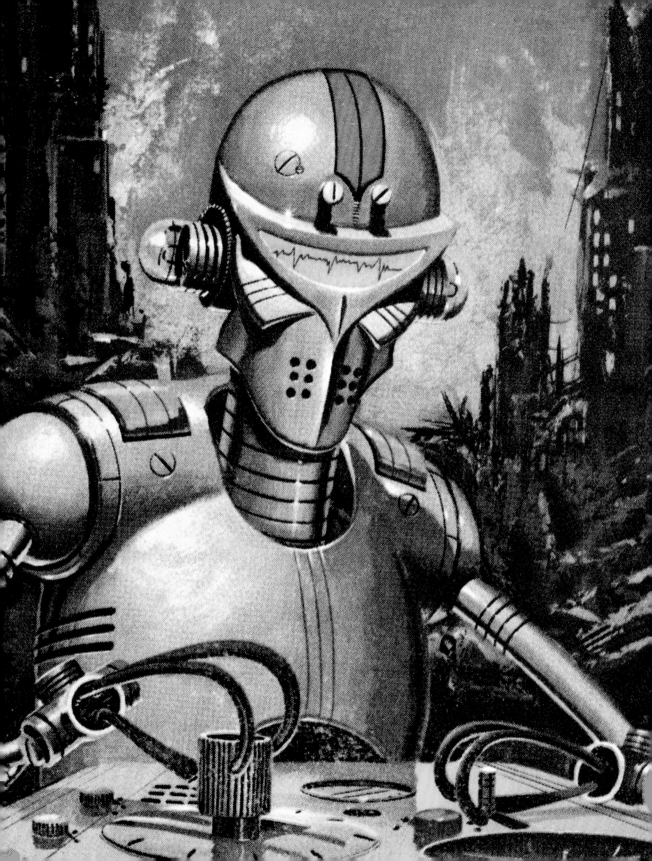

FANDOM AND POP CULTURE

SFF FANS HAVE ALWAYS BEEN PARTICULARLY ENTHUSIASTIC participants in their favorite genre, often with strong and passionate opinions about what science fiction and fantasy *is* and *should be*. We aren't just fans . . . we're *fandom*. And we change, shape, and grow the genre as actively as it changes us.

Sometimes those movements are right out in the open. Other times they're tectonic, big waves beneath the surface that only show their impacts much later–such as the fan fiction influences that pointed the way to a new kind of storytelling for two contributors. Or these movements are tangential at first, odd bits of pop culture lore, which like the Illuminati or the Voynich manuscript, slowly weave their way into science-fiction storytelling.

One thing is for certain–science fiction is culture, and culture is science fiction. (Or as Thomas M. Disch put it, science fiction is "the dreams our stuff is made of.") This chapter explores some of those lesser known interconnections . . . and how the active, participatory nature of SFF fan culture can bring them to the surface.

The Surreal Potential of the World's Most Mysterious Manuscript

There are a few things we know almost definitively about the Voynich manuscript. We know that it dates back to the fifteenth century and was created somewhere in Central Europe. We know it was once owned by Emperor Rudolf II of Germany (1576-1612), who reportedly purchased it for 600 gold ducats, which sounds like a lot. We also know that it is named after Wilfrid Voynich, the eccentric bookseller who acquired it in 1912.

The rest—the manuscript's origin, its history, its meaning—are shrouded in mystery.

The manuscript combines looping, handwritten text written in an unknown and probably invented language with bizarre botanical and figurative drawings of 113 nonexistent flowers, roots, and herbs; nude females in a variety of situations; pipes, chimneys, and tubes; and astrological and cosmological charts and symbols. Voynich enthusiasts typically divide the book into four sections— herbal, astrological, pharmacological, and balneological (a word that refers to the study of therapeutic bathing, and should really be used more often). Through the manuscript's entire history, the text has remained indecipherable, and the surreal drawings are equally enigmatic.

Likewise, the manuscript's full history is a mystery. It is not clear who Emperor Rudolf purchased it from, though it may have been the English mathematician and alchemist John Dee (1527-1608). Possibly, Emperor Rudolph believed the manuscript to be the work of Roger Bacon (1220-1292), an English philosopher. For a time, contemporary Voynichologists also theorized that

Originally published in Finnish in 2001, Leena Krohn's *Datura* appeared in English for the first time in 2013 with a publication by Cheeky Frawg Books, translated by J. Robert Tupasela and Anna Volmari. In a starred review, *Publisher's Weekly* praised the 2013 edition with the words "aficionados of the surreal will find this a contemporary masterwork."

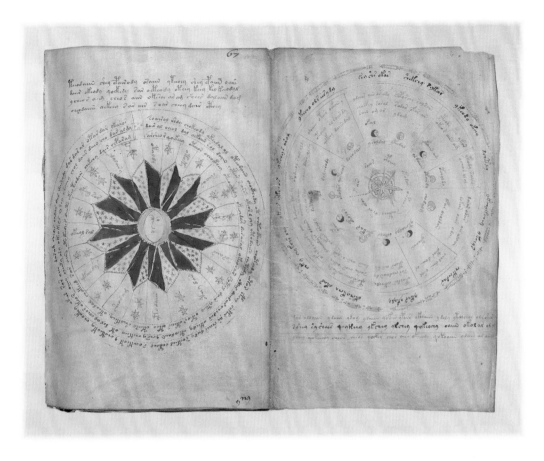

Bacon was the author, although this has since been debunked. The manuscript passed hands a few times after that. Its last known location was with Athanasius Kircher (1701-1680) in 1666. Then it disappeared from the historical record until Wilfrid Voynich obtained it from a Jesuit college near Rome in 1912.

Voynich was quite the colorful character himself. Born in 1864 Lithuania (in what was then the Russian Empire) to a Polish family, he was impressively multilingual, reportedly speaking twenty languages. He was a social revolutionary and a member of the Proletariat Party, which earned him a sentence without trial and a five-year exile to Siberia. He escaped from Siberia, bartered his way onto a boat, and made it to England, where he continued to rub shoulders with the political and intellectual counterculture and became a successful book dealer.

When a group of Jesuits decided to sell some of their library to the Vatican, Voynich traveled in secrecy to Rome and purchased some of the

All images from the Voynich manuscript are courtesy of Yale University's Beinecke Rare Book & Manuscript Library, where the "cipher manuscript" resides under call number Beinecke MS 408.

collection first–including the Voynich manuscript. He believed, or claimed to believe, that the manuscript was a tome of black magic, with "discoveries far in advance of twentieth-century science."

Considering Voynich's fascinating persona, and the fact that he once sold the British Museum a forgery, it was once hypothesized that the entire manuscript was a hoax fabricated by Voynich himself. However, carbon dating offers solid evidence that it definitely dates back to the Middle Ages. (*Unless* Voynich somehow obtained a large quantity of blank vellum from the early fifteenth century–implausible, but not absolutely impossible.) If it is the work of a practical jokester, the jokester in question most likely hailed from much more antiquated times.

Historians and Voynichologists have proffered dozens of theories as to the book's original authorship, but none have been proven. Likewise, cryptographers and codebreakers have spent the past one hundred years attempting to make meaning of the book's unknown and enigmatic language. As William Sherman writes in "Cryptographic Attempts," an essay that accompanies Yale's recent facsimile of the manuscript, "The quest has also exercised the minds of some of the greatest code breakers in history." Sherman goes on to detail some of these attempts, including work by William F. Friedman, "who would spend several decades as the U.S. government's top maker and breaker of codes."

Of course, attempts to crack the code are not only the domain of army cryptographers and scholarly medievalists. There are a hundred flourishing Internet communities and discussion groups where hobbyists and obsessives hash out a million theories of varying degrees of plausibility. Every few years, someone claims to have finally "cracked the code"–only to be refuted by their fellows. One of the first of these was William Romaine Newbold, a historian of medicine and philosophy. He announced his "breakthrough" in 1921 and went on a short but intense lecture tour. By 1928 his supposed cipher had been destroyed by skeptics and critics who pointed out his biases and errors.

These kinds of breakthroughs and retractions have happened a number of times over the past century. As recently as 2017, the *Times Literary Supplement*, a plenty reputable source, published an article by television researcher Nicholas Gibbs, who announced with no small modesty that he had finally found the solution. He'd identified certain common abbreviations of Latin words and then–following a circuitous chain of reasoning–concluded that the Voynich manuscript is in fact "a reference book of selected remedies lifted from the standard treatises of the medieval period, an instruction manual for the health and wellbeing of the more well to do women in society, which was quite possibly tailored to a single individual." The news spread quickly across the Internet, receiving glowing and credulous coverage on just about every pop culture blog there is, until experts weighed in with their knowledge of medieval literature. Their assessment: This makes no sense at all.

Perhaps the world's most mysterious manuscript will never be explained; perhaps it's better that way. We all need some mysteries, after all. As Josephine Livingstone wrote in *The New Yorker*, "Whether code breaker or spiritualist or amateur historian, the Voynich

speculators are linked by their common interest in the past, quasi-occult mystery, and insoluble problems of authenticity. . . . This single, original manuscript encourages us to sit with the concept of truth and to remember that there are ineluctable mysteries at the bottom of things whose meanings we will never know."

Leena Krohn, a remarkable writer of Finnish weird fiction, draws on these themes in her novel *Datura*, which features the Voynich manuscript as a through-line and a touchstone. The novel's narrator works as an editor and writer for *The New Anomalist*, an obscure magazine that specializes in the occult and paranormal. One of the subjects she's intended to cover is the Voynich manuscript, which she encounters for the first time with the typical bafflement: "It looked medieval and was richly illuminated: symbols, maps, circles, celestial bodies or maybe cells, it was impossible to know. Naked women with rosy cheeks bathing, and animals of unknown species, possibly frogs, salamanders, fish, cats, lions . . ." But our narrator has also begun dosing herself with the toxic seeds of the datura plant in an attempt to treat her asthma. Datura poisoning causes hallucinations, and as the story goes on, she finds herself increasingly untethered from reality.

But what is reality, anyway? That's what the narrator begins to question—and as aficionados of the inexplicable parade through her editorial offices, the answer grows ever less clear. She says, "This is what I think I've learned: Reality is nothing more than a working hypothesis. It is an agreement that we don't realize we've made. It's a delusion we all see."

If reality is a shared delusion, then perhaps the Voynich Manuscript is merely an artifact from another history's waking dream. As the narrator's connection to our own world grows more tenuous, it all seems like a hallucination, real and unreal. Toward the end she writes, "I wake up as if from another dream and look around myself for the first time. At times like that, all books are like the Voynich manuscript to me: ciphers, cryptographies, beyond all interpretation."

Krohn is far from the only storyteller to be inspired by the enigma of an unreadable book. The Voynich manuscript, or documents like it, has shown up in a multitude of works, particularly speculative ones. Another popular writer who was influenced by it is novelist and historian Deborah Harkness. As a doctoral student, Harkness studied the library of John Dee, who may have been one of the earliest owners of the Voynich manuscript. She's maintained a lifelong interest in the document, and a fascination with the mysterious and enigmatic that informs her fiction. Indeed, the narrative of her *New York Times* bestselling All Souls trilogy (which begins with *A Discovery of Witches)* hinges on the discovery of a rare manuscript.

In her introduction to the Yale facsimile, Harkness wrote of her first experience seeing the manuscript in the flesh, at Yale University's Beinecke Rare Book & Manuscript Library, where it goes by the moniker Beineke MS 408. "Perhaps my reaction to the Voynich manuscript was shaped by the fact that my interest in it was no longer as a Dee scholar but as a novelist. I don't know what I expected, but at first glimpse it was oddly anticlimactic: small, worn, and drab outside; cramped and confusing inside . . . At the same time, I could not stop turning the pages. . . . And yet the more minutes I spent with it the more I suspected that all the time in the world would not make the Voynich manuscript yield its secrets—at least not to me." ✦

Celebrity Robots of the Great Depression

—◈—

The United States during the 1930s is not exactly known for its autom-atons, but in-between the Crash and the New Deal, four humanoid robots toured the country and became Great Depression Rock Stars. First to set the stage was Britain's Eric the Robot, who debuted in 1929 at an exhibition of the Society of Model Engineers in London as a speaker replacement for the Duke of York. Built by Captain William Richards and Alan Refell, Eric's appearance was like an armored knight, and activated by voice

Fig. 1 et 2. —Machine à vapeur en forme d'homme, construite aux États-Unis.

control, he rose from his bench, bowed to the audience, and gave a four-minute address while turning his head, gesturing with his hands, and emitting blue sparks from his teeth.

After this famous premiere, Eric brought his mechanical chivalry to the United States, where he mysteriously disappeared. Richards replaced him with an improved second effort in 1930: George, whose multi-language program garnered him the reputation as an "educated gentleman" compared to "his rough-hewn awkward brother" in the press. Despite his gentle status and engineering advancements, George, too, vanished into the scrapheap of the unknown.

By 1934, audiences craved a more common man, and they got it with bad-boy Alpha. Also Britain-born, not much is known about this ruffian automaton with long metallic curls, other than he shot blank revolvers and cracked-wise with doe-eyed

George Moore's Steam Man (1893) by Georges Massias, an illustration of a steam-powered robot built by Canadian inventor and professor George Moore. The robot was life-size and exhibited widely.

dames. Before he landed in the U.S., his reputation was preceded as a Franken-stein-like creature who shot his creator, Harry May, upon activation. Surely, this false rumor didn't hurt ticket-sales.

By the end of the thirties, the U.S. had seen many a foreign robot come and go, but none successfully captured a genera-tion's imagination like Elektro the Moto-Man. Built by the Westinghouse Electric Corporation in Mansfield, Ohio, he was the U.S.'s first homegrown humanoid. With a seven-foot-tall gold-brushed aluminum body and color-differentiating photoelectric eyes, Elektro's stage presence seemed magical to the 1939 New York World's Fair attendees.

Millions waited three hours to catch Elektro's twenty-minute acts, where he walked the stage, taunted audience queries with provocative responses like "My brain is bigger than yours," counted on his fingers, and made jokes about operator errors. The real crowd pleasers were when he smoked cigarettes and blew up balloons.

But there was no legerdemain present in Elektro's performance, just a composition of the latest and greatest technologies. Under his golden aluminum skin was a metal skeleton containing camshafts, gears, motors, and a bellows system for lungs. His 700 word vocab-ulary was provided by a 78 rpm record player and was composed of forty-eight electrical relays that controlled the eleven motors that prompted his speech and twenty-six move-ments—all under voice control commands transmitted via telephone relay.

While all of his predecessors had been scrapped for war or disappeared, he enjoyed a much longer presence in the public eye, although it also became diminished over time. By the 1950s, Elektro went on revival at in-store promotions for all Westinghouse depart-ments. He even dabbled in acting, appearing as Sam Thinko in the B movie *Sex Kittens Go to College*, receiving stripteases from Vampira and Mamie Van Doren.

Eventually, Elektro retired at the Palisades Park in Oceanside, California and the fervor and enthusiasm he once enjoyed as "America's first celebrity robot" only remains in the black-and-white print of old newspaper and museum docent accounts. For those who want to relive the glory of the Moto-Man, a pilgrimage can be made to Ohio's Mansfield Memorial Museum, where Elektro's head and torso reside in its archive. ✦

Elektro, the cigarette-smoking robot. Image courtesy of the Mansfield Memorial Museum.

The Historical and Literary Origins
of *Assassin's Creed*

*A*ssassin's Creed is one of the top-selling video game franchises of all time, with eleven major games in the franchise as of 2018, and many more spin-offs. There was even a 2016 movie called *Assassin's Creed*.

The powerful franchise began in 2007, when the first game launched for PlayStation 3 and Xbox 360. But we can trace the concept's genesis much further back . . . to an obscure novel titled *Alamut*, published by Slovenian writer Vladimir Bartol in 1938,

A 2014 photo of the remains of Alamut Castle in the Alborz (Elburz) Mountains, northern Iran. Photo credit: iStockphoto/ivanadb.

and its historical influences: eleventh-century Persia (today's Iran), and real events that have been blurred by legend.

The novel is a fictional retelling of the founding of an Islamic order of assassins; it's also a commentary on fascism and totalitarianism, and the techniques that demagogues use to control their followers and manipulate the public. At the time of its writing in the 1930s, Europe was on the verge of crisis. Croatian and Bulgarian nationalists had just assassinated Yugoslavia's King Alexander I–perhaps at the behest of the fascist government in Italy. The ugly fervor of nationalism was taking hold across the continent. World War II was just a few years away.

Much like the magical realist authors of Central and South America, Bartol evaded censorship by cloaking his criticism in a fantastical tale, creating a world that on the surface might have seemed much different from his own, but when you read between the lines, there were plenty of similarities. Bartol even dedicated the novel to Italian dictator Benito Mussolini, a delicious bit of irony and politely cast shade.

Bartol did his research. In fact, he spent a decade learning about the history underpinning the legends of the assassins, and studying the religious and cultural context.

At the center of *Alamut* is real-life Ismaili

The ruins of Alamut Castle. Photo credit: iStockphoto/uskarp.

leader Hassan ibn Sabbah, who built a hilltop fortress called Alamut and created an elite squad of suicide attackers called the Assassins. Sabbah convinced his young warriors that paradise awaited them if they sacrificed themselves. He called his fighters "his living daggers." He rewarded them with drugs, booze, and beautiful women.

This historical reality was embellished generously by the Italian explorer Marco Polo, who reported the sect's existence to his fans back home. He may have exaggerated the full extent of the debauchery–there is some scholarly debate about whether his reports of drug use were totally accurate–but the sect's existence is confirmed, as well as their strategic political and religious assassinations. The ruins of their castle fortress, perched atop a massive mountain of rock, can still be seen today.

Bartol's *Alamut* is mostly told from the perspective of a young warrior named Ibn Tahir and a slave girl named Halima. Tahir assassinates a handful of Sabbah's rivals, leaders of competing sects. But he begins to turn against Alamut. Eventually he confronts Sabbah, who invokes the creed, "Nothing is an absolute reality, all is permitted."

In *Assassin's Creed*, those lines become "Nothing is true, everything is permitted," a manifesto that links the game's many iterations and installments. (William S. Burroughs also appreciated the line, which he used in *Naked Lunch*.) And the storyline of the first *Assassin's Creed* game also contains some parallels with Bartol's novel and the historic assassins, adding a dose of alien technology and other weirdness.

The novel found its fans here and there throughout the twentieth century, particularly in the war-torn Balkans of the nineties, where its themes of totalitarianism and zealotry struck home. Still, it was mostly forgotten until 2001, when Al-Qaeda's 9/11 terror attacks sparked the American public's interest in the motives of violent extremists. The real-life story of Alamut and the *hashshashin* (or assassins) seemed as if it might be relevant. Perhaps this 1938 novel that fictionalized eleventh-century Persia as a commentary on fascist Europe could offer some insight into the minds of twenty-first-century terrorists from Saudi Arabia?

Alamut enjoyed a brief renaissance and was translated into many more languages, and was published for the first time in English in 2004. A few years later, the first *Assassin's Creed* (2007) would be released to wide acclaim.

Judging from geopolitics, *Alamut*'s insights could neither solve the problem of terrorism, nor prevent the rise of fascist ideologues of any stripe. But its rich setting and compelling story may have helped to inspire a game with a powerful central narrative that continues to fuel a massive and successful franchise. ✦

Jack Kirby, the King of Comics

Just about every pop culture fan is familiar with Stan Lee (1922-2018), whose name is practically synonymous with Marvel Studios and the midcentury's comic book revolution. And while Stan Lee–who famously admitted he'd "take any credit that wasn't nailed down"–undoubtedly made enormous contributions to the genre, they were equally rivaled by those of his less-famous co-creator, Jack Kirby (1917-1994). As dedicated comic fans pay tribute to Kirby's contributions, he's never quite become a household name. The characters he invented are another story. As journalist and comics critic Jeet Heer writes in *The New Republic*, "If you walk down any city street, it's hard to get more than fifty feet without coming across images that were created by Kirby or inflected by his work. Yet if you were to ask anyone in that same stretch if they had ever heard of Kirby, they'd probably say 'Who?'"

In fact, Kirby was instrumental in developing the pantheon of superheroes currently filling theaters for summer blockbusters and fueling new forms of extended storytelling via Netflix's shows in the Marvel Cinematic Universe. His characters include Captain America, the Hulk, the X-Men, the Fantastic Four, the Avengers, and the Silver Surfer. He was both a storyteller and an artist, creating memorable storylines at the same time as he developed a unique and highly recognizable visual vernacular for superhero comics, bringing an energy and dynamism to the art that was previously lacking. He was massively prolific, creating an estimated 20,000+ pages of published art and 1,385 covers throughout his career.

Born to immigrant parents, Kirby grew up in a working class Jewish neighborhood in New York's Lower East Side. (His birth name was Jacob Kurtzberg; he began signing his comics Jack Kirby and later changed his name legally.) Both his Jewish heritage and his impoverished upbringing were essential aspects of his identity. As a child, he often participated in one of the neighborhood kids' favorite form of recreation: fighting. According to Rand Hoppe, curator of the biggest collection of Kirby images online, "Jack loved fighting so much that he once took a long subway trip to the Bronx to see if they fought any differently there." His first-person experience of hand-to-hand combat later proved immensely valuable as he choreographed and illustrated superheroes fighting for justice in the mean streets of New York.

Kirby enrolled at Pratt Institute to study art, but only lasted a week–they weren't interested in his artistic style and he couldn't afford the tuition anyway. Instead, he found work

at an animation studio, honing his skills as a draftsman doing gruntwork on cartoons like Popeye and Betty Boop. He moved into comics and worked on newspaper strips. It was then he began signing his name as Kirby.

Soon, Kirby went into business with Joe Simon, who he'd met in the comics business. The two of them formed their own studio and began developing multipage comics. One of the earliest of these was Captain America. This patriotic, flag-flaunting hero made his arrival in 1940, a year before America entered World War II. The cover of the first issue depicted Captain America punching Adolf Hitler in the face.

It's important to understand the cultural context here. While the United States' self-hagiography of its actions in World War II portrays a nation united against the Nazis, the reality was quite different. Then, as now, the United States was home to an appallingly large contingent of fascist and Nazi sympathizers. For their bold repudiation of Nazism, Simon and Kirby received enough death threats from fellow Americans that the police had to intervene. In his biography of Kirby, Mark Evanier describes one notable occasion: "Jack took a call. A voice on the other end said, 'There are three of us down here in the lobby. We want to see the guy who does this disgusting comic book and show him what real Nazis would do to his Captain America.' To the horror of others in the office, Kirby rolled up his sleeves and headed downstairs. The callers, however, were gone by the time he arrived." It's safe to assume that Kirby would certainly have punched those Nazis himself, if he got a chance.

In 1943, Kirby was drafted to fight in World War II. During the war, his commanders utilized his drawing skills (as well as his ability to speak Yiddish) and sent him into enemy territory to scout and draw maps. He remained traumatized for life by the horrors he observed during this time, and that brutality—as well as an all-stakes

New Gods #1 © DC Comics. The opening volume of Kirby's Fourth World series was published in 1971 and introduces characters Highfather, Lightray, Metron, and Orion. Image courtesy of DC Comics.

fight between good and evil–undoubtedly influenced the stories he told in the years to come.

Kirby's most prolific years came in the 1960s, during his collaboration with Stan Lee. The two worked ferociously to put Marvel Studios on the map, beginning with the Fantastic Four, which was a smashing success. The "Marvel Method" emerged, a stark contrast to how comics were typically created. Stan Lee, as the only writer on the team, would offer a very generalized outline, developed through a freewheeling discussion with Kirby, who threw out plenty of plot ideas. The artists would get to work, creating the panels. (Along with Kirby, Steve Ditko was one of these artists, and he also made really significant contributions.) This approach offered artists a lot of control over how the story was told–they made critical decisions on pacing and plotting. Then Lee would fill in the dialogue. Other studios had writers creating a complete script before handing it off to the artists.

The Marvel Method led to innovative and dynamic work, encouraging the story to evolve organically and letting artists participate more fully in the storytelling; it was an ideal format for Kirby, both an avid storyteller and an inventive artist, to grow and thrive. The method also created a number of problems, because it was not totally clear who contributed what to the end product. Conflicts over authorship eventually soured the partnership between Kirby and Lee; a sad turn of events, because each of them did their best work while under the other's influence. As novelist Jonathan Lethem writes, "Lee and Kirby *were* a kind of Lennon-McCartney partnership, in several senses: Kirby, like Lennon, the raw visionary, with Lee, like McCartney, providing sweetness and polish, as well as a sense that the audience's hunger for 'hooks'–in the form of soap-operatic situations involving romance and family drama, young human characters with ungodlike flaws, gently humorous asides, etc.–shouldn't be undernourished."

Concept art for a film based on Roger Zelazny's *Lord of Light*, designed by Jack Kirby and screenwriter Barry Ira Geller, and drawn by Kirby, with color later added by Heavy Metal Media, LLC. While the film was never made, the CIA used the concept art–and the movie-shooting–as a cover story to rescue six U.S. diplomats in Iran in 1979. The story is dramatized in the film *Argo*.

The work that emerged from Kirby and Lee's collaboration remains the foundation for much of what Marvel is still producing today. "The great Kirby and Lee comics of the 1960s were pivotal in remaking superhero comics into something more than children's fables, and one fundamental addition was the concept of a super-hero team," writes Heer. Under their influence, comics became more than action; they became vehicles for a powerful mythology. "Operatic, sprawling, and mythopoetic, the stories Kirby and Lee worked on remade superhero comics into a form of space opera, taking place in a teeming, lively, and imaginatively exciting universe."

Nevertheless, Lee and Kirby's irrevocable split over authorship and royalties was made more acrimonious by what Kirby saw as Lee's grandstanding. (A 1965 newspaper profile of the two that characterized Lee as "ultra-Madison Avenue" and Kirby as "the assistant foreman of a girdle factory" certainly didn't help.)

In 1970, in the aftermath of this breakup, Kirby shocked the entire comics world by making a switch to Marvel's number one rival: DC. This move was motivated in part by DC promising Kirby full creative control over his own stories. There he embarked on his most ambitious work yet. This series of titles, called The Fourth World comics, included *Mister Miracle*, *The New Gods*, and *The Forever People*. It was a complex and sprawling epic, overflowing with interwoven threads and dancing across genres–the innovative work of an auteur given free rein to explore his most genuine artistic impulses. Lethem describes it as "massively ambitious, and massively arcane." To DC's disappointment, it was not a commercial success.

"At DC, Kirby seemed to have flown off into his own cosmic realms of superheroes and supervillains without any important human counterparts or identities," Lethem says. "The feet of his work never touched the ground. The results were impressive, and quite boring."

Storytelling aside, it's not just his prolific creation of characters that earned Kirby the title the "King of Comics." His vibrant, boisterous, highly stylized illustrations influenced a generation of comic book artists. He pioneered foreshortening techniques, a part of the scene thrusting into the immediate foreground, bringing more depth to previously flat images. "There was something special about any story with Kirby art," writes biographer Mark Evanier in his Afterword to *Kirby: King of Comics*. "His work fairly crackled with life-affirming energy. Even with the bad printing and the sometimes-bad inking, it commanded your attention and your involvement."

Likewise, Kirby's intricate depictions of machines and technology–such as his rendering of Black Panther's futuristic techno-utopia of Wakanda–inspired creators like James Cameron, who called Kirby "a visionary." Cameron said of his own work on *Aliens*: "Kirby's work was definitely in my subconscious programming. . . . He could draw machines like nobody's business. He was sort of like A. E. van Vogt and some of these other science-fiction writers who are able to create worlds that–even though we live in a science-fictionary world today–are still so far beyond what we're experiencing." ✦

Valérian, the Popular French Comic Series That Inspired a Generation

*T*he Fifth Element (1997) is one of those delightfully polarizing movies that people seem to either love or hate; it's a weird spectacle, a baroque fever dream, both surreal and unforgettable. The narrative centers on an ancient alien evil that threatens to destroy a twenty-third century Planet Earth. The only weapon that can defeat it is comprised of four stones (expressing the classic elements, earth, water, air and fire) . . . plus Milla Jovovich. This narrative is often baffling and occasionally incoherent, but is carried by the charismatic performances of Gary Oldman, Chris Tucker, and a ruggedly handsome and wisecracking Bruce Willis, playing that guy he always plays–you know the one. A red-headed, waiflike Milla Jovovich is breathtakingly beautiful, making her status as the most supreme being on the planet a little easier to accept.

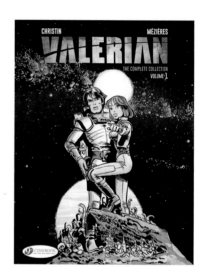

The film's greatest appeal is in its sheer spectacle. It's bizarre, exuberant, occasionally grotesque, a boisterous pastiche. As pop culture critic Emily Asher-Perrin wrote in a review for Tor.com, "It is loud and dark, funny and frightening, heavy-handed but full of mesmerizing and carefully rendered detail. It is the cinematic equivalent of Rococo artwork, of New Year's Eve fireworks, of a gorgeous rainbow cocktail that gives you the worst hangover of your life." Back in 2000, film critic Adam Smith wrote for *Empire,* "This is a film that looks unlike any you've seen before. Ever." Arguably, the descriptions still stands.

The film's director, Luc Besson, hired fashion designer Jean Paul Gaultier to create the over-the-top costumes. He also called on several immensely talented consultants to aid in the design of the film. One was Jean Giraud, the famous French concept artist and illustrator who also went by Moebius (see pages 118-119). The other

Valerian: The Complete Collection Volume I, which contains *The City of Shifting Waters* and *The Empire of a Thousand Planets.* Published by Cinebook in 2017.

was Jean-Claude Mézières, co-creator of the long-running smash-hit graphic novel, *Valérian et Laureline*, which chronicles the adventures of two time-traveling government agents. Valérian, the time-traveling space agent, meets and is saved by a peasant girl in eleventh-century France, who then joins him on his journey, traveling to the twenty-eighth century to become his partner.

Mézières's presence on the film was no coincidence. Besson had long dreamed of making these beloved French comics into a movie. In fact, he'd been a fan as a child, as the series first began in 1967. In 2016, he told an audience at San Diego Comic-Con that he began reading the comics when he was ten. "I wanted to be Valérian," he said, "but I fell in love with Laureline." Despite being a lifelong fan, Besson couldn't see a plausible way to make the movie. *Valérian*, a grand intergalactic space opera about time-traveling space agents, was not the kind of story one could easily film. Until, of course, CGI changed the game.

Besson credits James Cameron's *Avatar* with giving him the courage to finally tackle this project, his lifelong dream. "I thought to myself that the technology to make it was perhaps finally there. I'd already written several drafts of an adaptation a few years before then, but it was *Avatar* that made things possible."

Without any major studio backing, Besson assembled the funding himself, coming up with around $200 million to finally bring Valérian to the big screen—the most expensive non-U.S. studio movie ever made. *Valerian and the City of a Thousand Planets* hit theaters in summer of 2017. Fans of *The Fifth Element* were elated, ready to once again enjoy a space opera extravaganza brought to them by the brilliant imagination of Luc Besson.

The *Avatar* influence is obvious from the first moments of the film, which depict the idyllic island paradise of the alien Pearls, who are bald, slender, graceful, and almost translucently pale (and slightly blue-tinged, though maybe that's just the reflection of the sky and sea). Like *The Fifth Element*, the film is a massive visual spectacle, vibrant and frenetic, a million colors at once. Almost all of it is CGI. One of the earliest examples is a scene set in absolutely massive inter-dimensional market, an entire world somehow folded inside the atoms of ours. Writing for *Vanity Fair*, Richard Lawson calls the scene "an absolute marvel, clever and kitschy and suspenseful."

But *Valérian*'s sparkling eye candy and bizarre set pieces, while entertaining, feel entirely tangential to the story—and go on so long it becomes impossible to tell what the story is. "To pretend that there's a plausible or comprehensible narrative line to the film would be a punishable misrepresentation," wrote an unimpressed reviewer in the *Hollywood Reporter* (the trade paper wasn't a fan of *The Fifth Element*, either). One notable example is Rihanna portraying a shape-shifting "glampod" who, for some reason, treats our reluctant hero to several long minutes of exotic dance. There are deeply problematic aspects to some of the alien representations, which are offensive in much the same way as *The Phantom Menace's* worst offenders—with twenty years to do better. There is also a hearty helping of misogynist dialogue and a side of sexual harassment on the job, which comes across even more awkwardly because of the complete lack of sexual chemistry between the two leads.

It's a shame the movie didn't turn out better. But it did introduce the comic to a global audience, and it's a fun one to discover. *Valérian*'s originality made it a fan favorite. It's also surprisingly influential. In his 2007 introduction to the series, French critic and science fiction historian Stan Baretz wrote, "Catching it mid-run or discovering it today, in a world overflowing with heroic fantasy and virtual reality, *Valérian* might appear simple. Yet another spatio-temporal traveler juggling the mysteries of time and space? Wrong! In its time, *Valérian* was a groundbreaking series. It's the original archetype from which everything flows."

About that influence. The comparisons to *Star Wars* extend beyond the awkward depictions of aliens in *The Phantom Menace*. In fact, many of the film's reviewers compared it to the *Star Wars* saga. Like Peter Debruge, who wrote in *Vanity Fair*, "Written as a kind of cocky intergalactic lothario, Valérian ought to be as sexy and charismatic as a young Han Solo." (Spoiler alert: He isn't.) There are plenty of other similarities between the comics and *Star Wars*: the all-aliens-on-deck festival-like aura of an intergalactic cantina, a hero encased in a clear yet solid slab, a heroine in a metal bikini, and a people who wear high-tech helmets to cover their burned faces.

Mézières, the comic's artist, also noticed the resemblance. Stan Baretz wrote, "It was in 1977 during the International Science Fiction Festival that had seen the cream of the profession gather in Metz, France. Included in the film program: the premiere of *Star Wars* in France. At the end of the film, I remember Mézières laughing and telling me: 'It looked like an adaptation of *Valérian* for the big screen.'" One panel in *Pilote* #13 made Mézières's feelings clear; it shows Valérian and Laureline on a double date with Han and Leia, sharing a table in a dim cantina, a hodgepodge of aliens gathered round. Leia says, "Fancy meeting you here!" Laureline retorts: "Oh, we've been hanging around here for a long time!"

His co-creator, series writer Christin, was more diplomatic. "That's how it goes in sci-fi: it's all about copying from one another," said Christin in an English-translated interview with German newspaper *Die Welt*. "Or, in other terms, you borrow something from someone else and develop it further."

Barets casts a fair bit of shade in his writings on the topic, but concludes with savoir faire, "All creators thrive on influences, of course. Things, as the saying goes, are in fashion, and Mézières has become philosophical about it. He knows, though, that he is one of the fathers of modern science fiction iconography, one of the main inspirations of that pool of images from which all later illustrators drank, consciously or not."

Valérian's core conceit is a pure genre classic: the time traveling space agent and his smart, sexy companion. (*Doctor Who* first premiered in 1963, so we probably can't credit *Valérian* with the concept; it was simply the zeitgeist.) That's the fantastic thing about speculative fiction–it's a genre that begs, borrows, and occasionally steals, combining and recombining influences and still always managing to come up with something absolutely new. Some ideas are far too awesome to use only once. ✦

FRANK ROMERO

Beyond *D&D*: Lesser-Known Fantasy Role-Playing Games

In 1974, a small self-publishing venture named Tactical Studies Rules (TSR) released *Dungeons & Dragons*. While *D&D* continues to be the first game that comes to mind when thinking of tabletop role-playing, the 1970s spawned a number of imitators, contenders, and pretenders to *D&D*'s popularity.

Tunnels & Trolls is the second role-playing game ever published. Self-published by a librarian named Ken St. Andre in April of 1975 and republished by Flying Buffalo later that year, *T&T* represents St. Andre's fascination with fantasy role-playing and his reluctance to deal with the complexity he found in *D&D*. *Tunnels & Trolls* combat is decided by a roll-off between combatants. Perhaps the greatest innovation of *Tunnels & Trolls* is the amount of material supporting solo play, a revolutionary concept then and now.

That same year, TSR tried to replicate their success by publishing *Empire of the Petal Throne* by M.A.R. Barker, a Fulbright scholar and chair of South Asian Studies at the University of Minnesota. Barker went to Tolkienesque lengths to create the fantasy world of Tékumel, creating languages and writing thousands of pages of history. *Empire of the Petal Throne* provided a deep and complex setting hitherto unseen. Despite spawning five more games, five novels penned by Barker, and exerting influence on numerous other game designers, *Empire of the Petal Throne* remains undeservedly obscure.

Not all fantasy games involved wizardry and fighting men, however. In 1976, Fantasy Games Unlimited released *Bunnies & Burrows*, written by Dennis Sustare and Scott Robinson, and inspired by Richard Adams's novel *Watership Down*. Players took the role of individual rabbits contending with warren politics, human encroachment, and basic survival. While the rabbits in the game didn't swing swords or sling spells, they did use Bun-fu and participated in the first-ever skill-based system in a role-playing game. *Bunnies & Burrows* transcended the tropes that were rapidly becoming commonplace in the hobby and created a devoted fan base.

Perhaps the most notable non-*D&D* game published during the hobby's infancy was *RuneQuest*, written by Steve Perrin and released by Chaosium in 1978. *RuneQuest* introduced

a percentage-based combat and skill system. Set in the world of Glorantha, it allowed players to play as the same monsters they battled, including a race of intelligent ducks cursed by the gods. Despite not possessing the breadth of Tékumel, the fresh world that Glorantha provided paved the way for the complex worlds of the Forgotten Realms and the Dragonlance that *D&D* would come to use as its default settings.

While none of these the above games became as popular as *Dungeons & Dragons*, they each catered to the needs of players that *Dungeons & Dragons* hadn't yet served. The 1970s functioned as an incubator, sustaining an industry built on escaping the reality that grew out of the instability of the 1960s and early '70s. Role-playing games allowed players to create a fantasy world where good triumphed with the strength of arms and the hidden knowledge contained in a spell book . . . simply by throwing some funny dice. ✦

An original illustration by Ashanti Fortson, inspired by the fanciful world of *Bunnies & Burrows.*

MOLLY TANZER

Warhammer Fantasy Role-Play: A Grim World of Perilous Adventure

These days, when gamers hear "Warhammer" they tend to think of miniature wargames, usually either *Warhammer 40,000*, a far-future science-fantasy setting where *Dune* meets *Paradise Lost*, or *Warhammer Fantasy Battle*, which puts your typical elves, dwarves, men, and halflings in a gritty setting called "the Old World" that has more in common with the Holy Roman Empire than Middle-earth. But in 1986, Games Workshop released *War-hammer Fantasy Roleplay*, a pencil and paper RPG. *Warhammer Fantasy Role Play* is the grimdark cousin of *Dungeons & Dragons* and *Pathfinder*, taking its cues less from Tolkien and more from the *Conan* stories and Michael Moorcock's Elric saga. After all, the first edition of *WHFRP* tells us right on the cover that the players are entering "a grim world of perilous adventure." And it's true, they are.

The perils of *WHFRP* aren't just orcs, chimeras, and other fantasy beasts, however. Evil exists in the Old World, yes—but even at its worst, evil possesses

Warhammer Fantasy Role Play First Edition Core Rulebook from Cubicle 7 Entertainment Ltd.

motive. Evil can be understood, even if it is disgusting to the good (or those who are neutral).

The forces of Chaos, on the other hand, are incomprehensible. Chaos has no ultimate goal–by its very nature that is impossible–but if it did, it would be to strip away the warp and the weft of civilization itself. Four gods are responsible for most of Chaos's influence on the Old World: Tzeentch, the god of unending change; Nurgle, the god of plague and ruin, Khorne, the god of eternal war, and Slaanesh, the god/goddess of excess. Their agents are beastmen who prowl the wilds, sorcerers who traffic with demons, and sworn warriors who consider their mutations blessings. The kindly wizards of heroic fantasy have no place in *WHFRP*; to use magic is to risk being corrupted by Chaos, and thus your average citizen of the Old World is more eager to see a witch burn than to seek her out for a healing potion.

Indeed, man's inhumanity to man is the real danger of *WHFRP*, a theme echoed by the system's tendency to round dice rolls down, and always against the player's interest. Starting players choose "careers" that fit into familiar classes such as warrior, academic, rogue, or ranger, and yes, one can roll a herdsman, a scribe, or a nobleman . . . but one can also come into the game as a political agitator, a bounty hunter, a grave robber, tax collector, or rat catcher. Some of the advanced careers include assassin, demagogue, highwayman, slaver, and of course, witch hunter. And in the end, even a witch hunter with full plate armor or a templar with a horse (most players start with a hand weapon, "sturdy clothes," and maybe some pocket change) can–and will–be humbled by disease and madness.

The Old World is unforgiving. It's best not to get attached to anyone or anything–but then again, if a player flees, their opponent gets a free attack with a +10 bonus. No parrying allowed, and shields provide no protection. For anyone used to the brighter, more merciful worlds of *D&D* and *Pathfinder*, *WHFRP* can be a nice change of pace, nice here meaning "delightfully frustrating." ✦

Indeed, man's inhumanity to man is the real danger of *WHFRP*, a theme echoed by the system's tendency to round dice rolls down, and always against the player's interest.

Kentaro Miura, Grandmaster of Grimdark

While the term "grimdark" may have initially been coined as a pejorative, it has undeniably become convenient shorthand for describing works of dark fantasy characterized by moral relativism, gritty realism, and graphic violence. George R. R. Martin was hardly the first author to take this approach to fantasy, but his *A Song of Ice and Fire* catapulted the subgenre into the mainstream consciousness and is widely acknowledged at the quintessence of the form–here in the West, that is. Years before the 1996 publication of *Game of Thrones*, Japan witnessed the rise of its own grimdark champion in the form of mangaka Kentaro Miura and his revolutionary *Berserk*.

A richly detailed world inspired by medieval Europe, rife with intrigue, betrayal, and brutal combat, where mercenaries and knights are pawns in the schemes of nobles . . . schemes soon eclipsed by a monstrous threat growing in the darkness. A cultural touchstone that has inspired countless imitators and been adapted many times over, to television, video games, and the big screen. A creator's lifework that remains ongoing decades after its inception, provoking endless moans from entitled fans who resent the speed of the artist's output and the sabbaticals between new installments.

Yes, we're still talking about Miura.

Born in Chiba City in 1966, Miura began creating his own manga at a young age–his first comic appeared in a school publication when he was just ten years old, and by high school, drawing had become an obsession. While attending the Comi Manga School, Miura created a short comic about a hulking warrior taking on a shapeshifting Vlad Țepeș (AKA Vlad the Impaler). This initial iteration of *Berserk* won a prize from his art school in 1988, and after working on a few other projects, he returned to his prototype.

The first official volume of *Berserk* was published in 1990. It introduced readers to Guts, a mysterious wanderer with a really big sword and an even bigger vendetta against the grotesque monsters that hide amongst humankind. While Miura's art was impressive from the start, it wasn't until the series flashed back to Guts's past that the story transcended its roots to become something truly unique and phenomenal. This "Golden Age" arc, which is the heart of the *Berserk* saga, was first adapted as a twenty-five episode anime series in 1997 and then as a trilogy of animated feature films in 2012.

In "The Golden Age," the overt supernatural elements of *Berserk*'s early chapters fade into the background as Miura chronicles the heroic rise and tragic fall of the Band of the Falcon, a mercenary company led by the ambitious Griffith. Against a backdrop of medieval action and courtly intrigue, Miura focuses the story on Guts's complicated relationship with Griffith–and with Casca, the sole female captain in the Band. When the fantastical elements reassert themselves in the text it is to nightmarish consequence, and the grim fate of these three friends is the explosive conflict that has propelled *Berserk* for the last quarter century.

"Before Golden Age, I couldn't decide if I want(ed) to make a pure fantasy story or a piece of historical fiction," Miura told one interviewer. ". . . However, the moment when The Band of the Falcon took form in my mind, the name of Midland, a fictional country, emerged as well. The 'historical fiction' route stopped being an option, leading to *Berserk* turning into a fantasy story. And if so, I had to try using some trademark tropes of fantasy. Fairies, witch hunts, sorcery, pirate ships, et cetera. The representative features of medieval Europe."

Miura is very open about the influences that contributed to his meticulously rendered anti-heroes, their world of gloomy forests and mist-wreathed cities, and the hideous monsters of every conceivable shape and size. He cites everything from earlier manga titles like *Guin Saga, Violence Jack,* and *Fist of the North Star* to Paul Verhoeven films and the *Hellraiser* series to the works of Hieronymus Bosch, M. C. Escher, Gustave Doré, and Pieter Bruegel. Miura even admits to picking up a few things from Disney films and credits an unlikely source for helping him crack open the emotional core of the series when he began the "Golden Age" arc: "As I like *shōjo* manga (romantic comics aimed at a teen girl demographic) as well, I thought I could change my methods and put in some sad human relationships and an emotional story. Until then, I was exclusively going down the *Fist of the North Star* route, but couldn't compare with its author, Buronson-sensei. This is a good moment to try a different weapon . . ."

> A richly detailed world inspired by medieval Europe, rife with intrigue, betrayal, and brutal combat, where mercenaries and knights are pawns in the schemes of nobles . . . schemes soon eclipsed by a monstrous threat growing in the darkness.

From this witch's cauldron of inspiration, Miura continues to draw forth exciting new chapters as *Berserk* approaches its thirtieth anniversary. Having sold over forty million volumes around the world and with both a new video game adaptation and anime series released in 2016, *Berserk* continues to hold global audiences in its dark spell. ✦

The Ambitions of *BioForge*

◆—

Released in 1995, *BioForge* is a vaguely cyberpunk action-adventure game that was literally ahead of its time. Developed by Origin Systems to run on DOS (remember DOS?), the game's technical requirements were too extensive for most home computers. As a result, only the most dedicated of PC gamers with top-of-the-line hardware ever really got a chance to play it. Such are the risks of creation at the cutting edge!

BioForge is set sometime, somewhere in the far future. Your character awakens to discover himself stranded in an alien facility on an

abandoned moon. He has no memory of how he ended up here. Then it gets worse: He's apparently undergone a series of body modifications and is now covered in cybernetic implants and metal prosthetics. As he eventually discovers, he was kidnapped by a religious cult called the Mondites, with a penchant for body mods–a story that almost feels like it could be written by Brian Evenson, perhaps our greatest contemporary writer of weird fiction. There's also a hint of the thinking behind *Doctor Who*'s cybermen in the aliens' quest to conquer the galaxy by remaking themselves as robots. Of course, the cybernetic implants also come with an advantage–as the somewhat indestructible marriage of man and machine, your character has better chances for survival and escape.

You wander around this facility, piecing together your past through documents found on terminals or within logbooks scattered throughout the complex. There are several levels to explore, and rooms that contain appropriately cyberpunk alien technology. You solve puzzles to unlock new areas of the

BioForge official screenshot from Origin/EA digital catalog.

facility, and fight enemies using guns, melee weapons, and sometimes your wits. Meanwhile, you're on a search to figure out how you ended up here and what your captors are really up to . . . a foreboding sci-fi mystery with a touch of horror.

In 2013, *Giant Bomb's* Patrick Klepek interviewed Ken Demarest, programmer, producer, and director of *BioForge*, and Demarest shared some recollections from the game's development. "To some extent, it's a reflection of who I was back then," he said. "I cared about the technology, and that's really all I cared about." The technology was indeed cutting-edge—with running requirements that brought 1995 computers to their knees. But Demarest also fondly remembered his colleague Jack Herman's "over-the-top crazy writing." With that writing moved to journals and documents—not essential to the progression of the game, but simply there for players to enjoy at their leisure—Herman was free to explore the setting and backstory in whatever detail he pleased.

To be fair, beyond the fact that the game was so advanced technologically, the gameplay was decidedly clunky. The controls were awkward and the combat was slow and unwieldy, and sometimes unintentionally hilarious, as the characters continued to repeat the same dialogue over and over again while fighting.

Klepek believes that this clunkiness is in some way part of the game's appeal: "The reason the game was so much fun to play, even now, is due to all the rough edges and the randomness and the weirdness. . . . It was clearly a labor of love, a game like this wouldn't have existed without people who really wanted to make it."

Origin Systems was known for their innovative work, and *BioForge* was part of this tradition. Originally, it started out as an "Interactive Movie"—which in those heady days of the early 1990s, was destined to be the next big thing. The form of the interactive movie was as yet pretty undetermined, so the studio wanted to take a stab at it and maybe even do some genre-defining work. As Demarest put it, "'Go define what interactive movies can be, go do it.'"

Of course, interactive movies didn't actually turn out to be a thing, and what the team ended up making is pretty clearly a video game. ("It may not be an 'interactive movie,' but there's no doubt that *BioForge* is a compelling experience," wrote *PC Gamer* in 1995.) But the *idea* of an "interactive movie" is obviously fundamental to the far more cinematic video games of today, the best of which combine solid plots, engaging dialogue, strong character development, and gorgeous visuals. Demarest believes that *BioForge* was one of the first games to do scripted cut scenes, as well as fully 3-D texture-mapped characters.

BioForge still has its loyal fans. A MobyGames user review from the early 2000s calls it "overlooked, underrated and unexplored." Another terms it a "a highly underrated action adventure with a sci-fi feel to it." Another calls it "a grand action adventure with one of the best plots, and best character-descriptions in the history of computer games." In 2018, it's more of a historical artifact than anything else . . . but still a fascinating and significant chapter in video game history. ✦

The Massive Artificial Landscape of Tsutomu Nihei's *Blame!*

T hough far from a household name in the United States, Japanese manga artist Tsutomu Nihei (b. 1971)–considered a mastern of modern sci-fi manga–has long maintained an enthusiastic cult following, wowing aficionados and collectors with the strength of his artwork, which manages to fit a sense of devastating vastness into each small panel. His vision of the far future is influenced by cyberpunk and biopunk, with a visual inventiveness that's been invigorating and inspiring for creators beyond the bounds of manga and anime.

For instance, journalist Chris Priestman discussed Nihei's influence on video game design, citing games from Aloft Studios such as *NaissanceE*, "an adventure taking place in a primitive mysterious structure." Priestman writes, "What all these works have in common is that their creators have been inspired by *Blame!* and looked to transpose its design approach to a video game."

Recently, the reach of Nihei's work has grown significantly, since Netflix developed two of his manga series into anime features, both available to stream. *Knights of Sidonia* is a two-season show, with twenty-four episodes total. *Blame!* is a stand-alone film (106 minutes). The original graphic novels are also available in new, oversized editions from Vertical Comics.

Before he became a manga artist, Nihei was trained as an architect and also worked in construction. The influence is readily apparent in his work, which is filled with breathtaking

depictions of futuristic built environments that begin to feel like characters in their own right. "Nihei's art is simultaneously sparse and labyrinthine, his body of work defined by a unifying obsession with invented spaces," wrote Toussaint Egan for *Paste* magazine.

The effect is one of awe, alienation, and utter loneliness; humans both dominated by and disconnected from this massive artificial landscape their ancestors built long ago. Thematically, it's akin to Jack Vance's Dying Earth books—a civilization overshadowed by the weight of its history, a world in decay. Aesthetically, it's biopunk and cyberpunk, with cyborgs, aliens, and genetic engineering. This unique combination has been massively influential on the genre as a whole, its inspiration spilling over into fiction, film, and game design.

Nihei's first big work, *Blame!*, is set in a far-future megastructure the size of the world, or possibly even larger—its inhabitants are unable to measure or even estimate its total size. This self-replicating megastructure is simply called The City. It's a *smart* city, and in its own uncanny cyborg way, it is alive, and hostile. Once humans had the ability to control the machines with their minds, and thus the city. They lost that ability, and now they're refugees in the world they built, hiding out from the Safeguard, killer robots whose only job is to eliminate them. A mysterious young man named Kyrii (also spelled Killy) traverses this landscape, empowered by a lethal device (aka a gun) called the Graviton Beam Emitter, in search of a human who still possesses the "Net Terminal Genes"—which could allow humanity to take control of their world once more. But as with every quest story, the narrative is less about the destination and more about the journey, using Kyrii's perspective to explore the world.

As Jason Thompson wrote in *Manga: The Complete Guide,* "The amazing thing about *Blame!* is that it's such a good read even though it has almost no story or characters. It's all about the art and the experience of being there, of not knowing what will happen next, of the contrast between landscapes of endless sameness and bloody eruptions of chaos and gore."

The anime feature capitalizes on this

Blame! premiered globally on Netflix in May 2017 (and also appeared in theaters in Japan). The film was directed by Hiroyuki Seshita, with story and writing by Tsutomu Nihei. A sequel is underway.

by honing in on one story and one adventure among many (leaving the option open for a sequel or even a series). The movie centers on a handful of kids in an isolated, struggling village that's running out of food and on the brink of starvation. We see the story from their perspective, as the mysterious stranger named Kyrii arrives in town (after rescuing them from the Safeguards) and, while continuing to pursue his own search for the net terminal genes, also helps the village carve out a new means for survival. While the story may be small-scale, the world it depicts is just as massive as it is on the page, and the film's biggest strength is its wide panning shots of tiny humans miniaturized by the awe-inspiring scale of their empty and desolate surroundings.

Knights of Sidonia is set in a similarly artificial environment, but this one is a spaceship, traversing the desolate wilderness of empty space a millennium after the solar system has been destroyed. "Nagate Tanikaze has only known life in the vessel's bowels deep below the sparkling strata where humans have achieved photosynthesis and new genders," reads the cover copy from Kodansha Comics. Much like in *Blame!*, humanity is menaced by a hostile and alien life form–this time actual aliens–whose sentience and perspective is so foreign to our own that negotiation is impossible.

Nihei's third major work, *Biomega*, is also set on earth, in another brutal and decaying artificial landscape, which is in the process of succumbing to a zombie plague. Its synthetic android protagonist, immune to the zombie virus, traverses this apocalyptic world on a motorcycle in search of humans who are also immune.

With its preoccupation on the distant future, the built environment, and the aug-mented human in an artificial world, Nihei's work tackles the biggest questions of science fiction: What human thread connects us to the future, and what remains when every-thing is changed? But it's not all philosophical. With intensely choreographed fight scenes and breathtakingly gorgeous visuals, there's plenty of eye candy there, too. ✦

Kyrii is a hero of few words, a mostly silent and enigmatic figure–especially to the curious and grateful villagers. Their first introduction to him is via his Gravitational Beam Emitter, a rare, powerful weapon capable of blasting massive holes in the landscape.

Raëlism:
The Space-Age Message
of the Elohim

A great many of us earthlings–and presumably a decent percentage of this book's readership–have a fascination with the potential for extraterrestrial life. But who among us can claim that the existence of aliens forms the core of our religious views? Enter the Raëlians, the real-life believers in a theological doctrine centered on the premise that life on Earth is a result of alien experimentation, and that these technologically advanced beings walk among us still. They are called the Elohim.

The faith was established in 1974 by a French journalist and racecar test driver named Claude Vorilhon. During an initial close encounter with a kindly ET named Yahweh at the Puy de Lassolas volcano park, the alien shared with him the first of many messages to impart to humankind. Vorilhon was subsequently brought to a distant planet, where he learned that he himself was half-Elohim, as well as the Last Prophet to humanity that would herald the extraterrestrials' final return. Renamed Raël and introduced to other fellow ambassadors such as Moses, Buddha, Jesus, and Mohammed, Vorilhon became determined to spread the Elohim's message, as well as prepare us for the reemergence of our alien designers.

Thus a religion (though some would say cult) was born, one that has swelled to many thousands of followers across the globe (just how many thousands is a source of dispute). There is no sacred text in Raëlism, though Raël is himself an author of many books, including *The Message Given to Me by Extra-Terrestrials*, *Space Aliens Took Me to Their Planet*, *Sensual Meditation*, and *Yes to Human Cloning*. Oh, and their symbol is a swastika integrated into a Star of David, a conflation later obscured when the logo was redesigned during the church's effort to build an embassy for the Elohim in Jerusalem (the attempt was ultimately rebuffed by the Israeli government).

Raëlism is known for its disavowal of theism as well as its many pro-science and sex-positive stances and initiatives, which can be traced back to the movement's prin-

cipal tenet that human life is shaped in the alien Elohim's own image. Take Clonaid, for example, a project launched by Vorilhon and Raëlian bishop and chemist Dr. Brigitte Boisselier in order to advance cloning, and in 2001 Dr. Boisselier and Clonaid claimed to have secretly cloned the first human being. Another noteworthy endeavor is Clitoraid, a clitoral reconstruction mission started in 2006 that seeks to open a "pleasure hospital" in Burkina Faso to combat female genital mutilation. And then there's Go Topless Day, an annual (and self-explanatory) celebration in August timed to coincide with Women's Equality Day.

Blurring the boundaries between human and alien, pseudoscience and science fiction, self-promotion and legitimate activism, Raëlism might not be the largest or most famous UFO religion–it's certainly not the one with the most celebrity devotees–but it just might be the most forward-thinking. As for the future of the Raëlian movement, it depends on how enthusiastically we embrace the return of our extraterrestrial creators. Let's try not to disappoint them, shall we? ✦

CyberCity: Hackers, Virtual Reality, and the Games Of War

S o you know how the shockingly plausible scenario of *WarGames* aroused the concern of President Ronald Reagan (see pages 120-121), and led to the United States' first major cybersecurity initiative? Science fiction has always been majorly intertwined with the more forward-thinking elements of the U.S. military, and vice versa.

Today, the military is using virtual reality worlds to anticipate and prevent potential cyberattacks that seem like something cyberpunk writers like William Gibson or Neal Stephenson might have once dreamed up. With recent reports of Russian state hackers penetrating U.S. utilities like electrical grids, these fears are becomingly shockingly real.

One expert at the forefront of the video game/cybersecurity nexus is Ed Skoudis, owner of the company Counter Hack, and a highly sought-after instructor on cyber incident response. Skoudis's first claim to fame was a video game called *NetWars*, where the player's goal is to stop cyberattackers from . . . well, cyberattacking. Both corporate computer security experts and military defense personnel used *NetWars* as a training tool. But they also wanted something more; they wanted something that felt less like a video game and more like real life.

Skoudis recounts the conversation to Eric Molinsky on the *Imaginary Worlds* podcast. He'd been presenting *NetWars* on a military base when a commander told him, "What we need is something that teaches our warriors that cyber action can have kinetic effect"–i.e., that stuff cyberattackers do doesn't just affect our digital lives. Malicious hackers can impact our physical surroundings by targeting traffic signals, water treatment plants, hospital systems, the power grid. Skoudi took the commander's words to heart and began brainstorming a more tangible approach. The result is CyberCity, a "fully authentic urban cyber warfare simulator" built with the support of the U.S. Air Force.

CyberCity is a digital world, but it's a model of a real city, too. The model town, deep in Skoudis's lab (in an undisclosed location on a secret military base), is just 6' x 8', but it has all the amenities of a real town of 15,000 people–a bank, a coffee shop (with unsecured WiFi), an elementary school, a power grid, a water treatment plant, a hospital,

A sunny day in CyberCity. Photo taken by radio producer Eric Molinsky, host of the *Imaginary Worlds* podcast.

public transit, business offices and residential cul-de-sacs, and even a local newspaper.

While the model town might look like the kind of project a particularly obsessive hobbyist might build in his garage, it's connected to an advanced virtual reality. Molinsky says, "The city itself is built pretty cheaply—they just went to a hobby shop. But the power grids that run this model, that run the lights and the little train that goes around this town, they had to be tiny duplicates of the kind of equipment that Amtrak or Con Edison use." That power grid is hyperrealistic, designed by a real engineer who also designs power grids for military bases. And the residents of CyberCity have digital lives too, with email and bank accounts, and even a social networking site called FaceSpace.

So how do U.S. defense forces use this as training tool?

The assignments vary from day to day. Skoudis's team plays the role of cyberterrorists. They hack into the networks that power CyberCity, contaminating the water at the reservoir, targeting the natural gas pipeline, shutting off the lights, or derailing the local train. The cyber-defense trainees must figure out how to use cyber-warfare tools to stop them. They are training from all over the world—but as they solve the puzzles, they remain hooked into a live visual feed of CyberCity, a reminder that virtual actions have physical consequences. When real-life cyberattacks happen, there are lives at stake.

The charming verisimilitude of CyberCity is part of that psychology. On *Imaginary Worlds*, Skoudis offers a little tour of CyberCity's homey qualities: "There's fire hydrants, there are mailboxes. Now let's go over to the houses, over in the residential quadrant. There's a dog, there's a rug that's airing out, there's a rocking chair on the porch. I told you, it feels kind of like home."

There are also some fun nods to CyberCity's science fiction roots. For example, the DeLorean parked along a quiet street. In one mission, zombies invade the city. After the cyber-defenders prevail, they're supposed to hack into the billboards to let the CyberCity populace know the zombies are defeated and it's safe to emerge. (Don't panic—this was not a specific request of the U.S. military. Skoudis's team designed the zombie outbreak mission solely for their own amusement.)

But despite the quirky details, CyberCity is deadly serious.

"CyberCity provides insight into some of the Pentagon's closely guarded plans for cyber war," writes investigative reporter Robert O'Harrow Jr. for the *Washington Post*. "It also reflects the government's growing fears about the vulnerabilities of the computers that run the nation's critical infrastructure."

"It might look like a toy or a game," said Skoudis. "But cyberwarriors will learn from it." ✦

K. M. SZPARA

On the Internet, No One Knows You Aren't a (Gay) Wizard: An Ode to Fan Fiction

L ike many nineties kids, I grew up with Harry Potter. Literally. We were both eleven in 1997. We both wanted to be wizards. We both faced adventures during school–though mine involved fewer dragons. He had spats with teachers and friends, and experienced all the angst of growing up as a pubescent teenager. He was everything I wanted except for one thing. He wasn't *gay*.

I didn't know I was gay then, because I didn't even know I was a guy then. I was a teenage girl reading *Harry Potter and the Order of the Phoenix* by lamplight while Harry watched Draco Malfoy's every move on the Marauders' Map, by wandlight. But while an abundance of magic stopped technology from working at Hogwarts, in the muggle world, the Internet was taking off. On the Internet, Harry Potter could be gay. And so could I.

I'm not the only queer writer with this origin story–nor is *Harry Potter* the only fandom through which baby queers experienced personal revelations–but those stories go something like this: Many of today's twenty- to thirtysomething authors grew up during a time when Young Adult was beginning to take shape as a defined category and become part of the larger popular culture conversation, and during which the Internet provided a way for people to discuss their interests. Though fanfic has existed for much longer, through zines and other creative works, our generation experienced it with unprecedented speed and convenience.

Those of us with Internet access could spend hours online, often during which our parents had no clue what we were doing. I was privileged to attend a high school that instituted a laptop program, and, in the early 2000s, Internet safety extended to "don't use your real name online." So, while I was waiting for J. K. Rowling to finish writing the next *Harry Potter* book, I filled the void with wizarding worlds where Harry Potter and Draco Malfoy ventured from enemies to lovers. Where a magical war chewed them up and spit them out, jaded, angry, and mottled with scars. Where they were the only ones who could understand each other. Where they were G-A-Y.

Fanfic became an underground space where readers could bring themselves to light. So many characters were—and still are—cisgender, heterosexual, able-bodied, neurotypical, and white. Plenty of readers are all of those things, but many are not. I, for example, identify as a femme gay trans guy. I am also white, able-bodied, and neurotypical, but failed to find many characters like me growing up.

The only book in which I did was Anne Rice's Vampire Chronicles series. It blew my mind that her vampires were queer on the page—so many dog-eared scenes in my paperbacks—and yet it failed to make the impact *Harry Potter* did, despite Harry being straight and cisgender, because Anne Rice doesn't allow people to write fanfic. Technically, it utilizes copyrighted material. An author could issue takedown notices to fanfic authors, but most choose to ignore it, assuming no money is being made from their intellectual property.

Rice's fans are forced to exchange fanfic through private means, write for themselves or not at all. So while the characters are canonically queer, there's no means for fans to imagine *themselves* as queer vampires. To interrogate the world through her stories or reimagine her characters. To suggest that dandy Lestat de Lioncourt might experiment with his gender identity.

Fanfic became an underground space where readers could bring themselves to light. So many characters were—and still are—cisgender, heterosexual, able-bodied, neurotypical, and white. Plenty of readers are all of those things, but many are not.

When fans are allowed to experiment without constraints, however, magic happens. Take, for example, author thingswithwings' Captain America fanfic "Known Associates." Published in 2016, "Known Associates" is an approximately 300,000-word story about a queer Steve Rogers who identifies as a fairy and experiences bodily dysphoria once he becomes Captain America. Queer and trans people rarely see their experiences reflected authentically in mainstream fiction, which is why so many turn to fanfic. Thingswithwings utilized what Marvel didn't—and maybe couldn't: that while a souped-up muscle-body might be a fantasy for straight cis men, it could trigger gender dysphoria for a genderqueer person.

It's important to note that in 2018, "Known Associates," in all its queer glory, broke a barrier between original fiction and fan fiction when it was selected for the Tiptree Long List, which recognizes writing that "encourag[es] the exploration and expansion of gender." However, it's not the first penetration of fandom into mainstream fiction. Cassandra Claire is famous for having written *The Draco Trilogy*, which helped shape the fandom characterization of Draco Malfoy, whose arc in the *Harry Potter* series left many readers unsatisfied. Claire, a BNF ("big name fan"), went on to write *The Mortal Instruments*, a YA urban fantasy series, as Cassandra Clare. Though she deleted her fanfic from the Internet,

Clare set a precedent for writers moving between fan and original fiction.

In 2013, Rainbow Rowell published *Fangirl*, a contemporary YA novel about a college freshman who is a BNF in a fandom similar to *Harry Potter*. Furthermore, in 2015, Rowell published *Carry On*, the novel-length fanfic the protagonist of *Fangirl* is working on, wherein Simon Snow, teen wizard and Chosen One, fights an evil magical force, while falling in love with Tyrannus "Baz" Basilton Grimm-Pitch, another teen wizard who is also a secret vampire and secret queer.

While *Fangirl* is mainstream validation of how fanfic not only transforms original works, but also how readers and writers interact with their personal identities and the world at large, *Carry On* provides direct commentary on aspects of *Harry Potter* that Rowling didn't dig

as deeply into, such as the abuse Harry suffers at the hands of his caregivers and Dumbledore, as well as what it means to be a Chosen One. But beyond thematic exploration, Rowell queered the Harry and Draco analogue characters, as well as gender- and race-bent several secondary characters.

Fiction, both fan and original, has always provided me a space to explore what it means to be a queer and trans person, through my protagonists' stories. I was myself in fiction before I was myself in real life. And now I'm a grown-up writer, like so many of my peers. While I was getting to know the science-fiction and fantasy community of writers and publishing professionals, I hid my origin story. I was ashamed that I hadn't read all the straight cisgender white authors that were named on convention panels and in essays as the Science Fiction and Fantasy Canon. My canon was comprised of queer fanfic. I'm not ashamed anymore.

The Internet fan fiction generation is done with fanfic being treated like unoriginal, derivative work that's cast off as porn. It is worthwhile for many personal reasons, but also because it's taught a generation of emerging authors to experiment with stories. To write without worrying whether their plots are too tropey, their sex too gratuitous, their queers too unpalatable for the masses. To experience unabashed enthusiasm for characters. To bring all that to their original fiction and science fiction and fantasy at large. ✦

The Time of the Mellon Chronicles

T he fandom mailing list is likely as old as fandom itself. Letters and zines have always allowed fans around the world to build communities that shared the same passions. Once, physical mail was the only way large groups of fans could communicate with each other across such distances; but just as the Internet has greatly reduced the popularity of paper letters, it has also changed the way fans interact. Now, they share their thoughts on Twitter and Reddit, post drawings and photo manipulations on

The Return of the King stars Orlando Bloom (left) as Legolas Greenleaf and Viggo Mortensen (right) as Aragorn. Despite his boyish charm, the immortal Legolas is actually ancient; his 87-year-old friend Aragorn is youthful in comparison. Photo credit: Moviestore Collection / Shutterstock.

Tumblr or DeviantArt, and store their fan fiction on Websites like Archive Of Our Own.

And yet there was a moment, a brief springtime of the Internet, in which people tried to use the web the way it had once used the postal service. This was the time of Yahoo mailing lists.

This was the time of *The Mellon Chronicles*.

In 2001, Peter Jackson's blockbuster film *The Fellowship of the Ring* was released, inspiring both longtime *Lord of the Rings* fans and brand-new devotees. The *LOTR* fandom grew rapidly, obsessed with the beauty of New Zealand's Middle-earth, the unprecedented CGI, and the new life breathed into the characters by truly spectacular actors. Actors like Viggo Mortensen and Orlando Bloom, for example, who accidentally created one of the biggest crazes in the fandom: the bond between Aragorn and Legolas.

The Aragorn/Legolas Friendship (or A/L Friendship) became one of, if not the most, favored category of fics, due to the way Bloom and Mortensen's fondness for one another came through on-screen. One can hardly forget Legolas's first line in the film–yes, it's his second in the extended edition–as he tells off Boromir for disrespecting a "mere ranger." (*Sit down, Legolas,* Aragorn replies in Elvish, looking annoyed.) This was the first of many moments they shared throughout the trilogy, leaning on each other, exchanging smiles and glances that led many viewers to conclude that they were old friends.

Since Tolkien gave absolutely no background on Legolas–aside from him being the son of that mean old elf king from *The Hobbit*–fans had plenty of room for invention, and many chose to weave his story in with Aragorn's. Through individual "fic rec" lists on webrings, fans had unprecedented access to works exploring this new relationship. (Navigated by "previous" and "next" buttons, webrings allowed sites to promote themselves by attaching to other similarly themed Websites linked to a central hub, a useful construct back before the Internet was quite so easily searchable.) One of the most popular of these tales was *The Mellon Chronicles*; a collection of thirty-four stories containing over *one million* words.

In an interview on *Vice Motherboard* in 2016, the authors of *The Mellon Chronicles*, known by the pseudonyms Cassia and Siobhan, told the story of how it all started. They had collaborated before, having met via email while involved in the *Star Wars* fandom. Then, in 2002, Cassia wrote a short story called "Captive of Darkness" featuring a teenage Legolas being kidnapped by humans and eventually rescued by Elrond. Shortly after, using Cassia's backstory for the elf, Siobhan wrote a story in which an adult Legolas helps a young man named Aragorn. Inspired by the shared world, the two began collaborating regularly, emailing back and forth about plots and ideas, sometimes writing their own stories set in the shared universe, sometimes coauthoring a single tale. As emphasis on the central theme of the stories, they used the Elvish word *mellon*, meaning "friend," tying the chronicles together.

Cassia and Siobhan were surprised to discover that a Yahoo Groups mailing list had automatically been set up for the Website where they hosted their stories. They were even more surprised when the group reached over 2,000 members. Some asked permission to set their own stories in the *Mellon Chronicles* universe, or to use Cassia and Siobhan's original characters, essentially writing fan fiction *of fan fiction*. There was a CafePress page where one could buy mugs, T-shirts, and bumper stickers bearing the *Mellon Chronicles* leaf logo, or phrases like "Elf Girl" and "Ranger Girl."

Most of the stories in *The Mellon Chronicles* followed a format in which one character was injured or in peril (the series had a fondness for dark stories that included torture and abuse) and the other had to rescue him. This formula, known by fandom as Hurt/Comfort, allowed the authors to explore dynamics between characters and the structure of their relationships.

And while they certainly weren't the first or only fanfics to use the Hurt/Comfort trope as a springboard, the popularity of *The Mellon Chronicles* is often considered to have helped cement its use in the fan fiction community. Hurt/Comfort is also popular in romantic and slash fiction (the intimacy of caring for someone often serving as a lead-up to sexual intimacy), but Siobhan and Cassia never included romantic relationships in their stories and included a rule of "no slash or smut" in the mailing list. *The Mellon Chronicles* was considered, instead, to be a pillar of the Aragorn/Legolas Friendship community.

In 2003, an offshoot of the *Mellon Chronicles* mailing list was founded; the aragorn-legolas RPG. In this group, fans of *The Mellon Chronicles* could participate in a written, round-robin style role-playing game, playing either as canonical characters or inventing originals–mostly either elves or rangers–who often shared the member's username.

My name was Ciryatúre, a sea elf from the Grey Havens, one of the people of Círdan.

Although the series ended in 2005 and the accompanying fan conversations petered out, Siobhan and Cassia's work remains in archives around the Internet, and is still beloved by fans. There is a YouTube channel that hosts story trailers and other videos inspired by the series, and a "Mellon Chronicles" tag on Tumblr. Many of Cassia's early-aught photo manipulations can be found via image search, and there is still activity on the Yahoo group. And although the RPG is no longer running, its automatic moderator email still goes out periodically.

I am still a member of the group, and although I have moved on to other fandoms and participated in new RPGs, I have never quite been able to bring myself to unsubscribe. The friendship of Aragorn and Legolas, the friendship of these other fans, will always be too important to me.

And I am not alone. As of April 2018, there are still seventy-four others. ✦

An Interview with Hugh Howey

Hugh Howey is the *New York Times* bestselling author of *Wool*, *Sand*, *Beacon 23*, and over a dozen other novels. His works have been translated into forty-plus languages, and TV adaptations of *Wool* and *Sand* are in the works at AMC and SyFy. Howey worked as a bookseller while penning most of his novels. His two life dreams have been to write a novel and to sail around the world. He currently lives on a catamaran in Fiji, where he's continuing to write as he fulfills his dream of circumnavigating the globe.

DB: *Your mega-bestselling Silo series began as a self-published serial on Amazon, an innovative approach that allowed you to build a huge audience. (And yes, I still remember my brief moment of panic as I finished the first installment, a short story titled "Wool"; fortunately, there was more.) Can you talk about the way your work used a new publishing model to follow in the footsteps of other SF writers (and even non-SF writers) who utilized serialized storytelling?*

HH: The craziest thing about stumbling into success with *Wool* was later discovering that some of my heroes had done the same exact thing. Some of my favorite books growing up–*Ender's Game, Fahrenheit 451, I, Robot*–began their lives as short stories before they grew into novels. The same happened for me with *Wool*. At the time, I was concentrating on writing full-length novels, and I'd published five books before I wrote *Wool*. This story was nagging at me for years, and I didn't know when I'd find the time to fit it into my writing schedule, so I condensed it down and released the work as a novelette on Amazon.

The beauty of Amazon's platform, and the rise of e-books, is that the length of a story no longer took primacy over everything else. Short works of science fiction have had a long and important history, with countless magazines, anthologies, fanzines, and collections over the years. But now a short story could be purchased and consumed right alongside bestselling novels. On the same shelf. At any price. Nothing like this has ever happened before. It was a complete game-changer for all kinds of stories. Now you could publish hefty tomes that no publisher would risk printing, or box sets that the reader couldn't

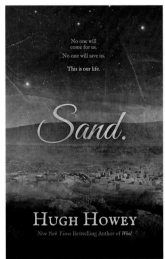

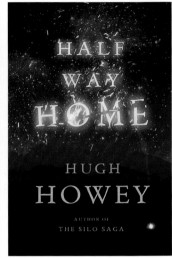

possibly carry home if it were physical. In a way, the limitations were dropped and it all became about the author telling the audience a story.

DB: *Do you think publishing a story in shorter installments shapes the way you approach the narrative? Does audience reaction impact how you develop the story (much like it might on a television series)? Do you think about plot arcs differently?*

HH: Absolutely! I never thought *Wool* would grow into a novel, much less a bestselling series. I wrote a short work and moved on, but readers didn't move on. They settled in and asked for more. They started a conversation. They asked questions. I dove back into the world I'd dreamt up and began telling more stories.

I've seen complaints from some writers about listening to audience feedback, and I've never understood this. Storytelling has traditionally been a live event. It's an oral tradition. You engage with the audience, feed off their energy, sense what's working and what isn't, and the story transforms over time and with the retelling. Dickens got this. He honed his craft with feedback from his readers. That doesn't mean you simply give readers what they think they want—it means you are in tune to their response to your work. It's like playing a concert as a musician. I think the modern concept of an author is akin to an artist making music in a booth, alone and without contact or input. I see it more like playing a guitar for friends and family, and then on a street corner with a hat, and then in small venues, and hopefully one day on the big stage. It should be vibrant, alive, and in the streets.

DB: *You've talked about your theory that dystopian and postapocalyptic stories such as the Silo series are part of a much, much older tradition of Survival Stories—which may actually have been the first stories, stories with a purpose. Can you expand on that a little?*

HH: We are storytelling animals, it's a central part of what we do. We gossip, joke, regale, thrill, terrify, all with the power of story. There are theories about why this is a universal trait, and how it helped us survive as a species, and most of these theories center around the bonding aspect of storytelling and the use of story as a warning device and learning tool. We tell kids if they wander into the forest, a witch might eat them. We tell stories of how the world got here and what our place in it is. Most world religions are simply us telling these ever-evolving origin stories of our existence.

As long as we look back, we see survival stories. They are probably the oldest stories there are. Stories of the hunt, of being cut off from the tribe, of being lost in the woods. These survival stories are about losing touch with our tribe and civilization. They challenge us to imagine how we might survive such travails, and also to warn us against getting lost in the first place.

The first survival stories were lost-in-the-woods stories. Makes sense, right? These people lived on the edge of a wilderness. It was a dangerous place. Wander off, and bad things might happen. When we pushed out to sea, we began telling deserted island stories. Again, we are cut off and must somehow survive. Again, we are playing out an ever present dread of losing our mates, our tools, our homes. *The Odyssey* is the grandest story in this tradition.

Westerns are survival stories, told about a new wilderness where the law was still unsettled, the land dangerous, the stakes high. Always pushing out on the edge. Until there was no more edge to push to. And then we looked skyward.

The Martian is a deserted island story. And every disaster flick is an attempt to find an edge where none exists. Now that we've covered the Earth and pushed into the heavens, the only way to tell survival stories is to tear everything back down. These stories are not new; they are a continuation of all that's come before. But now, to find the wilderness in which to get lost, we have to imagine civilization has crumbled. When people ask me why postapocalyptic stories are suddenly huge, I explain that these have been the oldest and most important stories we've ever told. When they ask when the fad will die, I tell them never.

DB: *What Survival Stories influenced you most? Particularly those outside the science-fiction canon?*

HH: *Gulliver's Travels* (though I often argue that this is one of the earliest works of science fiction), *The Tempest*, and *The Count of Monte Cristo* are a few of my favorite from fiction. But the ones that really drive me crazy and that I return to over and over are the true stories (and the root of our storytelling tradition): Callahan's *Adrift*, Krakauer's *Into Thin Air*, Shackleton's *South*. I find these stories vastly compelling. This is why literature exists, I would argue. We wouldn't have books without this human need. When writers in other fields look down on survival stories, I find them to be like those who dismiss our ancestors.

DB: *Here's another thread: The secret (and not so secret) history of science fiction is filled with collaborations and cross-pollinations between writers and musicians, drawing on each others' work to create truly compelling and atmospheric new worlds. You got a really neat opportunity to collaborate with the band Imagine Dragons, who created an original soundtrack for your novel* Beacon 23. *How did that come about? And what was the process like?*

HH: It was an absolute dream. The team behind Booktrack made it possible, and it was crazy to hear a favorite band take riffs and inspiration from one of my stories. This speaks to my feelings for fan fiction and collaborations in general, and it goes back to that analogy of the writer as a musician in a booth. Think instead on how most music is written, as a group of people jamming together. To me, that's the heart and soul of our craft.

Authors have clustered together over the centuries in salons, cafés, homes, and around fires and hearths. There have been famous friendships between writers who discussed each other's works and cross-pollinated ideas. It's a lot like jazz. You play the standards, you riff off one another, you jump in and add your instrument to the noise. I know it all sound flighty, but it's

an important concept. When you look at the comparison to jazz, you see fan fiction in a completely different light. So what if someone is playing a cover of your tune? Or mashing up your work? Or paying homage to your characters? Snap your finger. Join in. The way we attempt to protect books and shield stories is not the kind of art I want to be involved with.

DB: *Do you have any abandoned novels you don't mind telling us about? Or temporarily shelved novels you hope to return to one day?*

HH: So many. I'm pretty deep into a sequel for *Sand*, and the fifth book in my Molly Fyde series. I've got a YA series that I'm dying to get started, one that has consumed me since I jotted down the first few chapters. I won't have time to write all the books that I would like to. I think the last thing I publish will be all the fragments of ideas and outlines of the stories I wish were out there, just to get them out of my noggin and into the wide open.

DB: *And finally . . . as someone who's spent a lot of time in bookstores . . . what works or creators do you believe should get more credit and attention than they do—and why? What are* your *beloved cult classics?*

HH: Tastes are so subjective, so I have a hard time thinking my predilections should move others. One of my favorite works is a book I'm ashamed of loving, because of the legacy of its author. I think *Battlefield Earth* is a classic. But I don't urge everyone to go out and read it or agree with me. As a bookseller, I used to ask what other stories readers enjoyed and find something similar. I do find it confusing when I read a book like Max Barry's *Lexicon* and I look around and everyone in the world isn't also reading this book and going as bonkers as I am. Other times, I see a work becoming a hit and it doesn't resonate with me. That's the beauty of what we do as writers and our passion as readers: There's always a story for someone, and someone for every story. ✦

CHARLIE JANE ANDERS is the author of *The City in the Middle of the Night*, plus an upcoming young-adult trilogy. Her novel *All the Birds in the Sky* won the Nebula, Crawford, and Locus awards, and her short story "Six Months, Three Days" won a Hugo. She's also published a novella, *Rock Manning Goes For Broke*, and a story collection called *Six Months, Three Days, Five Others*. She was a founding editor of io9.com, and organizes the monthly Writers With Drinks reading series.

DARRAN ANDERSON is the author of *Imaginary Cities* (University of Chicago Press) and the forthcoming *Tidewrack* (Farrar, Straus and Giroux). He writes and gives talks on cities, architecture, and the future.

EMILY ASHER-PERRIN is the senior staff writer for Tor.com, and has been commenting on sci-fi and fantasy pop culture happenings in those wilds for the better part of a decade. You can find more odd Emily thoughts in collections like *Queers Dig Time Lords*, and around other hallowed corners of the Internet.

SYLAS K. BARRETT is a transgender actor, writer, and artist who has loved *The Lord of the Rings* since he was six years old. In addition to his theater work, he is a regular contributor on the *Is It Transphobic* podcast and runs the weekly column *Reading the Wheel of Time* for Tor.com.

JESSE BULLINGTON is the author of three weird historical novels: *The Sad Tale of the Brothers Grossbart*, *The Enterprise of Death*, and *The Folly of the World*. Under the pen name Alex Marshall he recently completed the Crimson Empire trilogy; the first book, *A Crown for Cold Silver*, was shortlisted for the James Tiptree Jr. Award.

SELENA CHAMBERS writes fiction and nonfiction from the swampy depths of North Florida. Her work has appeared in such publications as *Literary Hub*, *Luna Luna*, and *Beautiful Bizarre*, all with an emphasis on women creatives. She's been nominated for several awards, including a Hugo and two World Fantasy awards. Her most recent books include the weird historical fiction collection *Calls for Submission* (Pelekinesis) and *Mechanical Animals* (Hex Publishing), co-edited with Jason Heller. Learn more at: www.selenachambers.com.

JOHN CHU is a microprocessor architect by day, a writer, translator, and podcast narrator by night. His fiction has appeared or is forthcoming in *Boston Review*, *Uncanny Magazine*, *Asimov's Science Fiction*, *Clarkesworld Magazine*, and Tor.com. among other venues. His translations have been published or are forthcoming in *Clarkesworld*, *The Big Book of SF*, and other venues. His story "The Water That Falls on You from Nowhere" won the 2014 Hugo Award for Best Short Story.

MEG ELISON is a science fiction author and feminist essayist. Her debut novel, *The Book of the Unnamed Midwife*, won the 2014 Philip K. Dick Award. Her second novel was a finalist for the Philip K. Dick, and both were longlisted for the James A. Tiptree Award. She has been published in *McSweeney's*, *The Magazine of Fantasy and Science Fiction*, *Catapult*, and many other places. Elison is a high school dropout and a graduate of UC Berkeley. Find her online, where she writes like she's running out of time.

Bestselling author **NEIL GAIMAN** has long been one of the top writers in comics, and also writes books for readers of all ages. He is listed in the *Dictionary of Literary Biography* as one of the top ten living postmodern writers, and is a prolific creator of works of prose, poetry, film, journalism, comics, song lyrics, and drama.

WILLIAM GIBSON'S first novel, *Neuromancer*, won the Nebula, Hugo, and Philip K. Dick awards, and is considered a founding text of the cyberpunk genre. His many other books include *Pattern Recognition* (2003), *The Peripheral* (2014), and a collection of essays titled *Distrust That Particular Flavor* (2012). Gibson also coined the term "cyberspace," and his 1980s depictions of virtual reality have proven both prescient and influential.

LEV GROSSMAN is the author of five novels, including the No. 1 *New York Times* bestselling Magicians trilogy. A TV adaptation is now in its fourth season as the top-rated show on the Syfy Channel. *The Bright Sword*, Grossman's reimagining of the epic of King Arthur, is slated for publication next year. Grossman is also an award-winning journalist who spent fifteen years as the book critic and lead technology writer at *Time* magazine.

GRADY HENDRIX is the author of *Horrorstör* and *My Best Friend's Exorcism*. His latest novel is *We Sold Our Souls*. He's also the author of *Paperbacks from Hell*, the Stoker award-winning history of the horror paperback boom of the seventies and eighties.

JOHN JENNINGS is a professor of Media and Cultural Studies at the University of California at Riverside. Jennings is co-editor of the Eisner Award-winning collection *The Blacker the Ink: Constructions of Black Identity in Comics and Sequential Art*. His current projects include the art collection *Cosmic Underground: A Grimoire of Black Speculative Discontent*, the horror anthology *Box of Bones*, the coffee table book *Black Comix Returns* (with Damian Duffy), the supernatural crime noir story "Blue Hand Mojo," and the Bram Stoker Award and Eisner Award-winning, *New York Times* bestselling graphic novel adaptation of Octavia Butler's classic dark fantasy novel *Kindred*.

DAVID BARR KIRTLEY is the host of the *Geek's Guide to the Galaxy* podcast on Wired.com. His short fiction has appeared in books such as *New Voices in Science Fiction*, *The Living Dead*, *New Cthulhu*, and *Fantasy: The Best of the Year*.

MATTHEW KRESSEL is an author & coder, three-time Nebula Award Finalist, World Fantasy Award Finalist, Eugie Award Finalist, author of *King of Shards* and many shorts, creator of the Moksha submissions system, co-host of Fantastic Fiction at KGB reading series, and member of the Altered Fluid writing group. @mattkressel.

ROBERT LEVY is an author of stories and plays whose work has been seen Off-Broadway. A Harvard graduate subsequently trained as a forensic psychologist, his first novel, *The Glittering World*, was a finalist for the Lambda Literary Award and the Shirley Jackson Award. Shorter work has recently appeared in *Black Static*, *Shadows & Tall Trees*, *Wilde Stories: The Year's Best Gay Speculative Fiction*, and *The Best Horror of the Year*, among others. He can be found at TheRobertLevy.com.

NICK MAMATAS is the author of several novels, including *I Am Providence* and *Hexen Sabbath*, and dozens of short stories. His reviews and criticism have appeared in the *Village Voice*, *The Smart Set*, Germany's *Spex*, and many other publications.

ANNALEE NEWITZ writes science fiction and nonfiction. She's the author of several books, including *Autonomous*; and is the founding editor of io9.com

JEANNETTE NG is originally from Hong Kong but now lives in Durham, UK. She has an MA in Medieval and Renaissance Studies, which spawned her love for writing gothic fantasy with a theological twist. She used to sell costumes out of her garage.

MARK OSHIRO is the Hugo-nominated writer of the online Mark Does Stuff universe (Mark Reads and Mark Watches), where he analyzes book and TV series. He was the nonfiction editor of *Queers Destroy Science Fiction!* and the coeditor of *Speculative Fiction 2015* and is the president of the Con or Bust Board of Directors. When not writing/recording reviews or editing, Oshiro engages in social activism online and offline. *Anger is a Gift* is his debut YA contemporary fiction novel.

FRANK ROMERO has been playing RPGs since 1978, when he first played a wizard named Merlin (c'mon, I was seven!) using the *Dungeons & Dragons* White Box. He quickly moved on to Advanced *Dungeons & Dragons* and he has carried a set of emergency dice with him everywhere since then. He is also an original founder of Denver Comic Con and runs an actual play *Dungeon Crawl Classics* podcast in association with Mutiny Information Cafe in Denver, Colorado that can be found at http://mutinytransmissions.libsyn.com/.

EKATERINA SEDIA wrote several novels, *The Secret History of Moscow*, *The Alchemy of Stone*, *The House of Discarded Dreams*, and *Heart of Iron*, as well as the short story collection *Moscow But Dreaming*. Her short stories appeared in numerous anthologies and magazines. She also edited several anthologies. She cowrote a script for *Yamasong: March of the Hollows*, a feature-length puppet fantasy film featuring Nathan Fillion, George Takei, Abigail Breslin, and Whoopi Goldberg.

NISI SHAWL wrote the Nebula Award finalist *Everfair*, an alternate history about a nineteenth-century Utopia in the Congo; and the James Tiptree, Jr. Award-winning story collection *Filter House*. Tor.com publishes her monthly "Expanded Course in the History of Black Science Fiction" column. She co-edited the anthologies *Stories for Chip: A Tribute to Samuel R. Delany*; and *Strange Matings: Science Fiction, Feminism, African American Voices, and Octavia E. Butler*.

Content creator **STEPHEN SONNEVELD** won the Kennedy Center Outstanding Playwright Award; writes, produces, and performs in "The Don't Call Me Sweetheart! Show," a scripted radio comedy program broadcasting out of Chicago; and writes comics and children's books, such as the well-received *Greye of Scotland Yard*, and *Pandora's Lunchbox*.

Hugo and Nebula finalist **K. M. SZPARA** is a queer and trans author who lives in Baltimore. His short fiction and essays appear in *Uncanny Magazine*, *Lightspeed Magazine*, *Strange Horizons*, and more; his debut novel, *Docile*, is coming from Tor.com Publishing in Spring 2020. Kellan has a Master of Theological Studies degree from Harvard Divinity School, which he totally uses at his day job as a paralegal. You can find him on the Internet at kmszpara.com and on Twitter at @kmszpara.

MOLLY TANZER is the author of *Creatures of Will and Temper, Creatures of Want and Ruin*, and the forthcoming *Creatures of Charm and Hunger,* well as the weird western *Vermilion*. For more information about her critically acclaimed novels and short fiction, sign up for her newsletter at mollytanzer. com, or follow her @molly_the_tanz on Twitter or @molly_tanzer on Instagram.

PAUL TREMBLAY is the award-winning author of seven novels, including *The Cabin at the End of the World*, *A Head Full of Ghosts*, and *Disappearance at Devil's Rock*. His essays and short fiction have appeared in the *Los Angeles Times*, EntertainmentWeekly.com, and numerous "year's best" anthologies.

GENEVIEVE VALENTINE is a Nebula-nominated novelist and comic book writer. Her short fiction has appeared in over a dozen year's best collections; her nonfiction has appeared at the AV Club, NPR.org, the *Atlantic*, the *New York Times*, and others.

LASHAWN M. WANAK is a South Side Chicagoan living in Wisconsin with her husband and son. Her works have been published in Tor.com, *Apex Magazine*, and *FIYAH*, among others. She reviews books for *Lightspeed* magazine and is a 2011 graduate of Viable Paradise. Writing stories keeps her sane. Also, pie.

PENNY A. WEISS is professor and chair of the Women's and Gender Studies Department at Saint Louis University. She is the author of numerous books, including *Canon Fodder: Historical Women Political Thinkers* and *Conversations with Feminism: Political Theory and Practice*. Her most recent work is *Feminist Manifestos: A Global Documentary Reader.*

BRENNIN WEISWERDA received her MFA in directing for theatre and postbaccalaureate certificate in women's studies from Western Illinois University. She is a feature writer for the Washington Capitals Website *Russian Machine Never Breaks.*

CHRISTIE YANT writes and edits science fiction and fantasy on the central coast of California, where she lives with a dancer, an editor, two dogs, three cats, and a very small manticore. Follow her on Twitter: @inkhaven

SOURCES AND CREDITS

Cover: *Fortress on the Rocks* by Paul Lehr © 1998 the Paul Lehr estate. + **ix:** Art by L.B. Cole for *Contact Comics #12*, published by Aviation Press in July 1946. + **1-2:** *The King in Yellow* © by Vicente Valentine. + **2-3:** Fiolxhilde summons a daemon © 2019 by Jeremy Zerfoss. + **3-4:** Moon illustration © saemilee/iStock by Getty Images. + **9-12:** "Jane Webb Loudon's *The Mummy!: A Tale of the Twenty-Second Century*" © 2019 by Christie Yant; Mummy illustration © by rija_piliponyte/iStock by Getty Images. + **15-17:** *Sultana's Dream* concept art © by Isabel Herguera. + **20-21:** *The Golden Key* illustration © 2016 by Ruth Sanderson. + **22-23:** *The King in Yellow* © by Vicente Valentine. + **24-25:** *True Detective* stock image © 2014 by Anonymous Content/ Lee Caplin/Picture/Passenger/Kobal/ Shutterstock. + **26-27:** *The Inklings* © by Marc Burckhardt. + **28-29:** *Eagle and Child* © AmandaLewis/iStock by Getty Images; Echo Tree cover art © 2018 by Coffee House Press. + **29-30:** "Henry Dumas's Foundational Afrofuturism" © 2019 by John Jennings. + **32-33:** *The Lion, The Witch, and the Wardrobe* by C. S. Lewis, illustration by Pauline Baynes. © 1950 by C. S. Lewis pte. Ltd.. Reprinted by permission. + **34-35:** *Othertime* © 2019 by Jordan Grimmer. + **36-37:** *Gormenghast I* © by Ian Miller. + **38-39:** *Moderan* cover art © 2018 by NYRB Classics. + **40-41:** *Stronghold #10*, original illustration © 2019 by Jeremy Zerfoss. + **42-43:** *The Continuous Katherine Mortenhoe* cover art © 2018 by NYRB Classics. + **44-45:** Eye image © GeorgePeters/iStock by Getty Images; *Again, Dangerous Visions* cover art © 1972 by Doubleday, scanned by Thomas Pluck. + **48-49:** Street scene illustration © by Aleksandr Dochkin. + **52-53:** Cityscape illustration © by Aleksandr Dochkin. + **53-55:** "The Empress of the Sensual: Kathy Acker" © 2019 by Nick Mamatas; cover of US first edition of *Empire of the Senseless* by Kathy Acker, used by permission of Grove/Atlantic, Inc. + **54-55:** Kathy Acker, stock image by Associated Newspapers for editorial use © 1985 by Associated Newspapers/ Shutterstock. + **56-59:** "On Viriconium: Some Notes Toward an Introduction" © 2005 by Neil Gaiman. Reprinted by permission of Writers House LLC acting as agent for the author; Viriconium cover art © 2007 by Random House Publishing Group; Neil Gaiman photo © 2013 by Kyle Cassidy; M. John Harrison photo © by Hugo Glendinning. + **60-61:** "The Salvage Yard: Real-Life Experiences Revisited in Science Fiction" © 2019 by Darran Anderson; Canterbury Cathedral photo © 2009 by Edo Tealdi/iStock by Getty Images. + **64-65:** Original illustration © 2019 by Dea Boskovich. + **68-69:** "Funny Fantasy's Myth Conceptions" © 2019 by David Barr Kirtley. + **70-71:** *Phoenix* book covers © 1987 by Leisure Books. + **70-72:** "It's a Man's, Man's, Man's Apocalypse" © 2019 Grady Hendrix. + **72-75:** Foreword to John Shirley's *City Come a-Walkin'* © 1996 by William Gibson. Reprinted by permission of SLL/Sterling Lord Literistic, Inc.; 1980s landscape © by SavaSylan/iStock by Getty Images; William Gibson photo © GonzoBonzo/ Wikimedia Commons. + **76-77:** *Eclipse: A Song Called Youth Book One* cover © 2017 by Dover Books; John Shirley and Obsession photos courtesy of John Shirley and Paula Guran. + **82-83:** Thomas Olde Heuvelt photo © by Thomas Olde Heuvelt. + **86-87:** Karen Joy Fowler photo credit: Nathan Quintanilla. + **92-93:** Méliès's studio: stock image by Kobal/Shutterstock for editorial use, origin unknown. + **98-99:** *THX 1138* stock image by American Zoetrope for editorial use © 1970. + **100-101:** *THX 1138* theatrical release poster © by Warner Bros. and American Zoetrope Productions; *Star Wars Episode IV: A New Hope* (1977), stock Image by Lucasfilm for editorial use © 1977 by Lucasfilm/Fox/Kobal/Shutterstock. + **104-105:** Untitled/Mechanical Planet © 1971 by John Berkey. + **106-107:** *Battlestar Galactica* (1978-1979), stock image by MCA-TV for editorial use © 1978 by MCA-TV/Kobal/Shutterstock; *Battlestar Galactica* (1978-1979), stock image by Glen A. Larson Productions for editorial use, 1970s © by Glen A. Larson Productions/Universal TV/Kobal/ Shutterstock. + **108-109:** *Harkonnen's Flagship*, concept art from Jodorowsky's *Dune* © 2019 by Chris Foss/Artists Rights Society (ARS), New York/DACS, London. + **110-111:** *Jodorowky's Dune* (2013), stock image by City Film for editorial use © 2013 by City Film/Camera One/Endless Picnic/Snowfort/Kobal/Shutterstock. + **112-113:** *Dune V* © 1976 by H. R. Giger. Courtesy of the HR Giger Museum, Gruyères, Switzerland. + **114-115:** *The Tourist II, Biomechanic Bird Robot in His Room* © 1982 by H. R. Giger. Courtesy of the HR Giger Museum, Gruyères, Switzerland. + **116-117:** *The Tourist VI, Alien Heads* © 1982 by H. R. Giger. Courtesy of the HR Giger Museum, Gruyères, Switzerland. + **118-119:** Jean Giraud photo © 2000 by Alberto Estevez/EPA/Shutterstock. + **118-119:** "The Unicorn-Like Creations of Moebius, Concept Artist" © 2019 by Meg Elison. + **120-121:** *WarGames* (1983) stock image by MGM for editorial use © 1983 by MGM/ UA/Kobal/Shutterstock. + **124-125:** Dark Horse comics cover: "Alien 3" © 2019 by Twentieth Century Fox Film Corporation. High res image courtesy Dark Horse. + **128-129:** *Phase IV* (1974), stock image by Paramount Pictures for editorial use © 1974 by Paramount Pictures/Kobal/Shutterstock. + **129-131:** "Behold, the Science-Fiction Cosmic Horror of *Phase IV*!" © 2019 by Paul Tremblay. + **130-131:** *Phase IV* theatrical release poster © 1974 by Paramount Pictures. + **132-133:** "Night Skies" alien photo © by Rick Baker. Image courtesy of Rick Baker. + **134-135:** Moon rising over the farm © studio9400/iStock by Getty Images. + **136-137:** *Space Island One* stock photo for editorial use © 1998 by TBM/United Archives GmbH/Alamy Stock Photo. + **136-137:** "The Overlooked Genius of *Space Island One*" © 2019 by Charlie Jane Anders. + **138-139:** "The (Very) Secret Adventures of Jules Verne" © 2019 by Emily Asher-Perrin. + **142-143:** Film still from *James Cameron's Deepsea Challenge* © 2014 by James Cameron/ Millennium Entertainment. + **144-145:** Arcosanti interior photo © by Joshua Lieberman. + **146-147:** Hugh Ferriss (1889-1962) architectural drawing © by Hugh Ferriss estate. Image courtesy of Avery Architectural & Fine Arts Library, Columbia University. + **148-149:** *Star Wars Episode IV: A New Hope* (1977), stock photo for editorial use © 1977 by Lucasfilm/Fox/Kobal/Shutterstock. + **150-151:** Arcosanti, southern exposure. Image courtesy of the Cosanti Foundation. Photo credit: Ken Howle;

Blade Runner (1982) stock image for editorial use © 1982 by Ladd Company/Warner Bros./Kobal/Shutterstock. + **151-153:** "Reality Ahead of Schedule: The Designs of Syd Mead" © 2019 by Matthew Kressel. + **152-153:** *Reaching for Aquarius* by Syd Mead © 1969 by Syd Mead Inc. www.sydmead.com. + **154-155:** *Fortress on the Rocks* by Paul Lehr © 1998 the Paul Lehr estate. + **158-159:** *Wine of the Dreamers* cover art (1977) © by the Richard M. Powers Estate. + **159:** "The Surrealist Stylings of Richard M. Powers" © 2019 by Stephen Sonneveld. + **160-161:** *Cosmic Assembly* © by the Paul Lehr estate. + **162-163:** Bhen cover for *F&SF* © 2015 by David A. Hardy. + **164-163:** *The Silver Stallion* cover © 1969 by Ballantine Books; *On a Pale Horse* © 1983 Del Rey Books. + **166:** "On Fantasy Maps" © 2019 by Lev Grossman. + **166-167:** Fantasy map stock image © 2019 by VeraPetruk/iStock by Getty Images. + **171-172:** Steven Wilson press photo, credit Lasse Hoile. + **173-174:** *In the Court of the Crimson King* © 1967 by Island Records/Atlantic Records and cover art by Barry Godber; *The Rise and Fall of Ziggy Stardust and the Spiders from Mars* © 1972 by RCA/Sony. + **175-177:** "Astro Black" © 2019 by Nisi Shawl. + **175-176:** *Mothership Connection* © 1975 by Casablanca Records/Universal Music Group. + **176-177:** John Gilmore/Sun Ra Arkestra stock image for editorial use © 1990 by Sefton Samuels/Shutterstock. + **178-179:** The Who photo © 1975 by Jim Summaria. + **180-181:** Crowd at a music festival, illustration © 2017 by solarseven/ iStock by Getty Images. + **181-182:** "*Sweet Bye and Bye* and Speculative Fiction in Musical Theatre" © 2019 by John Chu. + **182-183:** Al Hirschfeld photo taken in 1955 by Carl Van Vechten, from the Library of Congress collection. + **183-185:** "X-Ray Spex, Poly Styrene, and Punk Rock Science Fiction" © 2019 by Annalee Newitz. + **184-185:** X-Ray Spex in concert, stock photo for editorial use © 1991 by Ian Dickson/Shutterstock. + **186-187:** Weezer official press photo © 2017 by Atlantic Records. + **188-189:** Outer space scene poster stock photo © 2015 by JDawnink/iStock by Getty Images. + **190-191:** Goldfrapp live, press photo © by Sonic PR/Daniel Roberts;

Moon Safari album cover © 1998 by Virgin/Caroline/Parlophone/Astralwerks. + **194:** "The Timeless Brilliance of Deltron 3030" © 2019 by Mark Oshiro. + **192-193:** *Deloused in the Comatorium* album cover © 2003 by Gold Standard Laboratories/Universal Records; At The Drive-In photo © 1999 by Jacob Covey. + **194-195:** *Deltron 3030* album cover © 2000 by 75 Ark; Del the Funky Homosapien © 2007 by Elliothtz. + **196-197:** Steven Wilson press photo, credit Hajo Mueller. + **198-199:** Janelle Monáe press photo/artwork © by Atlantic Records. + **198-200:** "*Metropolis* Meets Afrofuturism: The Genius of Janelle Monáe" © 2019 by LaShawn M. Wanak. + **200-201:** Janelle Monáe press photo/artwork © by Atlantic Records. + **202-203:** Alexander McQueen model stock photo for editorial use © 2006 by Giovannni Giannoni/Penske Media/Shutterstock. + **204-207:** "Plenty of Pockets: Fashion in Feminist Utopian SFF" © 2019 by Penny A. Weiss and Brennin Weiswerda. + **204-205:** *Herland* book cover from the 1979 edition © by Pantheon Books/Penguin Random House. + **206-207:** Woman on the Edge of Time book cover from the 1997 edition © by Ballantine Books/Penguin Random House. + **208-210:** "The Fashion Futurism of Elizabeth Hawes and Rudi Gernreich" © 2019 by Ekaterina Sedia. + **208-209:** Paco Rabanne chainlink outfit © 2009 by Peloponnesian Folklore Foundation; Paco Rabanne tunic: public domain image from the permanent collection of the National Museum of Scotland. + **210-211:** Peggy Moffitt wearing Rudi Gernreich stock photo for editorial use © 1968 by Sal Traina/Penske Media/Shutterstock. + **212-214:** "David Bowie's Queer Glam Futuristic Fashion" © 2019 by Meg Elison. + **212-213:** David Bowie in concert stock photo for editorial use © 1973 by Ilpo Musto/Shutterstock. + **214-215:** David Bowie in the Goblin King stock photo for editorial use © 1986 by Jim Henson Productions/Kobal/Shutterstock. + **215-217:** "Textile Arts Are Worldbuilding, Too" © 2019 by Jeannette Ng. + **216-217:** Original illustration © 2019 by Olivia Rose. + **218-219:** "Savage Beauty: Alexander McQueen" © 2019 by Genevieve Valentine. + **218-219:** Alexander

McQueen collection stock photo for editorial use © 1997 by Ken Towner/Evening Standard/Shutterstock. + **220-221:** Robot among city ruins illustration © 2012 by CSA Images/iStock by Getty Images. + **222-223:** *Datura* cover (art by Jeremy Zerfoss) © 2013 by Cheeky Frawg Books. + **227-228:** "Celebrity Robots of the Great Depression" © 2019 by Selena Chambers. + **228-229:** Elektro photo courtesy of the Mansfield Memorial Museum; Alamut ruins image © 2014 by ivanadb/iStock by Getty Images. + **230-231:** Alamut ruins © 2018 by uskarp/iStock by Getty Images. + **232-233:** *New Gods* #1 © DC Comics. + **234-235:** Lord of Light concept art © by Barry Ira Geller Productions, LLC, colors licensed to Heavy Metal Media, LLC, for their issue #276. + **236-237:** *Valérian* cover © 2017 by Cinebook. + **239-240:** "Beyond D&D: Lesser-Known Fantasy Role-Plaing Games" © 2019 by Frank Romero. + **240-241:** Original illustration © 2019 by Ashanti Fortson; *Warhammer Fantasy Roleplay* rulebook © Cubicle 7 Entertainment Ltd. + **241-242:** "*Warhammer Fantasy Role-Play*: A Grim World of Perilous Adventure" © 2019 by Molly Tanzer. + **243-244:** "Kentaro Miura, Grandmaster of Grimdark" © 2019 by Jesse Bullington. + **244-245:** *Bioforge* official screenshot © by Origin/EA digital catalog. + **246-247:** *Blame!* book cover © 2003 by Kodansha. + **248-249:** *Blame!* film stills © 2017 by Polygon Pictures/Netflix. + **250-251:** "Raelism: The Space-Age Message of the Elohim" © 2019 by Robert Levy. + **250-251:** Flying saucer image © 2016 by oorka/iStock by Getty Images. + **252-253:** CyberCity image © 2014 by Eric Molinsky. + **255-257:** "On the Internet, No One Knows You Aren't a (Gay) Wizard: An Ode to Fan Fiction" © 2019 by K. M. Szpara. + **256-257:** *Fangirl* first edition book cover © 2013 by St. Martin's Griffin. + **258-260:** "The Time of the Mellon Chronicles" © 2019 by Sylas K. Barrett. + **258-259:** *The Return of the King* stock photo for editorial use © 2003 by Moviestore Collection/Shutterstock + **262-263:** Self-published book covers courtesy Hugh Howey. + **264-265:** Mars landscape image © 2018 by dottedhippo/iStock by Getty Images.

INDEX

ACKNOWLEDGMENTS

First off, immense and heartfelt thanks to my editor at Abrams, David Cashion, whose unflagging enthusiasm for this book was instrumental in bringing it into being; throughout the occasional hiccups in the process, his kind support and steady guidance proved vital. And additional thanks to the entire team at Abrams, including executive editor Eric Klopfer, who worked heroically to help get this book to the finish line, along with managing editor Connor Leonard. Thank you, as well, to copyeditors Chris Cerasi and Drew Wheeler.

A huge thank you to designer Jacob Covey. There is such a special thrill to turning over a manuscript and seeing it transformed into a book–especially one that looks this amazing. I'm so grateful to have worked with you.

Big thanks to my smart and capable agent, Eddie Schneider, and the rest of the team at JABberwocky.

In addition to writing the foreword, Jeff VanderMeer has been an essential part of this project from the beginning–laying initial groundwork, providing foundational brainstorming, offering inspiration and ideas, and connecting me to several experts and rights holders. Thank you for everything, Jeff.

Of course, a project like this is built from the contributions of many. I'd particularly like to thank Diana Lehr and the Lehr estate for granting permission for us to use the gorgeous Paul Lehr painting that serves as this volume's cover art; Leslie Barany and Christopher Leich as representatives of the HR Giger and Hugh Ferriss estates, respectively; and Paula Guran and Thomas Pluck for providing high-res scanned images from their own collections.

I'd also like to especially acknowledge the contributions of Ashanti Fortson, Jordan Grimmer, Olivia Rose, and Jeremy Zerfoss, who created original illustrations for the book; it was a pleasure to collaborate with you. Thanks is also due to the interviewees who generously granted me their time and attention: Karen Joy Fowler, Thomas Olde Huevelt, Hugh Howey, John Shirley, and Ann VanderMeer. Finally, incredible thanks to every author who contributed an essay, including those whose efforts, due to tragic constraints of time and space, did not make it into the final book; I loved reading all of your writings, and I learned so much.

My deep appreciation also goes to administrative and research assistant Parker Bobbitt, who helped me conquer several deadlines.

Finally, all my thanks and love to my family, particularly my sisters Danelle and Daebrionne Boskovich, always patient listeners and encouragers; and my husband, Morgan Frew, a.k.a. my artistic consultant, main support, and sounding board for every scheme, who has always accepted deadline stress and working weekends as our way of life. And, of course, Emmett and Olive, my writing partners and very good dogs. ✦